IS DEMOCRACY EXPORTABLE?

Can democratic states transplant the seeds of democracy into developing countries? What have political thinkers going back to the Greek city-states thought about their capacity to promote democracy? How can democracy be established in divided societies?

In this timely volume, a distinguished group of political scientists seeks answers to these and other fundamental questions behind the concept known as "democracy promotion." Following an illuminating concise discussion of what political philosophers from Plato to Montesquieu thought about the issue, the authors explore the structural preconditions (culture, divided societies, civil society) as well as the institutions and processes of democracy building (constitutions, elections, security sector reform, conflict, and trade). Along the way they share insights about what policies have worked, which ones need to be improved or discarded, and, more generally, what advanced democracies can do to further the cause of democratization in a globalizing world. In other words, they seek answers to the question: is democracy exportable?

Zoltan Barany is the Frank C. Erwin, Jr., Professor of Government at the University of Texas and the Susan Louise Dyer Peace Fellow at the Hoover Institution at Stanford University.

Robert G. Moser is Associate Professor of Government at the University of Texas.

Is Democracy Exportable?

Edited by

Zoltan Barany

University of Texas

Robert G. Moser

University of Texas

CAMBRIDGE
UNIVERSITY PRESS

CAMBRIDGE UNIVERSITY PRESS
Cambridge, New York, Melbourne, Madrid, Cape Town, Singapore, São Paulo, Delhi

Cambridge University Press
32 Avenue of the Americas, New York, NY 10013-2473, USA

www.cambridge.org
Information on this title: www.cambridge.org/9780521748322

First published 2009

Printed in the United States of America

A catalog record for this publication is available from the British Library.

Library of Congress Cataloging in Publication data

Is democracy exportable? / edited by Zolton Barany, Robert G. Moser.
    p. cm.
Includes bibliographical references and index.
ISBN 978-0-521-76439-1 (hardback) – ISBN 978-0-521-74832-2 (pbk.)
1. Democracy – Developing countries.   I. Barany, Zoltan D.   II. Moser, Robert G., 1966–
JF60.I583   2009
321.809172′4–dc22   2008054780

ISBN 978-0-521-76439-1 hardback
ISBN 978-0-521-74832-2 paperback

Contents

Contributors

Zoltan Barany is the Frank C. Erwin, Jr., Professor of Government at the University of Texas and a Campbell National Fellow and the Susan Louise Dyer Peace Fellow at the Hoover Institution at Stanford University. He is the author, most recently, of *Democratic Breakdown and the Decline of the Russian Military* (Princeton, 2007), *The Future of NATO Expansion* (Cambridge, 2003), and *The East European Gypsies* (Cambridge, 2001).

Sheri Berman is Associate Professor of Political Science at Barnard College, Columbia University. She is the author, most recently, of *The Primacy of Politics: Social Democracy and the Making of Europe's Twentieth Century* (Cambridge, 2006) and has written numerous articles on European politics, political development, and the history of the left.

Nancy Bermeo holds the Nuffield Chair in Comparative Politics at Oxford University, where she directs the Oxford Centre for the Study of Inequality and Democracy. Her most recent books include *Federalism and Territorial Cleavages* (Johns Hopkins, 2005) with Ugo Amoretti and *Ordinary People in Extraordinary Times: The Role of the Citizenry in the Breakdown of Democracy* (Princeton, 2003).

John M. Carey is the John Wentworth Professor in the Social Sciences at Dartmouth College. His most recent book is *Legislative Voting and Accountability* (Cambridge, 2009). His research focuses on the design of constitutions and electoral systems, on legislative politics, and on political transparency and accountability. Current research, datasets, and citations to published work are available on his Web site at http://www.dartmouth.edu/~jcarey.

Daniel Chirot is the Job and Gertrud Tamaki Professor of International Studies at the University of Washington in Seattle. His books include *Why*

Not Kill Them All? The Logic and Prevention of Mass Political Murder (Princeton, 2006) co-authored with Clark McCauley and *Modern Tyrants: The Power and Prevalence of Evil in Our Age* (Princeton, 1996). He has also published work on social change, ethnic conflict, and Eastern European politics and history.

Steven E. Finkel is the Daniel Wallace Professor in Political Science at the University of Pittsburgh. He has published widely in the areas of political participation, democratic attitudes, and voting behavior. Since 1997, he has conducted numerous evaluations of the effectiveness of U.S. and other donors' civic education programs in developing democracies.

M. Steven Fish is Professor of Political Science at the University of California, Berkeley. He is the author of *Democracy Derailed in Russia: The Failure of Open Politics* (Cambridge, 2005), *Democracy from Scratch: Opposition and Regime in the New Russian Revolution* (Princeton, 1995), and the co-author of *The Handbook of National Legislatures: A Global Survey* (Cambridge, 2009) and *Postcommunism and the Theory of Democracy* (Princeton, 2001).

Edward D. Mansfield is the Hum Rosen Professor of Political Science and Director of the Christopher H. Browne Center for International Politics at the University of Pennsylvania. His research focuses on international security and international political economy. He is the author of *Power, Trade, and War* (Princeton, 1994) and the co-author (with Jack Snyder) of *Electing to Fight: Why Emerging Democracies Go to War* (MIT, 2005).

Robert G. Moser is Associate Professor of Government at the University of Texas. He is the author of *Unexpected Outcomes: Electoral Systems, Political Parties and Representation in Russia* (Pittsburgh, 2001) and is currently completing a book entitled *Mixed Electoral Systems in New and Established Democracies* with Ethan Scheiner.

Thomas L. Pangle holds the Joe R. Long Chair in Democratic Studies at the University of Texas. He serves on the Research Council of the International Forum for Democratic Studies of the National Endowment for Democracy and is the author of *The Ennobling of Democracy: The Challenge of the Postmodern Age* (Johns Hopkins, 1993) and the co-author (with Peter Ahrensdorf) of *Justice Among Nations: On the Moral Basis of Power and Peace* (Kansas, 2002).

Aníbal Pérez-Liñán is Associate Professor of Political Science and a member of the core faculty at the Center for Latin American Studies at the University of Pittsburgh. His research focuses on political stability and institutional performance in new democracies. He is the author of *Presidential Impeachment and the New Political Instability in Latin America* (Cambridge, 2007).

Marc F. Plattner is Vice President for Research and Studies at the National Endowment for Democracy, co-director of the International Forum for Democratic Studies, and co-editor of the *Journal of Democracy*. He is the author of *Democracy Without Borders?* (Rowman & Littlefield, 2008) and *Rousseau's State of Nature* (Northern Illinois, 1979), and the editor or co-editor of more than 20 books on contemporary issues related to democracy.

Adam B. Seligman is Professor of Religion at Boston University and Research Associate at the Institute for Culture, Religion and World Affairs there. He is the author of numerous books, including *The Idea of Civil Society* (Princeton, 1995), *The Problem of Trust* (Princeton, 2000), and *Modernity's Wager* (Princeton, 2003) and the co-author of *Ritual and Its Consequences: An Essay on the Limits of Sincerity* (Oxford, 2008).

Mitchell A. Seligson is Centennial Professor of Political Science at Vanderbilt University and a Fellow of the Vanderbilt Center for Nashville Studies. His most recent books are *The Legitimacy Puzzle: Democracy and Support in Latin America* (Cambridge, forthcoming), co-authored with John Booth; and *Development and Underdevelopment: The Political Economy of Global Inequality* (Fourth Edition, Lynne Reinner), co-edited with John Passé-Smith.

Jack Snyder is the Robert and Renée Belfer Professor of International Relations in the political science department and the Saltzman Institute of War and Peace Studies at Columbia University. His books include *Electing to Fight: Why Emerging Democracies Go to War* (MIT, 2005), co-authored with Edward D. Mansfield; *From Voting to Violence: Democratization and Nationalist Conflict* (Norton, 2000); and *Myths of Empire: Domestic Politics and International Ambition* (Cornell, 1991).

Acknowledgments

We are indebted to the entities at the University of Texas for having financed the April 2007 conference that brought the participants together in Austin:

- the Center for Middle Eastern Studies;
- the Center for Russian, East European, and Eurasian Studies;
- the Center for South Asian Studies;
- the College of Liberal Arts;
- the Graduate School; and
- the Lozano Long Institute for Latin American Studies.

We are also grateful to the contributors for making our work as organizers and editors pleasant and rewarding. Finally, we thank Regina Goodnow, Susanne Martin, and Curt Nichols, the three conscientious doctoral students in the Department of Government who helped to prepare the manuscript for publication.

Zoltan Barany and Robert G. Moser

MARC F. PLATTNER

Introduction

The question that provides the title of this volume has now returned to the center of public discussion, largely because of the severe difficulties in building democratic regimes following the successful military invasions of Afghanistan and Iraq. In the 1990s a fairly wide consensus had developed both in the United States and internationally, in favor of active efforts to assist those seeking to establish and maintain democratic institutions. Today, however, that consensus is fraying, and people once again are asking: Is democracy exportable? Can or should the United States or other democratic countries try to export it?

How one answers this question depends in substantial part on how the meaning of the word "export" is understood. It is clear that democracy cannot be exported in the way that food, or clothing, or machinery can be. In fact, organizations that are devoted to promoting the growth of democracy abroad do not like to characterize their own activity as being aimed at the "export" of democracy. The five-year strategy document adopted by the National Endowment for Democracy (NED) in 2007 even proclaims, "Democracy cannot be exported or imposed."

In disclaiming the idea that they are in the export business, democracy-promotion organizations acknowledge that there is a kernel of truth in the argument that democracy can take root only if it is homegrown. By its very nature, democracy is a political system that is founded on the consent of the governed. Obviously, if the people of a given country do not consent to be governed democratically, no outside efforts to implant democracy can succeed. One may go even further, and say, that unless the people of a country are willing to support and even defend democracy, no democratic system can long survive. The experience of decolonization in the twentieth century offered decisive proof that establishing a

1

democratic institutional framework is by itself insufficient to enable democracy to persist. The limits of what external support can achieve are recognized by the sensible proponents of democracy promotion as well as by its critics.

Many of the critics, however, go beyond emphasizing these limits and assert that the "export" of democracy is unwise or impossible. Some claim that democracy is an American or European or Western idea that does not fit other cultures or civilizations and, thus, is always in some sense imposed on other peoples. Others say that democracy can only arise "organically," that it requires a long gestation period of social, economic, and cultural change of the sort that first gave rise to democratic (or at least proto-democratic) government in Britain and the United States. Still others emphasize the importance of socioeconomic "prerequisites" for democracy – a certain level of economic development and of literacy, a substantial middle class, and the like.

Once again, there is something to these arguments – certainly, the overall correlation between levels of economic development and democratic stability still seems to hold. But, there is a massive problem with the contention that democracy cannot be exported – namely, that over the past two centuries it has been spreading around the world at a remarkable and accelerating pace. Moreover, in recent decades democracy has successfully taken root in countries with a wide variety of different cultures and different levels of economic development. Hence, the view that democracy can thrive only where particular cultural, historical, or socio-economic factors are present is no longer compelling.

Of course, one could argue that democracy's undeniable spread to something like half the world's countries has been propelled solely by internal factors. This seems highly implausible, however, given the fact that historically democracy has expanded in a series of "waves," and that countries in the same region have often democratized in quick succession. In any case, drawing a bright line between "exported" and home-grown political change is inherently difficult, especially in light of the high degree of international connectivity in today's world. Even in the distant past, various kinds of doctrines and institutional arrangements that first arose in one society have often been adopted – and adapted – by others. All the great world religions have been "exported" in this way. If we look at the alleged protagonists of Samuel P. Huntington's "clash of civilizations," we find that almost all of these civilizations are formed around religious teachings that had their origins elsewhere. The influence of these teachings radiated out through a variety of means ranging from the book to the sword. Does that mean that Islam should be regarded as an export item in Iran or Indonesia? Or Christianity in Italy or Britain?

It is not only religions that have been diffused in this way. In the last century, communism proved to be a remarkably successful export item in almost every region of the world. It was diffused through a variety of means, both military and intellectual, including direct assistance from Moscow to communist parties across the globe. Since the demise and discrediting of communism, however, it is democracy that has become the only political system with a plausible claim to universal legitimacy. As Amartya Sen has put it,

> In any age and social climate, there are some sweeping beliefs that seem to command respect as a kind of general rule – like a "default" setting in a computer program; they are considered right *unless* their claim is somehow precisely negated. While democracy is not yet universally practiced, nor indeed uniformly accepted, in the general climate of world opinion, democratic governance has now achieved the status of being taken to be generally right. The ball is very much in the court of those who want to rubbish democracy to provide justification for that rejection.

Another arresting formulation of the attractions of democracy comes from the Georgian political thinker Ghia Nodia:

> [W]hy do transitions occur? A major reason is imitation (which is what political scientists are talking about when they use terms like "demonstration effect" and "diffusion"). The greatest victory of democracy in the modern world is that – for one reason or another – it has become fashionable. To live under autocracy, or even to *be* an autocrat, seems backward, uncivilized, distasteful, not quite *comme il faut* – in a word, "uncool." In a world where democracy is synonymous less with freedom than with civilization itself, nobody can wait to be "ready" for democracy.

Even apart from its intrinsic appeal, the global legitimacy of democracy makes it an object of aspiration for people across the globe. Just as most people in most places today want economic growth and equality of treatment, they also want to be able to choose their own government and to have their rights respected. As Nodia puts it, "Democratic... models are not so much imposed by the West as sought by local elites.... The West need not feel guilty about 'imposing' its models on 'the rest': It is 'the rest' who recognize the centrality of the modern Western democratic project and want to participate in it."

The constellation of goals characteristic of modernity – self-government, individual freedom, political equality, the rule of law, and economic prosperity – along with the institutions that serve them, may indeed have first emerged in Britain and America, but they can hardly be considered an Anglo-American preserve. The British and American political models were, early on, presented most forcefully to the rest of the world by two Frenchmen – Montesquieu and Tocqueville, respectively. Clearly, the fact that democracy is now deeply rooted in almost all of Europe and in much of the Western Hemisphere results from the spread of these models, adjusted in various ways to national circumstances. Understood in this way, the "export" of democracy is an old, old story.

DEMOCRACY AND U.S. FOREIGN POLICY

As Thomas L. Pangle indicates in the essay that opens this collection, support for efforts to advance democracy abroad is also quite an old story in American history, with origins going all the way back to the beginnings of the Republic. At least since the First World War, the defense of democracy has been an explicit aim of U.S. foreign policy, and it has continued to be invoked through the Second World War, the Cold War, and the wars in Afghanistan and Iraq. The goal of making the world more democratic has been justified both on moral grounds and in terms of *realpolitik*. The moral argument holds that human rights and democracy should be extended because people everywhere are entitled to enjoy them. At the same time, by encouraging the spread of democracy we serve our own security interests by helping to bring into being regimes that are much more likely to be our allies than our foes. This dual case in favor of promoting democracy was given its most prominent and expansive expression in George W. Bush's second inaugural address:

> We are led, by events and common sense, to one conclusion: The survival of liberty in our land increasingly depends on the success of liberty in other lands. The best hope for peace in our world is the expansion of freedom in all the world.

> America's vital interests and our deepest beliefs are now one. From the day of our founding, we have proclaimed that every man and woman on this earth has rights and dignity and matchless value because they bear the image of the maker of heaven and earth. Across the generations, we have proclaimed the imperative of self-government, because no one is fit to be a master, and no one deserves to be a slave.

Advancing these ideals is the mission that created our nation. It is the honorable achievement of our fathers. Now it is the urgent requirement of our nation's security, and the calling of our time. So it is the policy of the United States to seek and support the growth of democratic movements and institutions in every nation and culture, with the ultimate goal of ending tyranny in our world.

It is hard to dispute the contention that, *in the long run*, the spread of democracy to other lands serves America's "vital interests" as well as its "deepest beliefs." Even in the short term, the imperatives of security and democracy promotion often point in the same direction. Yet, it cannot plausibly be denied that in other cases immediate and urgent security goals come into sharp conflict with the goal of advancing democracy in a particular country. Such situations are likely to produce compromises with our democratic beliefs. (The classic, if extreme, example is the alliance of the democracies with Stalin's Russia in the war against Nazi Germany.) This is a reality that the Bush administration has been forced to rediscover, as is reflected in its policy toward such key countries as Egypt, Pakistan, Russia, and China.

During the course of American history, the goal of advancing democracy has been pursued by the use of virtually every tool in the foreign policy arsenal: military force, financial assistance, economic sanctions, diplomatic pressure, covert action, presidential rhetoric, public diplomacy, and so on. But, since the 1980s, a new tool has been added – the open provision of financial support and training to prodemocratic groups abroad. This new approach, often referred to as "democracy assistance" or "political development assistance," has an interesting history of its own.

The story begins in the 1970s with the rise to prominence of the issue of international human rights. First given political salience in Congress, human rights were elevated to a central place in American foreign policy under the presidency of Jimmy Carter. This initiative, citing the official international acceptance of various human rights declarations as its justification, breached what had been the ordinary peacetime constraints against "interfering" in the internal affairs of other states.

Initially, however, the new boldness in asserting support for human rights abroad was not matched by equivalent efforts on behalf of democracy. That step was taken under the presidency of Ronald Reagan. In his historic June 1982 speech to the British parliament, Reagan noted the bipartisan efforts then underway to "determine how the United States can best contribute as a nation to the global campaign for democracy now gathering force." That speech led to the creation in late 1983 of the

National Endowment for Democracy (NED), a nongovernmental, but congressionally funded, institution that awarded its first grants in 1984.

In the NED's early years, the very idea of democracy assistance remained intensely controversial. The NED was set up as a nongovernmental organization precisely because it was felt that giving support to prodemocratic groups in other countries amounted to intervening in their internal affairs. This was widely viewed as something that government could not legitimately and openly do; it had to be done by a private organization at arm's length from the government. The NED also could draw on the precedent of the German political party foundations, which had long provided aid to their counterparts abroad and had played a particularly important role in assisting the transitions to democracy in Spain and Portugal. Yet, in the United States, despite strong bipartisan backing for the NED from the leaders of labor, business, and the two political parties, skepticism was widespread.

Hostility to democracy promotion was sometimes based on fiscal conservatism or on isolationism, but some of the sharpest opposition came from those most committed to a vigorous human rights policy. Today, the once-sharp split between the "human rights community" and the "democracy community" may seem difficult to comprehend, given the close interrelationship in both theory and practice between human rights and democracy. In part, this rift derived from the accidents of partisan rivalry in the United States, notably the disputes over Central America that roiled American politics in the mid-1980s. Democracy promotion came to be identified by some with the Reagan administration in the same way that human rights had been identified with the Carter administration.

These partisan divisions, however, were largely effaced by the end of the Cold War. The Clinton administration, upon taking office in 1993, made "democratic enlargement" one of the pillars of its foreign policy, and it proposed a large increase in the budget of the NED. In a move that symbolized the transcending of the rift between human rights advocates and democracy advocates, it reconstituted the State Department's Bureau of Human Rights and Humanitarian Affairs, which had been established under President Carter, into the Bureau of Democracy, Human Rights, and Labor. Differences between the human rights and democracy communities are still sometimes visible, especially in debates over the role of international institutions, but for most practical purposes the two communities today are strong allies. Whether in Russia, Burma, Zimbabwe,

China, or Uzbekistan, contemporary struggles for human rights are also struggles for democracy.

The new consensus in favor of democracy, of course, was powerfully influenced by the fall of the Berlin Wall and the demise of communism. These momentous events not only eliminated the old Cold War context, but brought about a real sea change in the way democracy was perceived. The worldwide prestige and legitimacy of democracy rose to unprecedented heights, and suddenly a wide range of individuals and institutions were in favor of promoting it. The change was remarkably swift. For example, career officers at the U.S. Agency for International Development (USAID), which previously had regarded itself as a nonpolitical, technical agency devoted to fostering economic progress in poorer countries, were initially horrified by the notion of becoming involved in political assistance aimed at supporting democracy. Their chiefs soon realized, however, that this was going to be a growth area of American foreign assistance and decided that USAID had better begin participating.

The new consensus in favor of democracy assistance was far from being an exclusively American phenomenon. Everyone was jumping on the bandwagon, including international and regional organizations as well as democratic governments. The UN secretariat now includes an Electoral Assistance Division charged with helping member states to carry out free and fair elections. A new United Nations Democracy Fund has been established to provide grants to nongovernmental organizations working to promote democracy. The United Nations Development Programme (UNDP), UNESCO, and other specialized agencies have instituted programs aimed at supporting democracy. Among regional organizations, it is not just the European Union (EU), the Council of Europe, and the OSCE that have gotten involved with democracy promotion. The same is true of the Organization of American States (OAS) and the Commonwealth. Even the African Union (AU, formerly the Organization of African Unity) and ASEAN, organizations that include nondemocratic member states and had traditionally been leery of any intervention in one another's domestic politics, have taken the plunge. Moreover, the EU and the bilateral assistance agencies of most major democratic countries now fund programs aimed at strengthening democracy in developing and post-communist countries.

In the 1990s, citizens and government officials in the new democracies were eager to receive "political development assistance," and external donors were eager to provide it. Especially in the post-communist countries, recipients tended to have no qualms about accepting democracy assistance, even if it came directly from Western governments. Very quickly, the amounts spent directly by government agencies began to dwarf the expenditures of nongovernmental organizations like NED. USAID's democracy and governance expenditures alone are now estimated to exceed $1 billion per year. Soon, democracy promotion itself became not only a very large enterprise but, as Michael McFaul has put it, a kind of international norm.

THE NEW CONTROVERSY

More recently, however, democracy promotion has started to become more controversial again – although spending on it has not declined and support for it in the U.S. Congress remains strong. I would say that the reemerging controversy has two sources. One, is what has been described as the "backlash" or "pushback" against democracy assistance. This comes largely from semi-democratic or "competitive authoritarian" regimes that, in the aftermath of the "color revolutions" in Georgia and Ukraine, see democracy assistance as a threat to their power. Foremost among the countries that have begun imposing tighter restrictions on domestic NGOs and their receipt of foreign funding are Chavez's Venezuela and Putin's Russia; others include Mubarak's Egypt, Mugabe's Zimbabwe, and Lukashenka's Belarus. These new restrictions are typically justified in terms of protecting national sovereignty or resisting Western hegemony. By making the provision of democracy assistance more difficult and harassing its recipients, these regimes have sown doubts in some quarters about its usefulness.

The second and by far the most important reason for renewed controversy is that democracy promotion is increasingly conflated with the unpopular war in Iraq. In one sense, this is very misleading, as attempts to establish democracy through invasion have been, and most likely will continue to be, exceedingly rare. In another sense, however, the efforts in Iraq and Afghanistan are part of a larger category, often labeled "post-conflict democracy-building," that has been growing in prominence. Most of the countries in this category have experienced severe internal conflict, and the attempt to reconstruct them has been taken up by the international community under the aegis of the UN, as in the cases of Haiti, Mozambique, Cambodia, Bosnia, Sierra Leone, East Timor, Kosovo, and Liberia. In addition to having undergone the trauma of civil war, many of these countries are desperately poor. None of them would be considered a very promising candidate for popular self-government. Yet, democracy-building has been an integral component of the international reconstruction effort in all these places. Why?

Part of the explanation is that elections can be a useful mechanism for resolving longstanding civil conflicts. But, the more important factor lies in the legitimacy democracy enjoys in the international community. Both the international organizations and the great powers that have taken the lead in responding to post-conflict situations would find it exceedingly awkward to evade their proclaimed commitment to democracy in a jurisdiction under their protection. Although the United States continues to do business with friendly dictators, these days one cannot imagine a U.S. president justifying – or U.S. public opinion accepting – a decision to hand a territory under U.S. control over to an unelected authoritarian leader. And, although the UN readily accommodates authoritarian regimes among its member states, it too feels compelled to try to leave behind functioning democratic institutions in places where it takes direct responsibility for post-conflict situations.

Building democratic institutions under such inhospitable conditions is a task fraught with complications. Restoring peace and security and rebuilding the state demand a whole array of capabilities and resources that go far beyond the demands of democracy assistance in more settled conditions. Experience gained in providing political development assistance to countries with functioning states has very limited relevance to places where almost every institution needs to be rebuilt from scratch. And, the record of the international community in dealing with such situations leaves a lot to be desired. Still, given the number of fragile states in the world, democracy builders are likely to face many more such tough cases in the future.

So, in some ways, democracy assistance today is paying the price for its past success. Increasingly, it will be operating in two quite different but equally challenging environments. One is a set of countries where fearful, but shrewd, dictators have learned some lessons about how democratic transitions unfold and how to thwart them. And the other is a set of countries where chaos threatens and almost nothing functions without external support. The difficulties will be great, but as long as democracy retains its unrivaled legitimacy and the United States remains the world's leading power, there is every reason to expect that democracy assistance will continue to be a significant feature on the international landscape.

A VARIETY OF PERSPECTIVES

As the preceding discussion has indicated, the question of "exporting" or promoting democracy is a complex one that raises a host of moral, theoretical, and practical issues. The chapters that follow examine some of the most important of these issues from a variety of perspectives and with a variety of different scholarly approaches. Some of the chapters are based on the analysis of large amounts of data, whereas others take a wholly qualitative approach. Some chapters focus primarily on the requirements of democracy itself; others deal more directly with the challenges of promoting it in other lands.

This book does not attempt to cover the full range of questions posed by the effort to promote democracy. Indeed, given the vastness and the complexity of the subject, it is hard to imagine how any single volume could offer a comprehensive study. The goal of this book is to accomplish something less ambitious but still of great value – namely, to illuminate some of the key issues that must be confronted in thinking about whether and how democracy promotion can be successful.

The opening chapter by Thomas L. Pangle examines the morality of exporting democracy by comparing the different views put forward by political thinkers from the ancient, Christian, and modern philosophical traditions. It aims not to provide a strict set of guidelines governing whether, when, and by what means the spread of democracy should be pursued, but rather to weigh the competing philosophical frameworks and to illuminate the moral and prudential considerations that can be used to answer these questions.

The next four chapters are devoted to an examination of some of the "structural preconditions" of successful democracy and what these imply for the enterprise of democracy promotion. The emphasis here is not on the socioeconomic factors that are sometimes viewed as prerequisites for successful democratization. Instead, these chapters focus on questions of trust, tolerance, religion, association, culture, and ethnicity. Adam Seligman in chapter five and Sheri Berman in chapter two explore from different angles the newly rediscovered concept of civil society and its relation to democracy, with Seligman reflecting upon the relationship of civil society to the tolerance of difference, and Berman stressing the necessity of understanding civil society in the context of the political institutions that shape its development.

In chapter three, M. Steven Fish investigates the impact of culture on both the propensity of different countries to successfully sustain democratic institutions and their receptivity to external efforts to assist them in doing so. This is followed by a chapter in which Daniel Chirot seeks to assess the problem posed for democracy by sharp ethnic and communal differences and the extent to which it can be surmounted by fostering tolerance and respect for individual rights.

The third section of the book consists of five chapters devoted to an examination of political institutions and processes. Chapter six by Robert G. Moser and chapter seven by John Carey look at two of the basic features of what political scientists often refer to as "institutional design" – namely, electoral systems and constitutions. Moser considers the extent to which electoral rules can be used to shape electoral and political outcomes in new democracies, whereas Carey investigates the impact of the processes by which constitutions are designed and adopted on the subsequent success and stability of democracy. In chapter eight, Zoltan Barany discusses a political institution that is essential for providing the secure environment that new democracies require, but is often neglected by students and promoters of democracy – the armed forces. Edward D. Mansfield and Jack Snyder devote chapter nine to testing two of the major claims made in favor of efforts to foster democratization – namely, that democracies are more likely to remain at peace with one another and that they are more likely to encourage economic prosperity and freer trade.

In the tenth chapter, Mitchell Seligson, Steven E. Finkel, and Aníbal Pérez-Liñán shift the focus from the questions of whether and how democracy should be promoted to the question of whether democracy promotion actually works. Reporting on the results of a larger study they have conducted of USAID democracy and governance programs, they conclude that the initial evidence suggests that these programs do have impressive achievements to their credit.

In this regard, their chapter stands out from most of those that precede it. On the whole, it seems to me, the prevailing tone of most of this book is one of relatively benevolent skepticism. None of the authors is an opponent of democracy. All would like to see democracy flourish and continue to spread. They do not shrink from making recommendations for ways to improve the work of democracy promoters. Yet, most of them seem to harbor more or less profound doubts regarding the ability of democracy promotion to accomplish its aims. In my own view, some of them (along with many other commentators on the subject) begin with an exaggerated notion of what democracy promotion can hope to achieve, and then come to conclude that it cannot meet this standard.

By contrast, the chapter by Seligson, Finkel, and Pérez-Liñán concludes that USAID democracy and governance programs have had a significant and favorable impact on the overall progress of democracy in the recipient countries. The record of success indicated by their analysis of the data is more robust than that of most government programs and, I would say, greater than most people engaged in the enterprise of democracy promotion would have anticipated. Given the increasing amounts of money being spent on democracy assistance worldwide and the growing scholarly attention to this field, there will no doubt be many subsequent attempts to measure the effectiveness of democracy promotion programs – and these may or may not give support to the optimism generated by the Seligson, Finkel, and Pérez-Liñán study. In any case, there is sure to be continuing debate not only about assessing the impact of democracy assistance programs, but also about the broader moral and political questions raised by efforts to spread democracy. This book is intended to provide readers with a useful entry point into that debate.

A MORAL IMPERATIVE?

THOMAS L. PANGLE

1 The Morality of Exporting Democracy
A Historical-Philosophical Perspective

Ours is an era in which democracy is bent on proliferating itself with
an energy that is breathtaking. The European Union, having mush-
roomed to twenty-seven member nations, is now committed to maintaining democracy among a vast Eastern population that within our
lifetime was once regarded as hopelessly under the heel of communist
totalitarianism. Prominent Europeans have suggested that there is no
reason why the spread of their democratic union should be limited by
European borders or culture. Lord Ralf Dahrendorf has suggested, in a
noted Munich address, that the union ought to have the ambition to
extend itself, not only to Turkey and Ukraine, but as far as Singapore and
New Zealand – following, as one commentator remarked, the tracks
of the British empire. Pierre Manent, a leading French political theo-
rist, has spoken with unease of the Europeans as having become dedicated to *"l'empire démocratique."*[1] The United States has for some time
been engaged in a less ambitious, but, in some ways, more active and
forceful policy of "democratization." But, as we all are keenly aware,
recent events, most obviously in Iraq, have aroused or deepened doubts,
and strengthened criticisms, of this far-flung and diverse enterprise. The
questioning is pressed through moral, but not solely through prudential
grounds. We have been acutely reminded of our need and duty to articulate answers to some basic ethical questions. Exactly what is it, about our
western liberal form of democracy, that gives us a right or duty to try to
transplant it as a replacement for existing regimes of a different character? How does such a policy avoid what will be, at best, a paternalistic,

[1] "Si le quiétisme européen forme un vif contrast avec l'activisme américain, ce sont deux
versions de ce qu'il faut appeler l'"empire démocratique' qui nous sont proposées avec une
égale conviction et une même implacabilité." (Manent, 2006: 15; see also 57–58).

soft form of imperialism on the part of democratic great powers? When, if ever, is it legitimate to use armed force in pursuit of this policy?

When we begin seriously to pursue these and kindred moral questions, we soon realize that our modern democratic principles, especially in their international expression, are the tension-ridden product of a succession of great historical contests down through the centuries. In each stage of this process, new or revived conceptions of domestic and international justice arose over and against, although in some sense incorporating, previously regnant, contrasting, and competing ideals and norms. If we are to become fully self-conscious, as we reflect on the grounds for exporting democracy, we need to recover, even to reenact, at least the major stages in this legacy of debate that shapes our tension-ridden moral thinking. In what follows, I want to contribute to such a recovery and reenactment.

THE TRADITIONAL SOURCES OF DOUBT CONCERNING
THE JUSTICE OF EXPORTING DEMOCRACY

First and foremost, this kind of genealogical inquiry brings into view a fundamental moral problem in democracy's tendency to export itself: a problem that our distinctively modern, liberal republicanism was intended to meet, or to mitigate. The problem is on vivid display in the original, massive historical example of a policy of exporting democracy: that of classical Athens, history's first great democratic power. Athens, in a relatively short time, forcefully brought into being or sustained well over a hundred democracies and democratic revolutions in the Mediterranean world. But, this classic example, of the policy of exporting democracy, reveals a policy that was a pillar of an overall imperialist strategy.[2]

Athenian democratic imperialism was not simply despotic, either in fact or by intention. In the pages of Thucydides, leading spokesmen for Athens articulate what one may call a semi-moral defense of their drive to hegemonic predominance, achieved in part through the imposition of compliant democracies on many subject peoples. The Athenian vindication must be called at most "semi"-moral, because the hard-boiled Athenian democrats explicitly dismiss, as hypocrisy, what they contemptuously term "the just discourse." That discourse is upheld by Sparta

---

[2] See Xenophon [writing as what is conventionally called "The Old Oligarch"], *Constitution of Athens*, 1.14, 1.16–18; 3.11; Kagan: 1969, 54–56, 72–73, 95, 100–101, 120–26, 347; Meiggs: 1972, 208–9, 220; Bleicken: 1994, chap. 15; Schuller: 1995, 310–23.

and her colonists – most notably the Melians. According to this "just discourse," polities have an obligation to respect one another's independence. This obligation is said to rest on two sorts of grounds (whose questionable compatibility points to deep conceptual puzzles). *Either* such obligation, as obedience to unwritten higher law, ought to trump, for each nation, its concern for its own good – and hence a nation's justice shines forth especially at moments of noble risk and sacrifice; *or* each nation's own truest, long-term good is thus most fully achieved as part of a genuinely common good, of all decent neighboring nations, living in a mutually supportive association.

Against either or both of these contentions, the Athenian democrats appeal to what they contend universal experience demonstrates: all humans, in their communities, are naturally and necessarily concerned chiefly with their own, predominantly exclusive, good (including not least the spiritual satisfactions of ruling); *and*, each community's clear-sighted pursuit of this good, given the ceaseless competitions for rule, and the unreliable or tenuous commonalities that characterize international life, requires that each seek to expand its political power as far as it can.

A quasi-moral element enters to elevate (and to deeply complicate) the Athenian self-justification, inasmuch as the Athenians proudly distinguish their empire from other empires, and do so not least on account of the specific virtues of their democratic regime.

To begin with, the Athenians argue that in acquiring empire, their democracy, in its leadership, has manifested an intelligence as well as enterprise in the pursuit of its own security and freedom that has entailed otherwise unavailable security and freedom for all the rest of democratic Greece – especially in the face of the Persian threat. The Athenian democratic empire thus represents a kind of common good.

Further, the Athenians proudly proclaim themselves "deserving of praise" because (as they put it) they "rule over others more justly than is called for by their power." In other words, they deny that sheer power is their sole concern. Indeed, they conceive of themselves as to some extent risking their power and security, out of a generosity toward their subjects. This noble generosity transfigures their concern for "honor" into a concern for a dignity or glory that entails the sacrifice of even prestige, at least among their contemporaries: they protest that (in their words) "from our decency we have unreasonably accrued infamy rather than praise."[3]

---

[3] Thucydides, *The Peloponnesian War* 1.76.2–1.77.3. All translations from this and other sources not in English are my own.

Above all, Pericles, in his famous Funeral Oration, boasts that the Athenians have forged what he calls a "model political regime" that would not have been possible without the resources and the invigorating challenges and responsibilities that empire alone brings. "Our regime," he says, "is called 'democracy,' on account of its being administered not for the few, but for the greater number"; but (he goes on to explain), "it is at the same time an elective and competitive meritocracy as regards ruling and honor." Whereas the best are honored by being elected to rule, "the rest of the citizens," Pericles says, "are not deficient in judgment concerning politics." Moreover, Pericles stresses that this democracy is exemplary, not only because it manifests the most effective governing virtues, but also because it understands how to employ the leisure and superfluity that, again, its imperial power alone has made possible. "We have proven," Pericles declares, that "we love the beautiful without extravagance, and we love wisdom without softness.... Summing up, I say that the city as a whole provides the education of Greece" (ibid. 2.37–2.41).

These last words suggest that it is especially by its own exemplary excellence that Athenian democracy, at the peak of its empire, is good for all Greece, including especially its subject states to which it has exported democracy. Those subjects can admire and learn what human flourishing is, from seeing such fulfillment realized in Athenian democracy.

Yes, but: must the subject democracies not, by the same token, see that this fulfillment is for only a few (the citizens who participate in Athenian democracy), and requires the subjection or exploitation of the vast majority who are citizens in the other, exported democracies? The exported democracies are obviously not supposed to learn how to truly model themselves after the hegemonic democracy (that would make them into rebellious challengers, like Syracuse). Even in the least demeaning cases, the "merit" for which the rulers in the subject democracies' are elected must include faithful servility to the Athenian ruling interest.

But, cannot the subject democracies find a noble consolation, if not satisfaction, in their recognized essential contribution to the more complete fulfillment of their hegemonic rulers, the Athenians? Pericles is so far from suggesting this, that he proclaims that "as regards what pertains to virtue," we Athenians "are the contrary of the many: for we" (he says) "acquire friends not by being done to, but by doing" (ibid. 2.40.4).

Pericles does not attempt to justify the servile status of the subject democracies that Athens has created. He averts his, and his audience's eyes, from that consequence of what he calls Athenian "virtue." The Periclean vision never reflects deeply on the tension between, on the one hand, the proudly frank and self-sufficient dismissal of "the just discourse," and, on the other hand, the passionate belief that a noble generosity, involving risk or even sacrifice of power and prestige, is a key part of what makes Athenian democracy deserving, as Pericles insists, of "everlasting" fame.

This massive moral problem has by no means negated the attraction of Periclean democracy down through the ages. Its appeal has persisted, reaching well into our own time – most conspicuously in the democratic theorizing of Hannah Arendt and Sheldon Wolin. Arendt and Wolin (and others) contend that a Periclean democracy, in spite or because of its finally having to acknowledge that its empire is – in the words of Pericles' last rather grim speech – "like a tyranny," nonetheless ennobles such inevitable resemblance to tyranny to the maximum possible degree.[4]

However: *Is* paternalistic empire, in some form, unavoidable for a great democratic power – even, or especially, insofar as it deliberately seeks generously to export democracy? That, I submit, is the great question posed by Periclean Athens for our discussion. Here we see manifested in its starkest form what I am going to call "the Athenian vector." By this term, I mean to designate what I am inclined to think is a general proclivity of energetic democracies: a democratic people's passionate collective aspiration to a noble preeminence in the world, achieved through international generosity, and hence leadership or rule – rule through which the democracy is spread and becomes exemplary, a "model," as Pericles says. Without this noble ambition, a democratic populace may tend to become petty or passive and even compliant – like most of the populaces in the numerous subject democracies fostered by Athens. But, on

---

[4] For Arendt, Pericles and his vision represent the exemplary form of political life ("Action"): see Arendt 1958: esp. secs. 27–28. Arendt's outlook informs Sheldon Wolin's assessment of Athenian imperialism (1996: 63–90, esp. 77–78; see also the editors' remarks on Wolin's position, 7–8). For another eloquent example, see the comments by Alfred Zimmern (who was to become not only a famous liberal professor of international relations, but a leading figure in the League of Nations and later in the founding of the United Nations) in his classic *Greek Commonwealth* (1961: 194–95 – supported by a quotation from a private letter from Arnold J. Toynbee): "Athens could no more step back than most Englishmen feel they can leave India. She had woken up to find herself an Empire and was resolved to play the part." And "the world is still blessing her for what she did with it." For "this it is which makes this short half-century perhaps the greatest and happiest period in recorded history." The Athenians "knew their work was right, that it was well and soundly laid, and that posterity would understand it." Such a democratic empire's defenders can rightly say: "Our society and intercourse is the highest blessing man can confer. To be within the circle of our influence is not dependence but a privilege. Not all the wealth of the East can repay the riches we bestow. So we can work on cheerfully, using the means and money that flow in to us, confident that, try as they will, we shall still be creditors."

the other hand, as the example of Athens shows, once this ambition is seriously aroused, it is in desperate need of some limitation – if not by an external force or a rival great power, then either by a higher principle, or by a balancing internal ambition.

THE "JUST DISCOURSE" AND THE "LAW OF NATIONS"

The most obvious candidate for the limiting higher principle is "the just discourse." That discourse, as it is articulated by the Melians, has as its cornerstone a trust in a divine providence that ultimately sanctions international affairs. The example of Thucydides shows that this trust is not without some powerful empirical evidence. The Spartans are indeed proven to be hypocrites, and the Melians are indeed crushed by the hubristic Athenians; *but*, in the pages of Thucydides' drama, this latter, minor Athenian triumph is followed at once by the beginning of Athens' slide into the Sicilian disaster, which foreshadows the Delphic oracle's prophecy of an eventual victory for the piously chastened Spartans – who, Thucydides stresses, never suffered from the plague, prophesied by another oracle, that tormented Athens periodically throughout the long war. Thucydides thus indicates the evidence that at least lays open the fundamental question: whether or not there exists providential divinity.

The wrestling with that question may be said to animate classical political thought. But, in post-classical Christian political theology, this fundamental question receives, of course, a dogmatic, affirmative answer that provides the basis for the distinctive Christian doctrine of the law of nations – the *ius gentium*. That doctrine, of an unwritten, but universally recognized legal code providing the basic norms of international conduct, has remained up through our time a cornerstone of all international legal thought in the West. The most important deployment of this Christian doctrine, in regard to the export of democracy, was by Edmund Burke, at the end of the eighteenth century, in his eloquent call for a policing international crusade – "a religious war," as he called it – to roll back the spread of democratic republics by the subversive influence and belligerent activities of the French Revolutionary regime.[5] For although regime change, even or especially through conquest, was defended as a legitimate last

---

[5] *First Letter on a Regicide Peace* (1839: 398–403); *Heads for Consideration on the Present State of Affairs in November 1792* (ibid.: 65–66); *Remarks on the Policy of the Allies with Respect to France* (ibid.: 102–3, 107–9, 114–18); Letter to Foreign Secretary Lord Grenville, Aug. 18, 1792 (1958–78: 176–77). See the helpful discussion of Burke's extracts from and comments upon Vattel's treatise *The Law of Nations* (reproduced in 1839: 132–41) in Welsh, 1995: 84–85, 127–28, 131–33, 137.

resort by traditional just-war theorists from Vitoria to Burke, these theorists were not prone to defend change to, or the spread of, democracy.
Why was the spread of democracy not welcomed by the Christian law
of nations tradition? The most serious reason was democracy's troubling
historical record, or the fear of what I have called "the Athenian vector" – which manifested itself not only in Periclean Athens, but also in
republican Rome after the rise of the popular Tribunes (in the regime that
was trumpeted as an inspiration for the future by Machiavelli); and then
later in the French Revolution. The history of more moderate democratic
republics was overshadowed by these most famous and influential examples. Democracy and its spread came to be welcomed by the Christian
doctrine of the law of nations only beginning in the nineteenth century –
and then, only in the wake of a revolution in fundamental democratic
principles and practice.

A NEW KIND OF DEMOCRATIC REPUBLIC

The revolutionary transformation of democratic principles and practices
was ushered onto the world stage by the American Founding. As James
Madison and Alexander Hamilton explain most capaciously in *The Federalist Papers*, the intention underlying the U.S. Constitution is the establishment of a new and radically un-classical, un-Periclean type of democratic republic. This republican innovation was rooted in the profound
renovation of monarchy that had brought about the English constitution
analyzed and celebrated as the paradigm of human liberty by Locke and
Montesquieu.

In the new republican theory, political life is no longer understood
in classical terms as the expression of humanity's "natural inclination" to
find fulfillment through participation in ruling – guided by, and dedicated
to, communally instilled and policed civic virtues. Instead, civil society is
understood to be essentially nothing more than the set of artificial con-
tractual arrangements, by which independent individuals seek to overcome their natural state, of chaotic, mutually destructive competition. In
this new perspective, "liberty" means chiefly, *not* participation in rule,
but rather security from interference by others. Liberty means chiefly the
security that allows each individual to pursue private interests – above
all, the accumulation of private property, or ever increasing economic
well-being.

The new democratic experiment is based on an abandonment of what
Madison calls "pure democracy, by which I mean" (Madison explains in
the Tenth Federalist) "a society consisting of a small number of citizens,

who assemble and administer the government in person." What is substituted, is what Madison calls the "extended" and "diversified" society, animated by numerous competing "factions," with "a government in which the scheme of representation takes place." "The true distinction," Madison explains in the Sixty-Third Federalist, "between" the classical republics "and the new American governments, lies *in the total exclusion of the people, in their collective capacity,* from any share in" direct participation in ruling. Elections maintain the citizenry's watchful and partisan ultimate control: but, the people's involvement in ruling is (in Madison's term) "filtered," through a tiny minority of select representatives (Hamilton, Jay, and Madison, 2001: 42–49, 329).

The implications for the foreign policy of this new kind of "liberal" republic (as John Adams christened it) are momentous. The vast populace, engrossed in and divided by the competitive acquisition of private economic power and comfort, is expected to be drawn away from the risky and costly collective political ambition that expresses itself in glorious foreign or imperial projects. In other words, the "Athenian vector" is to be controlled, not so much by a higher principle, as by a lower rival ambition, a privatized economic ambition. The citizenry's preoccupation with commerce is expected to promote a foreign enterprise that is vigorous, yet, much less warlike, much less aggressively imperialist. This results from not only the imperatives of peaceful economic interdependence brought by global trade and finance. As is stressed by Montesquieu, the more profound intended effect is a spiritual transformation, toward a secular humanism that softens – and, by the same token, corrupts, the older religious moralisms. As Montesquieu puts it in the key relevant passage in *L'esprit des lois* (20.2)

> Commerce cures destructive prejudices; and it is almost a general rule that wherever there are soft morals [*moeurs douces*] there is commerce; and that wherever there is commerce, there are soft morals.... One can say that the laws of commerce perfect the morals, for the same reason that these same laws destroy the morals. Commerce corrupts pure morals: that was why Plato complained of it; commerce polishes and softens barbarian morals, as we are seeing every day.

Somewhat later, Montesquieu writes (25.12):

> A more sure way to attack religion is by favor, by the commodities of life, by the hope of wealth; not by what reminds one of it, but by what makes one forget it; not by what brings indignation, but by what makes men lukewarm, when the other passions act on our souls, and those which religion inspires fall silent.

The frightful religious wars that had convulsed post-Reformation Europe made the founders of the new republicanism deeply wary of politics and political theorizing that looked for guidance to supra-rational revelation. As a result, the traditional Christian teaching on the "law of nations," which sought to constitute an international policing community of nations, was put into eclipse. The Christian doctrine was seen as introducing into international affairs self-righteously high, and conflicting, standards and claims, that legitimized, and thus promoted, mutual interference culminating in fierce punitive wars. All of this contradicted the mutual tolerance and the frank acknowledgment of competitive national economic interest that was now seen as the firmest basis for peace, achieved through maintaining a respectful balance of powers among nations.

Yet, ironically, the new liberal, commercial republicanism was deeply tinctured from the outset with its own crusading, and sometimes even benevolently imperial, spirit. For gleaming out from the new pragmatic liberal-republican idea was the promise or hope of an ever more universal "enlightenment," leading to an ever expanding global realm of liberal peace and prosperity. The collective national security interests of the liberal great powers dictated serious efforts to promote this expansion. But something nobler than collective national security was involved. From the beginning, the new liberal republicanism was also to some extent inspired with a humanitarian, moral internationalism.

John Locke, in the treatise in which he set forth the new principles in their classic formulation, left it at calling for revolutions and internal wars of national liberation – in the Turkish empire in particular (*Second Treatise of Government*, secs. 176, 192–96, 221–32). Some among the American Founders went further. Benjamin Franklin, America's first great diplomat, in proposing terms of reconciliation to the British on the eve of the American Revolution, insisted (to an astonished William Pitt) that the terms must include a change of regime in French Canada, replacing traditional French laws with liberal English laws and institutions. He explained the reason in the following words: "loving Liberty ourselves, we wish'd it to be extended among Mankind, and to have no Foundation for future Slavery laid in America."[6] Going a significant step yet further, Thomas Paine, the American Revolution's leading "ideologist," attacked Edmund Burke's Christian strictures against the French Revolution, and its export

---

[6] Franklin, 1959–: 21.560; see also 21.499 ("Canada: We cannot endure Despotism over any of our Fellow Subjects. We must all be free or none."); and 21.367, 382, 522, as well as James Bowdoin's Letter to Franklin of Sept. 6, 1774 (ibid.: 21.283).

of democracy, as revealing Burke's deep misunderstanding of the planetary moral implications of the American Revolution. What the American Revolution means internationally, Paine writes, is that:

> Government founded on a moral theory, on a system of universal peace, on the indefeasible hereditary Rights of Man, is now revolving from west to east by a stronger impulse than the government of the sword revolved from east to west. It interests not particular individuals, but nations in its progress, and promises a new era to the human race.[7]

The great puzzle and challenge that emerged was this: how can the liberal republican great powers – and in the nineteenth century this meant above all England and the United States – effectively export or promote their regimes abroad, for the sake of spreading peacefully independent self-government, without becoming paternalistically imperial, thus defeating the purpose, and perhaps even corrupting themselves in the process?

The most serious English response is articulated by John Stuart Mill, in his essay "A Few Words on Non-Intervention" (1965–81 [orig. publ. 1859]: 21.111–24, esp. 118–24). On the one hand, Mill strongly defends the right, and indeed the duty, of liberal great powers to conquer what he calls "barbarous" peoples. Such empire is intended, in his words, to "so break their spirit, that they gradually sink into a state of dependence" – and thus enter on the path from what Mill calls a "very low" to a "high grade of social improvement." The examples he applauds are British India and French Algeria.

But, on the other hand, Mill argues that where and when any subject people has reached the level of liberal political competence at which it initiates a serious democratic revolution against its rulers, then, he writes, "as a general rule" it "can seldom" be "either judicious or right" to "assist, otherwise than by the moral support" of "opinion." Mill gives two reasons for this policy of non-intervention. First, if a people, he says, "have not sufficient love of liberty to be able to wrest it from merely domestic oppressors, the liberty which is bestowed on them by other hands than their own, will have nothing real, nothing permanent." For "the only test" of "a people's having become fit for popular institutions," is that they "are willing to brave labour and danger for their liberation." Second, he

---

[7] *The Rights of Man*, Part Two, Introduction. See similarly Franklin's comments in his letter to the Committee of Secret Correspondence, 12 March 1777 (1959–: 23.473) and to Samuel Cooper, 1 May 1777 (ibid.: 24:6–7).

writes, "when a people has had the misfortune to be ruled by a government under which the feelings and the virtues needful for maintaining freedom could not develop themselves, it is during an arduous struggle to become free by their own efforts that these feelings and virtues have the best chance of springing up."

Mill hastens to add, however, that where a liberal great power finds itself fighting a war of self-defense against illiberal regimes, then it has a right and duty to ally itself with liberal revolutionaries in those regimes, and, what is more, has every right to make regime change or successful revolution a condition of the victorious peace. In addition, Mill argues that "in the case of a people struggling against a foreign yoke," intervention by liberal powers to help fight against the nonliberal foreign intruder is, in Mill's words, "always rightful, is always moral, if not always prudent." Mill closes his essay with a passionate call for England, or some other great liberal power, to make itself the head of what he calls a "heroic" armed coalition ready to fight any foreign intervention in any democratic revolution, thus ensuring what Mill calls "the almost immediate emancipation of every people which desires liberty sufficiently to be capable of maintaining it."

The more moderate keynote of the most thoughtful American response to the puzzle was struck by Alexander Hamilton, when he published his "Pacificus Papers" arguing against what he regarded as Thomas Jefferson's unwise advocacy of support for the French Revolution and its forceful export of democracy. Hamilton articulated what he thought was the proper American position as follows (1961–87:15.60):

> When a Nation has actually come to a resolution to throw off a yoke, under which it may have groaned, and to assert its liberties – [then] it is justifiable and meritorious in another nation to afford assistance to the one which has been oppressed & is *in the act* of liberating itself; but it is not warrantable for any Nation *beforehand* to hold out a general invitation to insurrection and revolution.

In the same spirit is Abraham Lincoln's response to the arrival in America of Lajos Kossuth, pleading for American help against the intervention of Russia in support of Austria's suppression of the Hungarian revolution of 1848. Lincoln (1953–55: 2.115–16) wrote and sponsored a set of resolutions that, although expressing deep moral admiration for Kossuth and his cause, nevertheless declared that, in accordance with what Lincoln called "our own cherished American principles of non-intervention," it "is the duty of our government to neither foment, nor assist, such revolutions" – even though (Lincoln added) "the sympathies of this country, and the benefits of its position, should be exerted in favor of the people of every nation struggling to be free."

THE MODERN DOUBTS, AND THE CHALLENGE FROM THE RADICAL LEFT

The whole picture is darkened and complicated, however, by the grave doubts that were raised, from early on, about the key premise of liberal internationalism – the premise that asserts the pacific tendency of commercial republicanism. Alexander Hamilton, who was unrivaled in the intelligent practical competence with which he promoted modern commerce and finance, nevertheless rejected with vigor this thesis that, as he put it in *The Federalist* "the genius of republics is pacific," because "the spirit of commerce has a tendency to soften the manners of men." "Is not," Hamilton counters (2001: 23),

> the love of wealth as domineering and enterprising a passion as that of power or glory? Have there not been as many wars founded upon commercial motives, since that has become the prevailing system of nations, as were before occasioned by the cupidity of territory or dominion? Has not the spirit of commerce, in many instances, administered new incentives to the appetite both for the one and for the other?

Much deeper and broader reservations along these lines had previously been introduced by Rousseau. Rousseau re-invoked the classical, participatory, pure democracy as a standard by which to judge, and to condemn, the emerging liberal republics. He decried the heartlessness and deep self-alienation that he was sure were the inevitable social and psychological consequences of the new liberal-commercial individualism. He contended that this spiritual deformation, working in tandem with the new normative theory of supreme national sovereignty, would have rendered international morals ever more ruthlessly inhumane. He predicted that this international commercial inhumanity would be armed with ever more horrific weaponry – funded by commercially acquired wealth, and made possible by the new philosophy's unleashing of scientific technology. Rousseau went so far as to contend that the modern commercial states were not less, but far more, prone to wage totally devastating war than were the ancient participatory republics.[8]

---

[8] *Social Contract*, 1.4; *Discourse on the Origins of Inequality*, in 1959–95: 3.178–79; *Project of a Constitution for Corsica, in ibid.*: 3.903; *Emile*, in ibid.: 4.848; *Considerations on the Government*

Rousseau's thought, transmogrified, inspired the radicals among the French Revolutionaries, who, led by Robespierre (1967: 10.226–37, 350–67), proclaimed the birth of an alternative, non-liberal democracy: a democracy of "fraternity," animated by "virtue" enforced through a deliberate policy of "terror." Compared to the earlier, liberal, and far less moralistic type of modern republic, this new form was much more aggressively dedicated to the transformation of the world in its own image. Here a moralistic version of the "Athenian vector" was unleashed. To what extent did this Jacobin democratic aspiration exemplify a spirit still akin to the American – ruder, no doubt, but perhaps to a significant degree also more "progressive?" To what extent were the Terror, the aggressive export of democracy,[9] and the eventual plebiscitary Napoleonic imperialism, unfortunate deviations from and betrayals of the Revolution's original, essentially still liberal, if more communal, democratic principles; and, to what extent were Robespierre and Napoleon – for the better, ultimately (as Hegel, Marx, and Nietzsche thought) or for the worse (as Hamilton and Tocqueville thought) – revelatory of something trans-liberal that is deeply embedded in the modern democratic movement? These questions lay at the heart of the debate in America in the 1790s between the Jeffersonian partisans and the Federalist condemners of the Revolution and its export of democracy.[10] And, one may doubt whether these questions are susceptible to definitive or unambiguous answers, in part

of Poland, in ibid.: 3.1013–14; "Extract from the Project of Perpetual Peace of the Abbé de Saint Pierre," in ibid.: 3.564, 568–74, 582, 584, 587–88; "Judgment on the Project of Perpetual Peace," in ibid.: 3.593–95; see also "That the State of War is Born from the Social State" (unpublished fragment, usually known as "The State of War"), in ibid.: 3.601–12; "Fragments on War" (unpublished), no. 3, in ibid.: 3.614; "War and State of War" (unpublished fragment), in ibid.: 3.1899–1904. Montesquieu, we may note, had already expressed grave worries about the tendency to arms races emerging among commercially powerful European nations: *Esprit des lois*, 13.17.

[9] See the French Convention's Decrees of Nov. 15 and 19, 1792, declaring military assistance to every people who wish to recover their liberty, and declaring that the French nation will treat as "enemies" any "people, who refusing or renouncing liberty and equality are desirous of preserving their Prince and privileged casts – or of entering into an accommodation with them," as quoted and discussed in Alexander Hamilton's second "Pacificus" paper (1961–87: 15.59–61).

[10] For a penetrating presentation of the issues, see Alexander Hamilton's two "Americanus" papers (1794), especially the beginning of the first, and the first two of his "Camillus" Essays (July 1795), as well as his second "Pacificus" paper (July 1793) – 1961–87: 15.55–63, 669–78; 16.12–19; 18.479–89, 493–501. Contrast Jefferson's letter to William Short of Jan. 3, 1793 (1984: 1003–6), speaking of the early stages of the Jacobin rule: "In the struggle which was necessary, many guilty persons fell without the forms of trial, and with them some innocent. These I deplore as much as anybody. . . . My own affections have been deeply wounded by some of the martyrs to this cause, but rather than it should have failed, I would have seen half the earth desolated. Were there but an Adam and an Eve left in every country, and left free, it would be better than as it is now."

because of the tension-ridden complexity of the evolving French Revolution and its principles or moral meaning, as conceived by the diverse array of its instigators and friends on the one side and its enemies on the other. Beginning with the French Revolution, and extending into the socialist-internationalist and Marxist eras, the core meaning of "modern democracy" – and perforce the meaning of its "export" – becomes profoundly contestable, between the liberal and the "fraternal" or "communal" versions. And, of course, this did not end with the French Revolution. Extending into the Marxist era, the core meaning of "modern democracy" – and perforce the meaning of its "export" – becomes profoundly contestable, between the liberal and the communal versions.

THE KANTIAN COSMOPOLITAN RESPONSE

It is in Immanuel Kant's political thought that we find the most influential attempt to resolve this contest, by forging a principled synthesis. Kant was committed to liberal republicanism or constitutionalism. But, Kant, a strong partisan of the French Revolution, was at the same time thoroughly penetrated by Rousseau's critique of previous liberalism. Kant set out to re-found liberal republicanism, and its internationalism.

Kant gave a sublime moral re-interpretation to the liberal ideas of permissive, and even amoral, but lawful, individual liberty and equality. Individual liberty and equality find their true meaning and justification as the pre-condition for the human dignity that consists entirely in rational moral self-legislation.

To be genuinely autonomous, this self-legislation must be freed from external coercion. Paradoxically, the liberal state truly accords with morality, precisely because the liberal state avoids, as much as possible, all legislation of morality. Paradoxically, it is out of the deepest respect for morality, as self-legislation, that the liberal state ought meticulously to limit its coercive, lawful policies to what is needed to promote the permissive external liberty, security, and prosperity of citizens. The heart of genuine moral progress must take place in the spontaneous realm of society and culture, which is generated and protected, but only minimally regulated, by the liberal state.

But, this moral progress requires that the inhabitants of liberal republics assume a cosmopolitan sense of responsibility, for to be genuinely moral, self-legislation must conceive of itself in universalistic terms. One's own moral maxims must respect the equal dignity of all other humans – regarded as co-legislators, constituting all humanity as what Kant calls a "kingdom of ends." But, this means that the cosmopolitan goal must be to include more and more of humanity in the actual moral and political liberation that is brought about only by liberal republican regimes and laws.

Thus, a foreign policy aimed ultimately at the spread, throughout the world, of liberal republicanism takes on unprecedented moral importance. Here, the Athenian vector finds it most moral expression. Yet, Kant's advocacy of this spread of liberal republicanism is complex.

Kant insists that to correctly understand the moral character of international relations, we need to begin from a wholly disillusioned recognition of what Rousseau has correctly diagnosed. As Rousseau taught, a worse-than-Hobbesian state of war naturally prevails among sovereign nations. In their mutually threatening sovereign independence, nations are driven into a worse version of the condition individuals are naturally driven into prior to their contracting to establish a lawful state governing their external relations. But, it turns out that Kant analyzes, in lurid detail, the ruthless lawlessness of this "natural state" among nations only to lay the foundation for its dialectical overcoming. For, once the ghastly character of the international "state of nature" is clear-sightedly grasped, sheer prudent concern for national security, reinforcing any decent statesman's underlying moral concern for human brotherhood, dictates, in modern conditions of frightful military power, the absolute need to begin to overcome the natural condition. Pragmatic as well as moral reason dictates moving toward some kind of social contract among the sovereign nations, aiming at a unified international power that wields international law with teeth in it.

Now, once this normative conclusion is drawn by prudent nations and their leaders, the whole international situation metamorphoses morally. Whereas in the international sphere as a state of nature, no party has a right to judge another, and no war is unjust (or, equivalently, every war is just); this is no longer the case when the more prudent, liberal nations have set out to forge what Kant calls a "league of nations." Once this progressive movement is underway, Kant teaches (1902: 6.349), any nation's "publicly expressed will (whether by words or deeds)" which is judged to "disclose a maxim" – "such as the violation of public treaties" – that stands in the way of this movement, constitutes that nation as an "unjust enemy" of world society. Then, the progressive states have a right, and a duty, to unite against such an enemy, and, if necessary, to change its regime by force to a more liberal regime. For, it is only a liberal republican regime that is reliably likely to recognize all these truths and to act upon them. Representative government that is responsible to a populace, whose prevailing concerns are personal liberty, security, and material prosperity, is government that is much less able to draw that populace into costly and dangerous warfare. Kant thus continues, like his earlier liberal predecessors, to count heavily on the pacifying effects of commercial republicanism. But, unlike his predecessors, Kant does so because he trusts, not simply commercialism by itself, but commercialism, in republics, set on the track toward international lawful organization through moral as well as pragmatic leadership.

So Kant contends that the envisaged "League of Nations" ought to have as the first of its "definitive articles" the following: "the civil constitution of every state shall be republican" – which means, Kant explains, a popular representative government under a fixed constitutional law with separation of powers. The "League of Nations" that Kant envisages is thus closer to today's NATO than to today's United Nations. Yet, Kant also insists that the League, or its "preliminary articles for perpetual peace," must rule out "interference by force in the constitution or government of another state" – so long, that is, as that state does not become an "unjust enemy" of world society. The principal reason Kant gives, is that armed intervention risks bringing back, through civil war, the anarchic state of nature with its horrific inhumanity.[11]

Kant provides the most powerful theoretical foundation for efforts at liberal world organization to enforce international law guided by and aiming to spread liberal-republican norms. The great question is, whether the hopes Kant inspired – for some sort of genuine liberal-republican world government – do not unwisely distract the liberal statesman's vision from the more realistic, because of the more modest projects of Kant's less moralistic and less hopeful liberal predecessors, with their quest for a more tolerant balance of sovereign powers. But, on the other hand, the great question for that earlier, less hopeful and less moralistic liberal thinking, is whether it can make sufficient room for what the American statesman Henry Clay, speaking of America's responsibility for encouraging liberal republicanism in Latin America, called "the magnanimity of a great and a generous people" (1961:2.524).

---

[11] "Perpetual Peace," in 1902: 8.343–47, 349–51, 354–56, 376n, and above all 368, 381, 386; *Metaphysical Principles of Right*, in ibid.: 6.344, 350–51, 354–55; "Universal History with Cosmopolitan Intent," Seventh and Eighth Theses; "Theory and Practice," in ibid.: 8.310–13; "An Old Question Renewed," in ibid.: 7.85–86, 91–92.

CONCLUSION

I have now laid out key relevant dimensions of the most important stages in the genealogy of our moral thinking about the export of democracy. By clarifying this complex moral ground in which we are historically rooted, we can better understand the manifold considerations involved in our passing judgment on the various kinds of liberal foreign policy that attempt to export democracy; at the same time, we can grasp with greater precision and depth of awareness why it is that our judgments are bound to remain divided by principled controversy – as well as perplexed by practical conundrums.

Let me close by suggesting some conclusions that seem to me to emerge from my attempt at a revivification of the tension-ridden moral tradition that unites and shapes us.

The soul of liberal republicanism has from its inception, in varying degrees, been animated by a dedication to the liberation of all humanity through the spread or export of liberal republicanism. I suspect that liberal republicanism cannot forswear this mission without losing its soul, its heart. But, precisely by recognizing this, we must recognize the dangers that lurk here. A liberal-democratic policy of seeking to spread democracies can all too easily become incoherent in practice: it can quickly come into conflict with a liberal respect for the self-determination of other nations – and with a liberal tolerance for the diversity of civic cultures.

Seeking to export democracy through military force runs this moral risk to a very high degree. Our tradition suggests that there is rarely, if ever, a case where war can be justified solely for the sake of spreading liberal republicanism. On the other hand, such coercive imposition would seem to be justified where, as in Japan after World War II, or as in the NATO intervention in Kosovo, it is the culmination of a last-resort remedying of some specific grave threat, or some specific atrocity – in a case where the disposing of that specific threat or atrocity is diagnosed as requiring the transformation of a particular nonliberal regime that is the cause.

Here, I submit, is the basis for the moral argument defending the rightness of the invasions aimed partly at bringing some version of liberal republicanism to Afghanistan and Iraq: these efforts at regime change can be morally justified as the necessary completion of the fight required to remove two specific nonliberal regimes that had proven themselves intolerably dangerous enemies of peace, as well as of basic human dignity, in their region and in the world.

But, here, there is also, arising out of our tradition, a strong counter-argument, based on a different evaluation of the evidence. The counter-argument contends, first, that the danger was not yet intolerable; and, second, that the foreseeable human suffering that would be caused by the military effort outweighed, as a cost, the likely human benefits. Our tradition thus provides grounds for a real contesting: in other words, this is a case where the moral status of the effort is truly debatable by people of good will on both sides. The debate is not so much over the character of the moral principles to be applied as it is over the interpretation of the evidence to which the application is being made – much of which is murky.

The debate over Iraq takes on another dimension, when one asks – perhaps prompted by Jurgen Habermas's reflections in his *Divided West* (2006) – whether a very great cost of the Iraq War was not the split within NATO: seen in world-historical terms, this is unquestionably a setback for the Kantian project of an ever-expanding league of liberal republican nations. I would suggest that there is more common moral ground than is being emphasized, by theorists like Habermas – and that there is, therefore, a greater basis and hope for repairing the split than may have at first appeared. Certainly, people of influence on both sides of the debate over the propriety of the War in Iraq share deeply in the awareness of, and the lament over, the long-term danger posed by this split in NATO.

But, of course, the two sides differ sharply over who, or what motivations, ought most to be blamed for this very regrettable split. On the one hand, influential voices among the Americans and the British, who went forward as a couple, conceiving themselves as vindicating international law and enforcing the resolve of the United Nations, tend to put the blame more on continental Europe, and especially France – for failing to live up to the moral resoluteness and comradeship in arms that NATO ought to embody. On the other hand, continental Europeans, who hung back, conceiving of themselves as upholding appropriate moderation, caution, and peacefulness, without cowardice, condemn the Americans, especially, for a hubristically unilateral moralism, leading to arrogance. Both sides, I submit, must strive harder to appreciate the possibly partial truth in the opposing point of view, and to recognize the likelihood of some degree of error in their own indignant outlook.

But, looking beyond the agonizing and bewildering contemporary case of Iraq, our tradition suggests the general proposition that, in the absence of a specific intolerable threat or atrocity, the project of promoting the spread of liberal democracy ought to be limited to much less aggressive, and largely non-belligerent tactics – and that these tactics ought to be considered as falling in a range of increasingly problematic intensity or intrusiveness.

The least aggressive, and hence least problematic, tactics are what we may call the "ideological" – including inter-governmental dialogue, exhortation, propaganda, cultural exchange, and educational efforts of all kinds directed at both subjects and rulers in nonliberal regimes. These are the sorts of tactics that the West has been employing most notably with China. Such efforts, on the part of liberal republican governments, would seem to be almost always legitimate, and indeed obligatory – as an expression of the highest defining goals of liberal republicanism and its self-expression and self-affirmation.

Requiring greater moral caution, with a view both to the dangers of destabilization, and to the respect that is due to nonliberal regimes that are relatively unwarlike and unoppressive, are attempts at exerting the pressure of peaceful, but costly, sanctions of all sorts – aimed at altering, gradually and peacefully, the behavior and even the character of specific nonliberal regimes. The most successful recent case is, of course, South Africa.

Demanding still greater moral circumspection are more intrusive policies, such as material and educational support for indigenous nongovernmental or semi-governmental democratic organizations and movements within nonliberal nations. These more intrusive tactics have been employed with some success in places like the Ukraine, Georgia, and other parts of the former Soviet Union, including Russia itself. The delicacy of this more intrusive agitation has rightly called forth the creation of a new breed of non-governmental organizations, which exploit the independent initiative characteristic of liberal civil society, and bring private citizen-groups together in coalitions and agencies that press for reform without introducing the heavy or threatening hand of liberal governments.

Finally, on rare occasions, liberal governments would seem to have both a right and a duty to provide even armed assistance to revolutionaries engaged in a civil war of national liberation – where such aid supplements and enhances, rather than supplants or dominates, native initiative and leadership, and where the revolutionary struggle has a likelihood of success, without the prospect of too high a cost in human suffering.

I conclude by stressing again that my closing reflections are meant to be suggestive rather than conclusive, and are aimed at provoking further reflection and discussion. My most serious goal has been to revive our

awareness of the dialectical philosophic tradition that can provide the theoretical basis for our case-by-case debate over how we ought to meet the
diverse particular challenges to our shared vocation of seeking prudently
to spread and defend our liberal democratic freedom. It is our philosophic
tradition, I want to stress in closing, that gives us our shared moral foundation; and the retrieval of this foundation may contribute substantially
to giving us, on both sides of the Atlantic, the common basis upon which
we can heal our present sad and dangerous – but, I believe and hope, not
lasting – spiritual division.

STRUCTURAL PRECONDITIONS

2 Re-Integrating the Study of Civil Society and the State

Today civil society is a hot topic both inside the academy and out. In the decades after the Second World War, scholars focused primarily on economic development, institutional arrangements, and long-term trajectories of historical change when trying to explain whether or not democracy existed in particular countries. But, beginning in the 1990s, those interested in the study and promotion of democracy rediscovered[1] the importance of civil society. Although one can find almost as many definitions of civil society as there are discussions of it, the term commonly refers to all voluntary associations that exist below the level of the state, but above the family.[2] As one well known treatment put it, "civil society is the realm of organizational life that is open, voluntary, self-generating, at least partially self-supporting, autonomous from the state, and bound by a legal order or set of shared rules" (Diamond 1999: 221). Civil society, in other words, encompasses a wide range of informal and formal societal relationships, networks, and interactions, including everything from bowling clubs to church groups, reading circles to NGOs (Bermeo 2000; Encarción 2003: 24; Foley, Edwards, and Diani 2001).[3]

---

[1] I say "rediscovered" because, as with almost all trends in political science, this one also returned to many of the insights and arguments of an earlier generation of scholars. See, for example, Kornhauser 1959; Arendt 1973; Neumann 1942; Mannheim 1980; Fromm 1941; Shils 1963; Walter 1964.

[2] This definition is, therefore, politically neutral: it says nothing about whether or not these associations have particularly laudable goals because this would make connecting them to successful democracy somewhat tautological. This is important to note as some have indeed tried to narrow this definition by excluding organizations and associations with explicitly antidemocratic or antiliberal views. In addition to making arguments about the benign effects of civil society tautological, this definition injects a great deal of subjective judgment into what is ostensibly an objectively defined phenomenon.

[3] My definition, therefore, differs somewhat from the one employed by Seligman in this volume.

This renewed interest in civil society was prompted by both scholarly trends and real world events. In the former category, the publication of several path-breaking works on civil society, particularly Robert Putnam's *Making Democracy Work* (1993), excited a social scientific community constantly on the lookout for new variables and paradigms. Meanwhile, the prominence of civic activism and organizations in the end game of communism combined with the contemporary importance of neo-liberal and communitarian thinking, increased civil society's attractiveness to policy-makers and activists across the globe (Carothers 1999; Ottoway and Carothers 2000).

For its promoters in particular, civil society was held up as both an indicator and a prerequisite for a healthy democracy, polity, and society. "Civil society was seen as the opposite of despotism" (Hall 1995: 1) and as embodying "for many an ethical ideal of the social order" (Seligman 1992, also Seligman in this volume). Civil society activity is said to produce the "habits of the heart necessary for stable and effective democratic institutions" (Bellah et al. 1985; Putnam 1993, 11). It is supposed to moderate attitudes, promote social interaction, facilitate trust, and increase solidarity and public spiritedness. Participation in civil society allegedly teaches citizens to be engaged and broad-minded, while at the same time training the activists and leaders what a democracy requires and laying the grounds for successful economic and social development (Diamond 1994; Edwards, Foley, and Diani 2001; Newton 2001; Seligman and Chirot in this volume). By the end of the 1990s, scholars had produced a wide-ranging literature that connected civil society to outcomes as diverse as the collapse of the Soviet Union, the nature of American democracy, and ethnic conflict (Fukuyama 1995; Harrison and Huntington, 2000; Putnam 1993, 1995; Varshney 2001, 2003) and the democracy promotion community was pouring money into all sorts of civil society programs (Hawthorne 2004; Hearn 2000; Ottaway and Carothers 2000; World Bank 2000).

Although the literature and practical programs produced by the rediscovery of civil society has been both incredibly rich and extremely useful, as with all trends, its claims and impact turned out to be somewhat overblown. Particularly problematic is a tendency to focus on civil society in isolation from the state and the broader institutional context within which it is embedded. This tendency has contributed to an overly optimistic picture of civil society and a misunderstanding of the role it can play in promoting progressive or beneficial social and political conditions. This paper will show how, under certain conditions, rather than promoting democracy and social harmony, civil society can play a key role in the rise of extremist and anti-democratic political movements and facilitate social conflict and even violence. In particular, it will argue that where states and political institutions are weak and/or lacking in legitimacy, civil society activity and organizations alone are unlikely to promote or protect democracy and, indeed, may often end up exacerbating political and social conflict. To illustrate such dynamics this paper will focus on a few particularly revealing and well-documented cases: the collapse of democracy in Germany and Italy during the interwar years, and the emergence of radical Islamism in parts of the contemporary Arab world. Although occurring at very different times and in very different contexts, these cases all demonstrate the importance of re-integrating analyses of civil society and the state. Only by so doing will we be able to understand, and, therefore, potentially be able to influence the fate of political regimes.

THE GERMAN AND ITALIAN CASES

The German Case

The German case is particularly intriguing for students of democracy and civil society because of the strength of the latter and the spectacular implosion of the former. By the late nineteenth century, German associational life had become so active that many contemporary observers spoke of the *Vereinsmeierei* (roughly translatable as "associational fetishism" or "mania") that beset German society. In fact, so pronounced was this trend that some joked that whenever three or more Germans gathered, they were likely to draw up by-laws and found an association (Nipperdey 1976; Sheehan 1995). Yet, despite the flourishing of civil society, Germany did not make a transition to democracy before the collapse of the old regime at the end of the First World War and its first attempt at democracy lasted only 15 years. Furthermore, during its 15 years of existence, the Weimar Republic was beset by societal conflict, which eventually spiraled into open violence and the coming to power of a totalitarian movement. Why didn't civil society have the beneficial effects civil society promoters predict? Why didn't Germany's vibrant and diverse associational life promote (or at least not destabilize) democracy and social harmony? The key lies in the relationship that existed between civil society, the state, and political institutions in the late nineteenth and early twentieth century Germany.

Beginning in the late 1800s, Germany experienced a large spurt of associational activity. In addition to the relative openness of the new

Reich's political system, this trend was spurred by the discontent and unease caused by rapid socioeconomic changes occurring during this time. Alongside the formation of a unified state, the country was experiencing an economic transformation – old businesses, hierarchies, and communities were being broken down by the relentless forward march of capitalism and individuals were being forced to confront a world where many old certainties and structures were crumbling. Concerned and confused by the changes occurring around them, many German citizens sought refuge in newly formed civil society organizations that promised to provide them with a new sense of community and efficacy (Blackbourn 1984; Wehler 1974; Winkler 1972). At the same time that all these changes were occurring, the political system of the Reich served to widen rather than bridge the cleavages that existed between German citizens. Its first long-standing Chancellor, Otto von Bismarck, deemed certain groups, particularly workers and Catholics, "enemies of the Reich." Through the *Kulturkampf* and the anti-Socialist laws, Bismarck isolated Catholics and workers respectively, increasing their distrust of the system and other groups' distrust of them. Furthermore, although the new Reich had universal suffrage, it was not a parliamentary system and the role played by political parties was, therefore, limited and warped in important ways. In particular, because parties could not directly form governments, incentives for permanent cooperation and compromise were diminished and the Reich's most popular and important party – the Social Democratic party (SPD) – was blocked from exerting power commensurate with its support, alienating it and its supporters further from the political order and increasing their suspicion of other political and social groups. Liberal parties, meanwhile, remained informal collections of notables with little in the way of grass-roots organizations and this hindered their ability to connect with their natural middle-class constituencies, leading many in these groups to look for alternative ways to become involved in the life of their country. Many of these individuals found civil society organizations much more congenial and effective vehicles for the expression of their concerns and demands (Eley 1994; Koshar 1986). A particularly important manifestation of this trend was the growth of nationalist organizations, which, as Geoff Eley has argued, are best viewed as "symptoms and agencies of change." They were formed as distinctive organizations within a space that the difficulties and obsolescence of an older mode of dominant-class politics had "opened up" (Eley 1994: xix). These nationalist associations developed relatively broad-based appeals, were fairly "democratically" organized, stressed equality and community, and opened up new channels for participation in public life.

Thus, by the turn of the twentieth century, one could already see a distinct and troubling pattern emerging in Germany: the growth of civil society during periods of strain and in response to the failure of mainstream political institutions. In particular, as national political institutions proved unable and unwilling to address citizens' needs, many turned their energies and attention away from them and towards civil society groups instead. Under such circumstances, associational and civil society activity served not to integrate citizens into the larger national polity or bridge differences among them, but rather divided citizens further, and often helped mobilize groups against each other.

This pattern continued and indeed became even pronounced after the First World War. The full democratization of Germany in 1918 opened up a new phase in the country's associational life; one of feverish activity on all fronts. As during the Wilhelmine era, however, Weimar's rise in associationalism did not indicate an increase in social cohesion, consensus, or stability, but rather the reverse. Particularly worrisome was what was going on among the middle classes. The country's liberal parties proved unable to adjust to the hurly-burly of democratic politics and, as a result, the middle classes grew increasingly alienated from politics. This trend was furthered by the Great Inflation of the early 1920s and other economic problems the Weimar Republic faced. "By the end of the 1920s the economic position of the independent middle class had deteriorated to such an extent that it was no longer possible to distinguish it from the proletariat on the basis of income as a criterion" (Jones 1972: 25). Economic hardship made the middle classes increasingly resentful of those groups – especially workers – that they felt were benefiting disproportionately from the system and that had their own designated political champions (i.e. the SPD and the Communists). This led middle class groups to be even more frustrated with the seeming inefficiency of their "own" liberal and conservative parties, and as a result support continued to drain from them. As mainstream liberal and conservative parties lost support, in turn, splinter parties arose to attract particular parts of their constituencies. By 1928, these splinter parties (appealing, for example, to agrarians, Bavarians, and other specific groups) were collectively outpolling their more established forebears.

Middle class Germans were not simply leaving traditional liberal and conservative parties in response to their frustration with the Weimar Republic's trajectory; they were turning to the civil society sphere.

During the 1920s, middle class Germans threw themselves into their sports clubs, community groups, and patriotic associations, searching for the sense of purpose and efficacy that both political parties and national politics seemed unable to provide. This civil society activity, in turn, served to draw citizens even further away from their fellows and traditional political activity and thus only compounded the Weimar Republic's problems. By siphoning off much of the German public's best intentions and energy into civil society groups that tended to reinforce rather than bridge social and political cleavages, civil society helped further undermine Weimar's already fragile social and political contract. As one analyst put it: "Spurred by growing political tensions, social organizations helped to lead an unprecedented surge of apoliticism that escaped the control of bourgeois elites. . . . [M]any spokesman for Weimar apoliticism argued that social organizations would do more than cushion political strife – they would bind together a moralistic, antisocialist, 'folk community' of disparate classes and strata. . . . [T]he middle and late 1920s . . . thus saw not only an acceleration of tensions that had originated in the Empire but also an unprecedented rupture between the social and the political authority of the local bourgeoisie" (Koshar 1986: 166).

By the end of the 1920s, a vacuum had opened up in German politics, and when the Great Depression hit, the country found itself in a very precarious political situation. Its citizens, particularly its middle classes, were politically frustrated and dissatisfied. Its mainstream liberal and conservative parties were disintegrating. And, its civil society was highly developed, yet, largely segmented and, to a large degree, alienated from mainstream political life. This situation turned out to be tailor made for a disciplined, politically savvy, extremist movement to exploit.

Indeed, during the late 1920s and early 1930s, the Nazis worked hard to infiltrate and exploit the rich associational life developed by the Weimar Republic's middle classes. It was precisely the dense networks of civil society organizations that had developed over previous years that provided the Nazis with cadres of activists who had the skills necessary to spread the party's message and increase recruitment. Indeed, these bourgeois "joiners" and the organization they were tied to were a critical component of the NSDAP's success. In the words of historian Peter Fritzsche, "path breaking work in recent years on the rise of National Socialism has stressed the importance of local newspapers, municipal notables, and voluntary associations, and points to the buoyancy and vigor of civic traditions. Had bourgeois community life been overly disorganized and fragmented, the body of new evidence indicates, the Nazis would never have been able to marshal the resources or plug into the social networks necessary to their political success" (Fritzsche 1990: 13).

The Nazis recognized that the skills of the joiners and the connections and resources of civil society associations could be put to evil purposes as well as good ones. Accordingly, they made particular efforts to recruit people who had a wide range of associational memberships and used these activists' connections and their organizational abilities to advance the party's cause. It is not an exaggeration to say that civil society organizations served as a sort of "fifth column," allowing the Nazis to infiltrate and master significant sectors of German life before emerging to capture the country's national political structures.

In short, civil society in Germany was not able to overcome the social and political cleavages and conflicts that plagued the country since its formation. Indeed, civil society reproduced and reinforced these cleavages and helped mobilize citizens against each other. Civil society attracted many frustrated and alienated citizens and provided them with the skills and connections necessary for engaging in anti-system activity and even violence. The Nazis understood this potential of civil society and took great care to infiltrate civil society associations and attract these frustrated, alienated, and mobilized individuals and use them to build an antidemocratic political movement. Without such an active and well-developed civil society, in other words, the Nazis most probably would never have been able to so quickly gather steam as a political movement and most probably would not have been able to so quickly destroy German democracy and rise to power as quickly and efficiently as they did.

The Italian Case

The Italian case exhibits many disturbing similarities to the German one. Most importantly, in both, it would be impossible to understand the collapse of democracy and the rise of totalitarian movements without paying careful attention to the relationship among civil society, the state, and political institutions. In particular, in Italy as in Germany, expanding civil society activity during the late nineteenth and early twentieth centuries reflected and reinforced political discontent and did little to bridge the country's increasingly treacherous societal cleavages. Civil society also played a crucial role in facilitating the rise and rule of Fascism.

Although finally possessing a unified state, the new Italy that came into being in the 1860s was hardly a unified nation. Opinions varied greatly on the legitimacy of the new order and social suspicions and

divisions were pronounced. These problems were mirrored in the organization of the country's political life. Three main groups dominated the
new Italy: Liberals, Catholics, and Socialists. As was the case in Germany
and other parts of Europe, Italy's liberals were a fairly elitist bunch, suspicious of the dawning era of mass politics and unable or unwilling to reach
out to broad swathes of Italian society. Partially as a result, the liberal
party did not develop into a modern, mass organization, and its ability
to mobilize large numbers of Italians for significant political projects or
goals remained limited. Middle class associational life in many ways mirrored the structure and problems of liberal political life. To a large extent,
liberal organizations were narrowly focused; indeed, it seems that many
members of the Italian middle classes turned to civil society to recreate
the hierarchies and social distinctions that were being rapidly eroded by
socioeconomic and political change. The result was a bourgeois associational sphere that was largely provincial, restricted in membership, and
often "structured around a single notable, or family or larger group of
notables" (Banti and Lyttelton in Bermeo and Nord 2000).

Catholics and Socialists, meanwhile, developed much more vibrant
and extensive civil society networks than did liberals. However, they,
unlike the liberals, were alienated from the new state. In the case of
the Catholics, this was because the formation of a unified Italy robbed
the Pope of much of his temporal power and sovereignty; as a result,
he issued an injunction banning Catholics from participating in national
political life. In the case of the Socialists, this was because Italian socialists, like their counterparts in Germany and many other parts of Europe,
were discriminated against by the state and ruling elites and were, in any
case, inherently suspicious of the reigning "bourgeois, capitalist" order.
Thus, although the number and range of associations generated by or
affiliated with the Catholic and Socialist spheres grew throughout the
nineteenth and early twentieth centuries, these organizations served primarily to strengthen in-group ties and loyalties rather than bridge them.
In addition, as these associations expanded and provided a growing range
of services, they decreased participants' contact with and reliance on the
state. As one observer notes, Italian civil society during this time exhib-
ited a "striking paradox." The groups created around political languages
that denied legitimacy to the liberal state were the very same ones most
successful at building national organizational networks, a feat the liberals
themselves were unable to reproduce (Banti 2000: 55).

But, it wasn't just political groupings that generated civil society activity in late nineteenth and early twentieth century Italy. And, as in

Germany, much associational activity fed not off progressive or democratic sentiment, but was rather generated by discontent with the reigning order and a sense that the state was unwilling or unable to solve the country's myriad problems (Absalom 1995; Patrucco 1973; Seton-Watson 1967). The most important manifestation of this tendency was the rise of nationalist organizations that claimed to speak for all "true" Italians (rather than just one sector of society as did the major political groupings) and called for a new, refounded, reinvigorated, and internationally more assertive, Italian state (Cunsolo 1990; De Grand 1978; Thayer 1964).

These patterns continued and became more pronounced after the First World War as the problems of the Italian state intensified. Although on the winning side, the immense political divisions caused by Italy's entry into the war poisoned political life, discontent was furthered by many Italians' sense that they were "robbed" by the postwar settlement and by the daunting task of reconstruction faced by the country. These and other problems contributed to the chaos that followed the war (the *bienno rosso*). From 1918 to 1920, Italy was wracked by growing social unrest, massive strikes and rising political mobilization and dissatisfaction. Indeed, by the beginning of the 1920s, the country appeared to many as ungovernable and growing numbers of Italians had come to conclude that the reigning order was unable to protect much less promote their interests. As one observer notes, "it seems fair to say that [by] the early 1920s the majority of Italians of all classes [had] lost confidence in the liberal regime" (Tannenbaum 1972: 35).

This was the perfect breeding ground for a savvy revolutionary movement. In 1919, the Fascists were a small urban group with 870 members; by 1921, Fascism was a mass movement with over 300,000 members widely distributed across the country. The reasons for this transformation are many (Berman 2006: chapter 6), but it would be hard to understand the movement's rise without paying careful attention to its relationship with civil society. As Riley and other scholars have noted, there is a strong correlation between areas Putnam identifies as high in associationalism and the strength of fascism in interwar Italy (Kwon 2004; Riley 2005; Tarrow 1996). The causal mechanisms underlying this correlation are similar to those operating in Germany: Italian fascists infiltrated and absorbed existing civil society organizations and adopted skills and relationships developed in the associational sphere for their own use. In particular, Italian fascists targeted patriotic and agrarian associations, drawing them into the movement and using them as the base upon which a truly national, grass-roots, mass organization could be built (Riley

2005: 298–301). Many of the techniques that enabled fascism to grow so rapidly – fund-raising, outreach, and targeted social assistance programs – were borrowed from civil society organizations (Riley 2005: 301). In short, "a relatively strong associational sphere, far from constituting a barrier against the development of an authoritarian party, provided the materials out of which the fascist party was constructed" (Riley 2005: 301). In addition to facilitating fascism's rise, Italy's fairly robust associational life also seems to have played a role in determining how fascism ruled. In particular, it may help to explain why fascism developed in a totalitarian rather than authoritarian direction. Unlike Spain, for example, where civil society was much less developed, when the Italian fascists came to power they faced a relatively large and extensive civil society sphere. They, therefore, worked to absorb or co-opt as many of these organizations as possible, politicizing or "fascistizing" ever larger sectors of Italian society. The result was a much more inclusive, grass-roots, and mobilizing regime than existed in Spain (Riley 2005).

ISLAMISM

Although dramatic, the German and Italian cases are hardly unique. In fact, if we look at the most often discussed contemporary anti-system movement – Islamism[4] – we can see some similar dynamics. In particular, crucial to an understanding of the rise of Islamism is an appreciation of the failures of many Arab states and mainstream political organizations and an awareness of how successfully Islamists have exploited civil society to further their own ends. As in the German and Italian cases, the expansion of civil society in parts of the Arab world is both a reflection and a cause of local states' declining effectiveness and legitimacy. Civil society, moreover, has served as a base from which Islamists have launched an impressive challenge to the status quo.

As with the interwar European cases, we have to go back in time to understand the contemporary situation. A good place to begin is in the 1950s and 1960s, with the heyday of the ambitious, Pan-Arabist nationalist states in much of the Arab world. In Egypt, for example, this was the period during which Gamal Abdel Nasser undertook a wide range of social

---

[4] Of course, Islamism is not to be equated with fascism and National Socialism because the latter were unequivocally antidemocratic, whereas the former is a much more heterogeneous political movement. Indeed, one of the most important current debates regarding Islamism is the degree to which some groups within the movement are fully committed to democracy. On this debate, see Berman 2008.

and economic development projects and entertained dreams of international glory for the Egyptian state. By the late 1960s, however, many of these dreams were proving to be chimeras. Internationally, the loss of a war to Israel led many to question the legitimacy and efficacy of the state, whereas domestically the economy was leaving much of the population discontented and even desperate. Since the 1970s, Egypt's economic situation declined, and unemployment and underemployment rose dramatically. Making a bad situation worse, was the dramatic rise in population across much of the Arab world and Egypt in particular. Between 1980 and 1995, the Middle East had the highest population growth in the world, twice as high as East Asia and even higher than sub-Saharan Africa. Not surprisingly, population increases have dramatically outpaced the growth of per capita income and GNP. Particularly worrisome has been the extremely rapid increase of the region's "youth rate." In Egypt and the Arab world, approximately 40 percent of the population is under 15 years old.[5]

Rapid population growth made it impossible for the Egyptian state to live up to the promises it had made to citizens in return for political support. The government had tried to guarantee education and subsequent public employment, but economic decline made such pledges unsustainable, and indeed, by the 1980s, Egyptian society was becoming flooded by large numbers of secondary school and university graduates who could not find a job. The ones who were fortunate enough to get a job, meanwhile, found that their real wages actually decreased over time. As one analyst comments,

> the regime's ultimate retreat from the entitlement program stirred intense resentment among would-be recipients who had come to regard state benefits as their "due." In sum...the regime deliberately fostered youth dependence on the state but – under conditions of resources scarcity and under-development – ultimately failed to deliver on its promises. The exhaustion of the statist model... contributed to the rise of a frustrated stratum of educated, underemployed youth 'available' for mobilization by opposition groups (Kepel 1985: 11; Wickham 2002: 11–12, chapter 3).

Alongside the slowdown in state employment, the "safety valve" provided by migration to the oil rich states of the Gulf also began to close. Up

---

[5] The rate for the developed world is 20% and for the developing world in general 35%. A generally accepted estimate identifies 25% as a sustainable number for the long term, and views anything over 35% as "high risk." There has, however, been some progress made on this front in the last years.

through the early 1980s, Egyptians flooded to places like Saudi Arabia, Kuwait, and the Gulf, but falling oil prices, political disturbances, and the Gulf War severely limited this option (Wickham 2002: 42–43). The cumulative result of these trends was a massive rise in unemployment, particularly among the educated.

Thus, by the final quarter of the twentieth century, the Egyptian state had been battered by military defeat and the collapse of pan-Arabism together with economic failure and overpopulation. It could no longer provide jobs, social services, or a sense of hope and direction to its citizens, and proved unable or unwilling to respond to the numerous challenges it faced. The government remained relatively resistant to the dramatic liberalizing trends occurring in many other parts of the world and, indeed, had a tendency to retreat further into an authoritarian and repressive cocoon as problems mounted.[6] Not surprisingly, therefore, it became increasingly estranged from its citizens. Surveying the scene in 1995, one observer noted sorrowfully "At the heart of Egyptian life there lies a terrible sense of disappointment" (Ajami, 1995: 79).

This situation turned out to be tailor made for a disciplined, politically savvy, anti-system movement to exploit. Islamist groups moved into the political, social, and economic voids left behind by the Egyptian state (Bayat 1998; Wickham 2002; Zaki 1995). Islamist organizations became the center of community life in many parts of Egypt, especially in poorer areas. They did this by providing social goods that the state either could not or would not provide. Islamists offered citizens everything from health care and housing to education and employment help. In addition, Islamists worked hard to infiltrate existing civil society organizations. Beginning especially in the 1970s, Islamists came to dominate the student unions of many campuses as well as many of Egypt's most important professional associations. For example, by the early 1990s, the Muslim Brotherhood – the largest of Egypt's Islamist groups – had gained control of the doctors', engineers', scientists', pharmacists', and lawyers' syndicates in free and fair elections, and here too provided their constituents with a variety of much-needed services (Ibrahim 1995, 1996; Wickham 2002). Islamists have been so successful in running these organizations and using them to provide services and a voice to their members that some scholars have argued that under their influence "professional

[6] There was some economic liberalization (the *intifah*) and occasional relaxations on political controls. But, the former came nowhere close to solving the country's economic problems and the latter were never allowed to develop far enough to significantly threaten the regime.

syndicates [became] perhaps the most vibrant institutions of Egyptian civil society" (Esposito 1999: 100–1; Wickham 2002: 2; Zubaida 1992: 8).

Varied and extensive civil society activity allowed Islamists to gain insight into the needs and demands of a wide range of citizens and craft their appeal and programs appropriately. As one observer noted, Islamist groups are "seeking to gain the support of the average Egyptian one by one, inch by inch, through the provision of welfare facilities, Islamic schools, Islamic clinics, technical schools, economic institutes for profit, social insurance, monthly payments for the poor," and so forth (Kifner 1986). Involvement in civil society has also directly benefited Islamist movements, by allowing them to improve the efficiency, flexibility, and responsiveness of their organizations. Infiltration of and participation in civil society associations has helped the movement recruit and train new leaders and it has also used its position in civil society to tap "members' knowledge and organizational skills, financial resources, and access to mosques, newspapers, publishing houses, professional associations, and political parties, to mobilize opposition to government policies or the state" (Al-Sayyid 1995: 289; Dekmejian 1995: 97–98; Denoeux 1993).

But, perhaps the most important, if intangible, way in which civil society has helped Islamism is by enveloping their supporters in a dense associational web that provides them with an alternative view of how the world can and should be organized. By so doing, Islamists have helped build a sense of community and collective identity among their supporters, deepening their commitment to the cause, and their willingness to sacrifice for it. In a country such as Egypt, where political participation and social activism has generally been discouraged, membership and participation in Islamist associational life has also provided many with their first meaningful opportunity to play an active role in the life of their communities and society. For example, as one scholar notes (in an assessment that fits in well with the encomiums to civil society so often found in the literature): "Islamists challenged dominant patterns of political alienation and abstention by promoting a new ethic of civic obligation that mandated participation in the public sphere, regardless of its benefits and costs" (Wickham 2002: 120; Denoeux 1993: 25; Ibrahim 1980: 448).

A similar pattern to the one that played itself out in Egypt can be found in other parts of the Muslim world. Just as in Egypt, by the late 1960s, the implicit social construct struck between many Arab governments and their citizens began to fall apart (Anderson 1997; Dekmejian 1995; Ibrahim 1993, 1995; Khashan 1997; Maddy-Weitzman 1997; Norton 1993; Sivan 1990b). Economic decline set in across much of the region;

demographic trends exacerbated economic problems and created a large pool of unemployed, frustrated youth along with destabilizing urban migrations; and the military impotence of Arab regimes against Israel was brutally revealed. States proved unable or unwilling to respond to these challenges and, so, lost popular support and legitimacy. Islamist groups stepped into the political space thus opened, and managed to go a long way towards satisfying the basic economic and social needs of many citizens.

In Algeria, for example, the Islamic Salvation Front (FIS) rose to a position where it was poised to win national elections in 1992 as the result of a dynamic similar to the one we saw in Egypt. By the mid 1980s, Algeria was in dire economic straits and more than 60% of the population was under twenty-five years of age. The state had largely abdicated its public responsibilities, and as a result most Algerians were left without basic services or hope for the future. The Islamist movement moved into the breach, using an extensive associational network to provide the social services, community and recreational groups, and economic support that Algerians desperately needed (Entelis 1996; Esposito 1999: 182; Kepel 2002: chapter 7; Maddy-Weitzman 1996). Such activities and programs helped the movement attract widespread support while further undermining the state's legitimacy, a pattern displayed when an earthquake hit the country in 1989. "The Islamists were the first to respond and did so effectively. They, rather than the government, supplied blankets and medicine, and this scored further points while the government reinforced its image of ineffectiveness" (Esposito 1999: 176).

Algerian Islamist organizations also provided citizens with some of the country's few genuine opportunities for political involvement and debate. As one participant recalls, in such associations, Algerians could meet to discuss "all the problems that the Algerian nation was confronting. We spoke about everything... the economy... all aspects of life" (Esposito 1999: 174). Not surprisingly, the Islamists were able to use such success in civil society to mobilize supporters and construct a powerful political machine. "When [the FIS] became a legal entity in 1989, [the movement's civil society] associations became the support network of the new party" (Davis 1992: 11). The FIS was able to attract "a broad base of support across the country... [and bring] a level of organization and ideological commitment, lacking in other sectors of society, as well as an impressive record of social responsibility and welfare" to the struggle against the existing regime (Esposito 1999: 182). Only the suspension of voting and the imposition of martial law prevented the FIS from taking full control of the country.

Lebanon represents another variation on this theme. Here the state was never as powerful or centralized as its Egyptian or Algerian counterparts, but its collapse was even more spectacular. As the country descended into civil war in the 1970s, Islamists, and Hezbollah in particular, moved in to provide desperately needed services to hundreds of thousands of Lebanese – especially Shi'ites, the country's largest and poorest religious group. Hezbollah-affiliated associations supplied citizens with medical care, hospitals, housing, clean water, schools, and more. In addition to providing desperately needed material aid, Hezbollah also sponsored a wide range of recreational and communal associations that helped it attract supporters, spread its ideology, and gradually reshape society from within. At one Hezbollah-supported facility, for example, an American visitor observed, "disabled veterans spend[ing] their days weaving baskets, taking computer classes and carving souvenirs with the group's logo that features an AK-47 machine gun clutched in a raised fist." Its civil society activities allowed the movement to "keep tabs on the recipients' political feelings and religious observance" (MacFarquhar 2001; Trofimov 2001), and helped it win "the hearts and minds of new supporters" while building its backing "from the grass roots up" (Esposito 1999: 156; MacFarquhar 2001; Norton n.d.; Trofimov 2001). Similar dynamics were noted after the 2006 war between Lebanon and Israel, when Hezbollah moved quickly to help reconstruct areas destroyed by the fighting and exploit the state's weakness to bolster its own political support.

In Palestine, meanwhile, Amaney Jamal has convincingly shown how the ineffective and clientalistic governing institutions of the PLO have helped generate civil society organizations that parallel the problems and pathologies of the ruling regime – they are undemocratic, vertically structured, and buttress rather than undermine authoritarian tendencies (Jamal 2007).

CONCLUSIONS

Although different in critical respects, even a cursory examination of the interwar European and contemporary Middle Eastern cases reveals some striking similarities. Most obviously, it shows that a vibrant civil society is neither an indicator of nor a precursor to healthy democracy. This conclusion is not, however, probably surprising today as numerous recent studies have revealed a much more complex relationship between civil society, democratization, and consolidation than was initially believed. For example, studies of first, second, and third wave democratizers have not found an expanding associational sphere to be a particularly good predictor of democratization nor have successful democratizations been uniformly characterized by particularly strong or vibrant civil societies (Bermeo and Nord 2000; Encarnación 2003; Howard 2003). Others have found that authoritarian and democratic regimes generate different types of civil society (Jamal 2007). This essay contributes to this emerging reconsideration of the role and nature of civil society, arguing, in particular, that in situations where states and mainstream national political institutions are either unable or unwilling to respond to the needs and demands of their citizens, civil society may step into the gap. This civil society activity, furthermore, whereas often oppositional, may be neither democratic nor peaceful. In fact, it might very well be in the service of radical or undemocratic movements, which exploit legitimate criticisms of an existing order in the service of something much worse. In addition, the interwar European and contemporary Middle Eastern cases reveal that civil society can provide many of the resources radical movements need to build effective, flexible, and responsive structures and organizations. In interwar Germany and Italy, as well as in some parts of the contemporary Middle East, radical and undemocratic movements used civil society associations to recruit and train activists for anti-system activity and even violence. Similarly, in interwar Europe and parts of the contemporary Middle East such groups have used their extensive web of civil society contacts and affiliates to learn about the needs and concerns of a wide range of citizens – information that they then used to devise effective and flexible responses to them. Last, and perhaps most importantly, the dense associational web in which Nazis, Fascists, and Islamists wrap their supporters helps keep them isolated from other members of society and mobilized and committed to the cause – a situation that undoubtedly helps explain why supporters of such movements are often willing to engage in illegal and even violent activity.

What the cases discussed here seem to indicate, in short, is that under certain conditions civil society is likely to be associated not with peace, prosperity, and democracy (as many of its boosters argue), but rather with social conflict, anti-democratic tendencies, and even violence. The most important difference between civil and uncivil polities, this examination seems to indicate, is not to be found in the levels or internal nature of civil society activity, but rather in an examination of political institutions.

In other words, if the tendency within social science during the high point of the third wave was to turn to an examination of civil society to understand why some countries are peaceful and prosperous, whereas others are marred by violence, conflict, and political instability; this writer agrees with the more recent tendency within political science to shift back in the other direction – to pay renewed attention to the role played by the state and other traditional political institutions in hindering violence and instability and promoting social cohesion and democratic behaviors (Fukuyama 2004; Jamal 2007).

This is not to say, of course, that states and traditional political institutions cannot be the promoters of violence and instability – the German, Italian and Egyptian cases show that very well (Chirot in this volume). But, it is also true that without strong and responsive states and political institutions, societies are more likely to be marred by violence or at least social conflict. Indeed, going back to Max Weber, states have long been defined by their monopoly over the means of violence. Where they begin to lose this, conflict and even violence is the likely result.

An interesting contemporary case of this is India – a relatively long lived and stable democracy where, as Ashutosh Varshney has shown, civil society has indeed played a role in containing ethnic violence. In particular, Varshney found that by facilitating intergroup communication, restraining politicians, and providing an institutionalized forum for managing tensions, inter-(as opposed to intra-) ethnic associational networks helped defuse potential ethnic conflicts before they exploded into violence (Varshney 2001, 2003). This is an important (and heartening) finding; however, it is also incomplete without a careful consideration of the relationship between ethnic violence and the state. For example, it is now clear ethnic rioting in India was often aided and abetted by agents and institutions of the local state. For example, during the 2002 riots (in which over 2,000 Muslims were killed), local politicians willfully turned a blind eye to the emerging violence; police forces helped identify and perhaps even kill victims; and local governments willfully obstructed efforts to bring perpetrators to justice. As one police official noted, "In districts where Muslims were killed on a large scale, the police were collaborating with the rioters. In districts were there were very few deaths . . . the senior police official had decided to uphold the law and protect innocent people. If you want to understand riots in India that is all you need to know" (quoted in Luce 2007: 255). Making matters worse was the initial reaction of the national government. The prime minister's refusal to visit the scene of the violence for a month after it occurred served to at least implicitly

condone the killers' actions and the government's subsequent inability or
unwillingness to provide adequate help to the hundreds of thousands dis-
placed by the riots. This only fed a growing sense of grievance on the part
of Muslims (which may, in turn, have led some to turn to Islamic organizations for support and perhaps even to violence [Johnson 2007, Luce
2007: 159–62]). In short, even in democracies, when states and other
political institutions prove unwilling or unable to enforce the "rules of
the game," social conflict and even violence may result.[7]

This was certainly the pattern in the German, Italian, and some Middle
Eastern cases, where there was an almost inverse relationship between
the strength and legitimacy of the state on one hand, and civil society
on the other. As each country's political institutions proved incapable of
channeling and redressing grievances, civil society grew to compensate
and became an alternative to politics for many disaffected citizens, drawing them even further away from mainstream political life as well as from
their fellow citizens. This created a context in which conflict and societal
violence was, if not certain to explode, then not at all a surprising occurrence. Relatedly, the cases examined here show that civil society organizations are often the product of societal divisions and conflicts rather than
instruments for bridging them (Seligman and Chirot in this volume). In
interwar Germany and Italy and also in parts of the contemporary Arab
world we saw that associational life was often generated by circumscribed
socioeconomic and/or political groupings and developed out of a sense of
grievance and fear and a desire for self-protection.[8] In such situations,
civil society developed in a way that reinforced existing cleavages and
often mobilized citizens against each other. This dynamic is not limited
to the cases examined here. As one recent survey of the development of
European civil society, for example, concluded "The nineteenth-century
experience illustrates that negative incentives were the origin of much
associational life. Civil society everywhere was rooted in fears and conflicts.... Threats, insecurities, and the voids left by collapsed institutions
are ... powerful incentives for civic organization (Bermeo and Ertman in
Bermeo and Nord 2000: 250).

---

[7] This conclusion is consistent with the work of scholars such as David Laitin and James
   Fearon and Stathis Kalyvas and Mathew Adam Kochner who argue ethnic civil wars and
   political violence are a consequence of a particular kind of (weak) state rather than racial,
   religious, or other societal divisions (Fearon and Laitin 2003; Kalyvas and Kochner 2007).
[8] This is consistent with the findings of Putnam's recent work, which concludes that the
   more diverse a community is, the less likely its citizens are to trust each other and join in
   civic activities together.

Reflecting realizations like these, already the wheel has begun to turn within the scholarly community, with more and more analyses focusing on the potential "dark side" of civil society. But one would be just as wrong to focus unsparingly on the negative potential of civil society as some earlier scholarship was to uncritically praise civil society's overly democratic and beneficial impact. Instead, if we want to understand under what conditions civil society is likely to promote or hinder violence, social conflict, or democracy, we need to turn away from analyses that study it in isolation or that see it as a positive, beneficial alternative to states and mainstream political institutions. Not only can civil society never replace states and mainstream political institutions, it is only in examining the relationship between the two that we can begin to understand whether and when societies are likely to find themselves marred by violence and instability.

These conclusions have important implications for the way we think about democracy promotion. As in the scholarly community, recent years have seen a spate of works questioning the value of civil society promotion programs. Studies have found that outside funding of civil society organizations may facilitate and even promote a wide range of pathologies, including unaccountability and corruption (Carothers 1999: chapter 8; Glasius, Lewis and Seckinelgin 2004; Jamal 2007; Mendelson and Glenn 2002; Ottaway and Carothers 2000). More fundamentally, research on civil society promotion programs has begun to recognize that thinking about civil society in isolation from the development of state and political institutions diminishes the efficacy of democracy promotion efforts overall. For example, students of democracy promotion have come to recognize that in societies where particularistic identities trump national ones and states are unable to protect individuals and enforce the rules of the game, promoting high levels of participation and advocacy is unlikely to generate the type of vibrant, bridging, liberal civil society associated with successful democracy; instead, patrimonial, segmented forms of associational life are more likely to be the result (Carothers 1999: 223; Chirot in this volume; also Seligman 1992: 5, 27, 69). In addition, there is some concern that encouraging the growth of civil society organizations, especially those engaged in service provision, in the context of weak states, may only weaken the latter even further. As one scholar has argued, in the case of Bangladesh, many NGOs have come to substitute "for absent or inadequate government provision in health, education and rural development. The state has meanwhile increasingly 'discarded' its responsibilities for service provisions and citizen accountability through the 'franchising out' of key state functions to NGOs and the private sector, which now cater – inadequately – to citizens as consumers" (Lewis in Glasius et al 2004: 114; Rieff 1999). Finally, and perhaps most importantly, research shows that promoting civil society organizations in countries where states and political institutions are weak is unlikely to have a great impact on the development of democracy, because such organizations alone are unlikely to be able to solve the problems many newly democratizing countries face (Carothers 1999: 223). As one study put it, if civil society organizations advocate goals that existing states can't carry out, increasing support for such organizations is unlikely to make much impact (Mendelson and Glenn 2002: 16–7; see also Jones and Weinthal 1999: 1268).

In conclusion, both scholars of political development and analysts of democracy promotion would do well to reintegrate thinking about civil society and political institutions (Berman 1997, 2004; Diamond in Diamond and Plattner 1996; Foley and Edwards 1996; Whittington 1998). This makes, of course, perfect intellectual and practical sense. We have now rediscovered something that many of the best classical scholars of civil society knew very well: that the evolution and nature of civil society can only be understood through a careful consideration of the political context within which it develops (Seligman 1992). Such a conclusion does, of course, complicate things for scholars and practitioners because it asks them to move from a focus on social relations *or* the state to an appreciation of their interaction and mutual dependence. However, it is only by so doing that we will be able to better understand, and, therefore, potentially influence the fate of political regimes.

3 Encountering Culture

When assessing how a country's culture affects the potential for democracy promotion by external actors, we must take two crucial matters into account. The first is the extent to which the culture of the recipient country is conducive to democracy. Does the country that external actors aim to help have a culture that favors open politics? If so, democracy-promotion efforts start with an advantage. If not, would-be promoters of democracy – no matter how sound their programs, competent their personnel, diligent their efforts, and pure their intentions – will probably find themselves frustrated. Factors other than culture – for example, level of economic development – shape the environment in which democracy-promoters work. Even if a country's culture does not necessarily favor democratization, a relatively high material standard of living may bolster democracy's prospects. Still, democracy promotion may be a better investment where the local culture is conducive to open politics than where it is not.

But, the conduciveness of the culture to *democracy* is not the only relevant cultural issue. So too must we examine the disposition of the culture of the polity in question to *would-be external democratizers*. Here, the key question is the extent to which the predominant form of nationalism in the recipient country is friendly to interventions from the outside and specifically to interventions by the providers of assistance.

Thus, as we encounter culture, we must grapple with two separate dimensions: the disposition of the society toward democracy and the disposition of the society toward the providers of democracy assistance. Before considering these matters, however, a brief discussion of culture is in order.

CONCEPTUALIZING CULTURE

Culture is a contested concept. Often in discussions of the influence of culture on politics we speak of *political culture*. A multitude of definitions is available. In their classic and still-influential study, *The Civic Culture*, Gabriel Almond and Sidney Verba (1963) broke political culture down into three components: cognitive orientations, or what people know about politics; affective orientations, or how people feel about politics; and evaluative orientations, or how people judge politics. Other writers have conceived of political culture differently. But most, like Almond and Verba, consider political culture a matter of psychological orientations and, in particular, people's attitudes toward politics (for example, Eckstein 1992; Putnam 1994).

Such a conception of political culture is sound. It has guided many prominent works. Yet, a shadow of ambiguity stills hangs over political culture. The source of ambiguity is this: By political culture, do we mean specifically political-psychological orientations, or do we mean any psychological orientations that may be of relevance to politics? The first is largely limited to the factors Almond and Verba studied, such as people's attitudes toward the political system, the way they think of their own role in that system, and how they assess their own influence and that of others on public policy. The second concept is looser. It may refer to any politically relevant psychological orientations. It might include not only how people think about politics, but also how they think about the origins of the cosmos, their status with regard to other people and groups of people, and so on. These factors may have implications for politics, but they are not by nature exclusively political. They have nonpolitical aspects, manifestations, and effects.

In practice, we often blur the distinction between political culture (meaning broadly-shared political-psychological orientations) and culture in general (meaning broadly shared psychological orientations). We often include as part of "political culture" any aspects of culture that are potentially relevant to politics. We pick aspects of "culture" in general and, upon hypothesizing that they might have some impact on the political question of concern, consider them elements of "political culture." Thus, some scholars call religious beliefs or authority relations in the family *aspects* of political culture, when they really mean that these things are *determinants* of political culture. Writers thereby conflate what determines the way people think about politics, on the one hand, and the way people think about politics, pure and simple, on the other. By so doing, writers construct a causal chain leading from culture in general to political culture in particular, usually without realizing that they are building causal arguments into their definitions. This move may contribute to conceptual fuzziness and protract the dreary debate over what political culture is, whether it really exists, and whether it can be defined clearly enough to be used in a comparative analysis.

Here, I conceive of culture in the broad sense, meaning that I include aspects of culture that may have manifestations and effects outside as well as inside the political sphere. In particular, I wish to specify, and explicate the effect of, several aspects of culture that are relevant to democracy promotion.

Furthermore, I regard culture as broadly shared psychological orientations, not the practical manifestations of those orientations. Some scholars working within a poststructuralist or postmodern tradition define culture in terms of "practices," including and especially "speech acts" and "discourses." To my way of thinking, practices are behaviors that reflect psychological orientations; they are not psychological orientations themselves. Whether behaviors determine psychological orientations or the reverse is another matter. Here, I note only that I believe that psychological orientations have a life of their own and are not fully determined by practices. I further hold that broadly-shared psychological orientations are real and observable; that they may differ meaningfully from one society to another; and that they are not merely products of the observer's imagination.

What I consider culture, moreover, is distinct from institutions. Some social scientists have recently claimed that much of what is typically considered culture is better conceived of as institutions (Helmke and Levitsky 2004). They have argued that the unwritten rules and expectations that govern patron-client relations, for example, although sometimes considered facets of culture, are actually institutions – informal rather than formal ones, but institutions nonetheless. These scholars may discipline and sharpen the concept of "culture" – although they also risk distending the concept of "institution." Even after shrinking the realm of culture as they expand the ambit of institutions, however, such scholars normally concede that people's values remain aspects of culture rather than institutions. One may add that values are a type of broadly shared psychological orientations.

In sum, I retain the old-fashioned identification of culture with broadly shared psychological orientations. I reject the postmodern conception of culture as discourses and behaviors. I restrict my understanding of culture to what even advocates of expanding the notion of "institutions" to cover informal rules regard as properly in the realm of "culture." Yet, rather than focus on political culture per se, I consider culture more broadly, without the modifying adjective. I am interested specifically in those components of culture that shape societies' receptivity to democracy and to external efforts to promote democratization.

ASSESSING CULTURAL DISPOSITION TOWARD DEMOCRACY

Myriad facets of culture may influence the probability of democratization. Yet, two aspects are vital: tolerance and equality. Most foundational theorists of democracy, including Montesquieu, Mary Wollstonecraft, Thomas Jefferson, Benjamin Constant, John S. Mill, and Alexis de Tocqueville, as well as contemporary thinkers such as Benjamin Barber, Stephen Holmes, Seymour Martin Lipset, Carole Pateman, John Rawls, Robert Putnam, Giovanni Sartori, and Ian Shapiro, stress tolerance and/or equality in their accounts of, or assumptions about, the values that underpin democracy. These writers represent a wide range of thought, yet, they all regard either tolerance or equality, or both, as the essential values of open government. Without tolerance, there can be no perpetual process of open, peaceful competition, which is the essential procedural feature of democracy. Without equality, there can be no decision rule that is consistent with rule by the demos, because anything but one person, one voice implies a hierarchy that privileges one type of human being over another (and, therefore, some groups over others) and thereby yields rule by a part (e.g., aristocracy, oligarchy, monocracy) rather than by the whole (i.e., democracy). Equality is, therefore, the essential substantive feature of democracy.

Tolerance and equality need not be absolute for democracy to exist. They are never absolute in practice, and democracies function anyway – although one may argue that no democracy has ever been absolute (or complete), either. What is more, one may argue – indeed, writers argue a great deal – about what aspects of tolerance or equality are most important for democracy. Equality is especially contested, as some writers emphasize equality before the law, whereas others stress equality in the distribution of resources or capabilities.

Still, the principles of tolerance and equality are central to democratic theory, and habits that embody and advance tolerance and equality are central to democratic practice. Thus, psychological orientations that esteem tolerance and equality are more likely to aid robust democratization than psychological orientations that do not. The more widespread and the deeper people's commitments to tolerance and equality, the more conducive the culture to democracy.

Tolerance

An individual who does not believe that those with whom he or she disagrees have the right to a voice will not oppose the exclusion of those voices from the political arena, and, therefore, will not oppose leaders who exclude them. Conversely, a person who holds that even opinions he or she finds objectionable should enjoy a hearing will be inclined to resist leaders who try to silence dissent. The more widespread the notion that all voices have the right to a full hearing, the more widespread the spirit of tolerance; and the more widespread the spirit of tolerance, the more tolerant society as a whole is. The more tolerant a society is, the lower the likelihood that one citizen will seek to silence or exclude another and the greater the likelihood that rulers who seek to silence opinions or repress groups will encounter substantial popular resistance.

The notion of tolerance implies an object – that is, something one tolerates. It is more difficult to tolerate something that is potentially abhorrent than something that is not. Attempts to measure tolerance, therefore, aim to assess whether people forbear controversial or unorthodox things. It is easy to imagine a plethora of forms of tolerance that might be germane to political behavior. One's acceptance of members of racial or religious groups that differ from one's own may be relevant; so too might one's acceptance of people whose lifestyles and opinions differ from one's own.

Whereas such matters have been investigated in many societies, information that is usable for cross-national analysis is not plentiful. Ideally, we would have an abundance of cross-national data on matters such as whether one believes that people with unorthodox views should have the right to express them. Some researchers have used such queries and generated interesting data (for example, Ottemoeller 1998). Unfortunately, such studies have been limited to a single country or a small number of countries (Weldon 2006). The World Values Survey (WVS), however, does cover a large portion of the world, and it asks questions that may tap into tolerance. Here, I use data from the most recent wave of surveys, which were conducted during 1999–2004 (*World Values Survey* 2007).

The data provided by the WVS are a blunt instrument. People's recent experiences may affect how they respond to questions and, of course, even basic beliefs may change over time. The question is not whether the WVS is a perfect source of information on people's beliefs and attitudes; it is not. The question is whether the WVS is better than nothing or than anecdotal evidence alone; it certainly is that.

Although numerous questions in the WVS elicit responses that shed light on tolerance, three items are especially revealing. One offers respondents a list of qualities that may be important to instill in children. Of particular interest is the proportion of respondents who mention "tolerance and respect for other people" as an important quality in children's upbringing. Whether or not people see tolerance as an essential part of childhood socialization may reflect the value people assign to tolerance. Responses from the survey are reported as whether tolerance and respect for others was or was not mentioned as an important quality in a child. Here, I use the proportion of respondents who *did mention* this quality as an indicator of tolerance.

The second item asks respondents what kinds of people they would not like to have as neighbors. Of interest is the proportion who mentioned "people of a different race." Distaste for having neighbors of a different race may be a sign of intolerance. Responses are reported as whether or not respondents mentioned people of a different race as potentially undesirable neighbors. I consider the proportion of the respondents who *did not mention* people of a different race as unwelcome neighbors as an indicator of tolerance.

The third item concerns whether homosexuality is justifiable. On this item in the WVS, responses were recorded differently than with the other two items just mentioned. Respondents were asked to rank the behavior on a scale of 1 to 10, with 1 standing for "never justifiable" and 10 for "always justifiable." In many countries, large majorities selected "1," meaning "never justifiable." Indeed, in the world as a whole, "never justifiable" is by far the modal response. Here, I treat the proportion of respondents who *did not offer the response "never justifiable"* as an indicator of tolerance.

Each of these three items offers a distinct angle on tolerance. The first, by querying people about tolerance *per se*, offers the most direct evidence of the value that people assign to tolerance. The second and third items provide more indirect approaches. One assesses racism and the other gauges attitudes toward deviance on a controversial and sensitive matter of personal behavior.

Scores for each country range from 0 to 100 on each item. I take an average of the three items and create a "Tolerance Index." Each of the three items is weighted equally. The index is obviously a crude indicator. It is intended only to give us a glimpse, through squinted eyes, of an aspect of culture that cannot easily be measured.

Table 3.1 presents the raw data and the Tolerance Index for individual countries. The numbers reveal considerable cross-national variation in each of the three survey items as well as in the index. Countries are listed in the order of their Tolerance Index scores.

Two criteria determine whether a country is included in the analysis. First, the WVS must provide data for the country for all three of the items that go into making up the index. This rule narrows the field to roughly three-score countries. Second, the country must at some time in the recent past have had a political system that was not fully open. Because the subject at hand is democracy promotion, there is no need to examine countries in which democracy has been thoroughly institutionalized (and, therefore, presumably does not need to be promoted by external actors). To assess whether a country qualifies as an established democracy, I examine the "freedom ratings" issued by Freedom House on an annual basis for each of the world's countries. These data are not the only source of information we have on the status of political regimes, and they are not uncontroversial. But, they are the most widely used and respected source, and they will be used here. In addition to providing numerical scores, Freedom House lumps countries into three categories: "free," "partially free," and "not free." To make it into our sample, a country must have failed to rate as "free" – that is, it must have rated as merely "partially free" or "not free" – for at least one year since 1984. In other words, we are considering only countries that have not enjoyed uninterrupted open government for the past quarter-century. The WVS includes thorough coverage of Western Europe and North America, so dropping the old democracies reduces the universe of cases by about half. We are left with a sample of 30 countries.

For many major countries the WVS does not provide complete data. Russia, Ukraine, Brazil, Columbia, Ghana, and Senegal are examples of countries for which data are lacking. These omissions are unfortunate, because these countries are among the most interesting candidates for democracy-promotion. Still, the available sample includes a substantial array of countries and does not systematically over- or under-represent particular regions. It provides fodder for some rudimentary cross-national comparison.

In any event, the use of cases here is intended merely to illustrate how data may be used to investigate matters relevant to culture and

TABLE 3.1: Indicators of tolerance

Country	Valuation of tolerance: Percent who mention tolerance and respect for other people as an important quality in children	Racial acceptance: Percent who do not mention people of other races as undesirable neighbors	Acceptance of social deviance: Percent who do not consider homosexuality as never justifiable	Tolerance Index
Argentina	70	96	64	77
Chile	76	91	65	77
Moldova	78	91	44	71
Philippines	60	79	71	70
Singapore	70	95	45	70
Mexico	71	85	52	69
Peru	73	89	44	69
South Africa	74	76	54	68
Venezuela	80	85	39	68
Bosnia	72	87	28	62
Macedonia	75	81	27	61
China	73	85	18	59
S. Korea	65	65	47	59
Albania	80	70	23	58
Tanzania	84	83	7	58
India	63	58	50	57
Kyrgyzstan	66	82	20	56
Vietnam	68	68	26	54
Zimbabwe	78	80	5	54
Jordan	67	80	3	50
Nigeria	59	70	22	50
Pakistan	53	94	4	50
Uganda	57	82	9	49
Iran	59	76	10	48
Turkey	61	68	16	48
Algeria	54	72	8	45
Indonesia	63	65	6	45
Saudi Arabia	56	62	17	45
Bangladesh	71	28	4	34
Egypt	65	34	0	33

democracy promotion. The analysis does not aim to provide definitive statements on the status of the countries themselves. Doing that would require more fine-grained data and more elaborate methods than I use here, as well as more extensive investigations of individual cases.

Spirit of Equality

Like tolerance, spirit of equality is difficult to measure. Again, however, the WVS provides some data that facilitate investigation.

To assess the spirit of equality, we must ask: Equality among whom? This question is a bit more circumscribed than what we asked when assessing tolerance, which was: tolerance of whom? Whereas there are many types of people or personal behavior that someone might or might not tolerate, the realm of groups among which one might or might not favor equality is more limited. At least in the modern era, the spirit of equality has advanced far enough that surveyors do not bother asking whether all people should be regarded as equal before the law or whether God loves all people equally. Presumably the spirit of equality is sufficiently widespread that overwhelming majorities everywhere (or in most places) would say that they do not feel innately inferior (or superior) to other people.

However, one area of equality and difference – that of sex – indeed remains a subject of study included in the WVS. Here, we cannot rely upon direct questions about whether one sex is better than the other. In the realm of gender as well as others, few people are likely to profess belief in innate superiority, and surveyors do not pose questions about whether respondents regard one group as inherently better than another. But, the WVS does ask whether one sex deserves to be favored under certain circumstances, and there is wide cross-national difference in the answers.

The spirit of equality between the sexes is more tractable to cross-cultural analysis than is the spirit of equality among other groups. It is difficult to ask, for example, whether this or that racial group or class deserves preferential treatment and elicit results that are commensurable across cases, because societies' racial and class compositions themselves differ widely. But, everywhere there are males and females; everywhere they live with one another; and everywhere they appear in approximately the same proportion (which is rough parity). Further, the two types of people, taken together, exhaust the population; everyone (or very nearly everyone) falls into one group or the other.

The WVS asks respondents whether one sex deserves preferential treatment in certain situations. So, too, does it pose other questions about whether one sex is more capable than the other in some realms of life. The answers provide a glimpse at an aspect of the spirit of equality.

Three items yield data that are particularly useful. The first item asks if, in times of job scarcity, "men should have more right to a job than women." Respondents are asked either to agree or disagree with the statement. I treat the proportion of respondents who *disagree* with the statement as a measure of spirit of equality.

The second item asks whether "university is more important for a boy than for a girl." For this item respondents are asked whether they "agree strongly," "agree," "disagree," or "strongly disagree" with the statement. I treat the proportion of respondents who "disagree" or "strongly disagree" with the statement as an indicator of spirit of equality.

The third item asks whether "men make better political leaders than women do." As with the previous item, people are asked to offer one of four responses. Again I treat percentage of those who "disagree" plus those who "strongly disagree" as the measure of spirit of equality.

Table 3.2 shows the data. The sample of countries is the same as that for which tolerance was assessed earlier. The right-most column presents an average of scores for the three items, here labeled the "Equality Index." Like the Tolerance Index, the Equality Index is a rough and ready indicator. Countries are placed in the order of their scores on the Equality Index.

Tolerance, Equality, and Overall Disposition toward Democracy

To assess overall cultural disposition to democracy, we may construct a table that incorporates both tolerance and spirit of equality. Table 3.3 provides such a scheme. Tolerance is represented on the vertical axis and spirit of equality on the horizontal axis. Scores on the Tolerance Index, shown in Table 3.1, and the Equality Index, shown in Table 3.2, are used to rank countries as "high," "medium," or "low" on each dimension.

The table has nine cells. Cell 1 contains the countries that score high on both tolerance and equality. These countries have the most favorable cultural conditions for open government. Cells 2 (high tolerance/medium equality) and 4 (medium tolerance/high equality) also present generally favorable cultural conditions. Cells 3 (high tolerance/low equality), 5 (medium tolerance/medium equality), and 7 (low tolerance/high equality) present ambivalent cultural conditions. Cell 9 (low tolerance/

TABLE 3.2: Indicators of Spirit of Equality

Country	Employment: Percent who disagree with the statement that men should have more right to a job than women	Education: Percent who disagree/strongly disagree with the statement that university is more important for a boy than for a girl	Political leadership: Percent who disagree/ strongly disagree with the statement that men make better political leaders than do women	Equality index
Peru	66	78	73	72
Argentina	60	82	61	68
Bosnia	47	81	66	65
Venezuela	52	84	58	65
Tanzania	54	82	55	64
Singapore	53	84	48	62
South Africa	55	79	52	62
Zimbabwe	54	81	45	60
Chile	51	68	58	59
China	40	87	46	58
Macedonia	34	85	56	58
Mexico	55	64	55	58
Albania	31	81	45	52
Indonesia	39	81	37	52
Uganda	48	76	31	52
Vietnam	43	72	41	52
Kyrgyzstan	39	72	42	51
S. Korea	26	73	47	49
Moldova	37	71	36	47
Pakistan	18	74	50	47
Turkey	31	70	36	46
Algeria	20	69	29	39
India	28	50	36	38
Philippines	15	62	37	38
Iran	22	57	30	36
Nigeria	30	55	20	35
Jordan	12	61	13	29
Bangladesh	16	37	32	28
Egypt	0	69	16	28
Saudi Arabia	9	37	24	26

TABLE 3.3: Cultural disposition to democracy, assessed by scores on tolerance and equality

		Equality		
		High	*Medium*	*Low*
Tolerance	*High*	Argentina, Chile, Peru, Singapore, South Africa, Venezuela	Mexico, Moldova	Philippines
		(1)	(2)	(3)
	Medium	Bosnia, Tanzania, Zimbabwe	Albania, China, S. Korea, Kyrgyzstan, Macedonia, Pakistan, Vietnam	India, Jordan, Nigeria
		(4)	(5)	(6)
	Low		Indonesia, Turkey, Uganda	Algeria, Bangladesh, Egypt, Iran, Saudi Arabia
		(7)	(8)	(9)

low equality) represents the least auspicious conditions for democracy; cells 6 (medium tolerance/low equality) and 8 (low tolerance/medium equality) also present generally unfavorable cultural environments.

All but one of the cells contain at least one case; only cell 7 is empty. As a preliminary statement, one may say that countries in cell 1 and, more ambiguously, cells 2 and 4, present favorable cultural environments for democracy. The countries in cells 3, 5, and 7 present ambiguous cultural environments. Those in cells 6 and 8 have cultures that may not be conducive to open government. Cell 9 contains the countries that, in cultural terms, may be the most resistant to democracy.

The categorization of particular countries should be regarded as merely preliminary. The data used to place countries in categories are highly imperfect, and my selection of indicators from among the available data certainly may be challenged. But, our exercise may illustrate one way of establishing some baseline expectations about the amenability of cultures to democracy in a comparative context.

ASSESSING CULTURAL DISPOSITION TOWARD EXTERNAL DEMOCRACY PROMOTION

The disposition of a country's culture to democracy may be an important determinant of the probability of robust democratization, but, it is not the only aspect of culture that would-be promoters of democracy must weigh. Even societies whose cultures are high on tolerance and/or equality may have other cultural traits that make them bad places for foreign promoters of democracy to work. In addition to considering whether a culture is favorably disposed to democracy *per se*, external promoters of democracy must consider whether a culture is open to help from the outside. The crucial issue is the character of nationalism. To what extent is the country's nationalism amenable to foreign involvement? More specifically, how receptive is nationalism to the involvement of actors from the countries that underwrite democracy promotion?

The first, more general matter concerns the extent to which a country's nationalism promotes freedom from external involvement in domestic politics. People in some societies are, on average, more psychologically disposed to regard foreign influences with suspicion than are people in other societies. The *character* of nationalism, not its *strength*, is the issue here.

The narrower question regards the orientation of nationalism to the specific external actors involved in advancing democratization. The lion's share of democracy-promotion efforts originate in and are associated with a handful of countries located in North America and northwestern Europe, a group I will refer to collectively as the "northwest." Thus, the orientation of the nationalism of the target country to influence emanating from the northwest is of special concern.

The following discussion first addresses the general issue of types of nationalism. It then considers specifically the orientation of nationalism toward the providers of democracy assistance.

Nationalism, Prickly and Smooth

Measuring the quality of nationalism precisely is impossible. But, a broad comparative perspective, combined with a willingness to suspend our scientific skepticism long enough to allow some common sense to seep into our analysis, makes possible some useful generalizations.

Although opinion may vary, many observers would agree that French, Chinese, and Russian nationalists are more jealous of national autonomy than Italian, Thai, and Indonesian nationalists. The question is not about the strength of nationalism. After living in Italy in the 1980s, this author came away convinced that no people are more enamored of their own country – and less interested in everywhere else – than Italians. Yet, contemporary Italian nationalism is not especially suspicious of foreign influences. French nationalism is quite different. In France, laws endeavor to purge the national language of foreign words and circumscribe foreign influence on popular culture. Such regulations, at least on the scale that they are present in France, are unimaginable in contemporary Italy. Italians love their country as much as the French love theirs. But, it is difficult to imagine a broad, sustained public consensus emerging in Italy on the need for an independent national nuclear deterrent.

The character of nationalism has real implications for international interactions. French nationalism poses a permanent challenge to the European Union (EU) and its institutions. Italian nationalism does not. It readily accommodates European transnationalism. Relatively speaking, French nationalism is prickly to the foreigner's touch; Italian nationalism is smooth.

Asia provides fodder for similarly crude but apt generalizations. As George Kennan noted: "The Chinese, to my opinion, are the French of Asia. The two peoples are similar in a number of respects. They are both proud people. Both are conscious of being the bearers of a great cultural tradition. They don't really, in either case, like foreigners; or at least they don't particularly appreciate the presence of foreigners in their midst. They like to be left alone" (Ullman 1999; see also Gries 2005). Here, we have a perfect depiction of prickly nationalism. On the other hand, Thai nationalism, for example, looks nothing like what Kennan described. Thais fervently love their country, but their nationalism is much more likely to manifest itself in blissful celebrations of the monarch's birthday and pride in the accomplishments of Tiger Woods (who the Thai press refers to as a "Thai golfer") than in guarding against foreign intrusions and snubs. Chinese nationalism tends to be prickly, Thai nationalism tends to be smooth.

I have had the pleasure of conducting extensive field work in the two largest countries that took part in the wave of democratization that covered the last quarter of the twentieth century. In Russia, I take for granted that some members of the elite whom I interview assume that I am a CIA agent. Even some people I would count as friends distrust my poking my head into their country's politics. They doubt that I am merely the university-affiliated observer I claim to be (and in fact am). In Indonesia, by contrast, I have never felt that anyone doubted that I am who I say I am – or, for that matter, would much care if I were not. Now, the red-and-white bicolor inspires as much loyalty and emotion among Indonesians as the red-white-and-blue tricolor does among Russians. Nationalism is every bit as strong in Indonesia as it is in Russia. Furthermore, contempt for the U.S. government is, if anything, even stronger in Indonesia than in Russia. It is aggravated by religious grievance against a perceived global assault on Islam by the United States. But, Indonesians are not generally inclined to regard foreign influence with suspicion, whereas Russians are. Russian nationalism is prickly, Indonesian is smooth.

The texture of nationalism's skin is not necessarily immutable. One hundred years ago, German nationalism was prickly. The hard lessons of the past century smoothed it out. Russian nationalism has been prickly for centuries. But, relatively speaking, it is pricklier during the first decade of the twenty-first century than it was at the time of the USSR's demise.

Still, at least within a specific historical stage, it is possible to make cross-national comparative generalizations about the character of nationalism. Given that we are concerned with a specific time period, namely the early twenty-first century, such generalizations can be made – although they should be taken with a grain of salt.

The texture of nationalism does not necessarily affect the likelihood of democratization. Neither type of nationalism is inconsonant with open government. Democracy thrives in the presence of prickly nationalism in France and smooth nationalism in Italy. Similarly, neither type of nationalism necessarily safeguards open government. Democracy has faltered in both prickly Russia and smooth Thailand. China's prickly nationalism might be bane or boon to democratization. In fact, it might cut both ways – or have little effect at all. The same may be said of Indonesia's smooth nationalism.

Yet, whether nationalism is prickly or smooth *does* affect the potential effectiveness of democracy-promotion efforts by outside actors. Countries with prickly nationalism are often bad bets for democracy promotion. Regardless of their intentions, democracy-promoters will be widely regarded with suspicion. Association with them may undermine the forces the outsiders endeavor to help, because those forces will be widely regarded as friends of interlopers. For this reason, serious political actors in the target country may even shun contact with the external democracy-promoters.

To be sure, someone in the target country will always be delighted to accept outside assistance. Americans and Europeans engaged in the democracy-promotion business often point to this fact to justify their operations and to argue that they should work in every country possible.

They hold that even if recipients publicly downplay their association with foreigners, they really do need, appreciate, and benefit from the help. But, democracy-promoters sometimes do not seem to realize that the only forces who are eager to take the help and suffer the consequences to reputation may be political flyweights, bit players who specialize in collecting foreign aid. The hazard is especially acute in countries with prickly nationalism. Where nationalism is smooth, the cost of association with foreigners may be negligible and serious political actors may indeed welcome and benefit from external assistance.

Nationalism and the Democracy-Promoters

The general character of nationalism is one aspect of a culture's receptivity to external democracy promotion. A distinct, albeit related, issue is how receptive the nationalism of the target country is to the specific foreign actors engaged in democracy promotion. The national origins of the democracy-promoter are of crucial significance. If the foreign organization originates in a place that local nationalism regards with suspicion, the efforts of the promoters may be fruitless or even counterproductive. If the nationalism of the target country is generally friendly to the place from which the outsiders hail, the cultural milieu for democracy promotion will be less problematic.

Virtually all democracy-promotion efforts originate in the northwest. The United States is the leader. The U.S. Agency for International Development (USAID), which is part of the Department of State, as well as the nongovernmental National Democratic Institute (NDI) and the International Republican Institute (IRI), lead the American pack in terms of resources and global coverage. The Soros Foundation's Open Society Institute (OSI) is deeply engaged in the post-communist region and, in recent years, has opened offices elsewhere as well. The Asia Foundation, headquartered in San Francisco, supports democratization in East, Southeast, and South Asia. Dozens of other American organizations, and some Canadian groups, including the Canadian International Development Agency (CIDA), also attempt to advance democracy abroad. Some engage in multiple tasks, with democracy promotion being only one of several things they do. Others concentrate mainly or exclusively on democratization.

Most of the other agencies are headquartered in northwestern Europe. Germany is Europe's leader. Each of its main political parties has an international arm that partners with actors abroad who share the principles of the respective German party. The main organizations are the Social Democratic Party's Friedrich Ebert Foundation, which aids social democrats (or their rough equivalents) in developing countries, and the Christian Democratic Party's Konrad Adenauer Foundation, which does the same for Christian Democrats (or whatever pro-democratic right-center organizations there are to work with). British and Scandinavian organizations also figure prominently. The U.K. Department for International Development is involved in governance and democracy promotion. The Westminster Foundation for Democracy and the Commonwealth Parliamentary Association focus especially on strengthening legislatures, as does the Swedish organization, Sida. On the level of broader Europe, the EU has established a directorate for the promotion of democracy, and the European Commission has set up agencies for human rights and democratization.

Not all countries that have the resources to engage in democracy promotion do so. Whereas many groups from the United States, the United Kingdom, Germany, and Scandinavia labor to advance democratization abroad, other rich democracies are bereft of such outward-bound agencies. Cross-cultural variation *within* the advanced industrialized world may account for differences in policy. That matter cannot be addressed here, but it is interesting to note that proselytizing democracy is largely a Protestant affair. Although the French, Italians, Japanese, and Taiwanese extend substantial foreign aid, democracy promotion does not figure prominently in their foreign agendas. The French government has recently forayed into the realm of "governance." But, its program, which is carried out by the ministry of foreign affairs, explicitly aims first and foremost "to re-legitimize the state" in developing countries. Its efforts on behalf of better governance are fully integrated with its technical and development assistance. The French government, as well as other French agencies, shies away from promoting democracy *per se* (*Stratégie gouvernance de la coopération française* 2007).

Thus, given that the bulk of democracy promotion efforts emanate from the northwest, the orientation of the recipient country's nationalism toward the northwest is of special importance. If nationalism in the recipient country is well-disposed toward the northwest, the promoters of democracy will encounter less cultural resistance than where nationalism is suspicious of the northwest's intentions.

Assessing the Quality of Nationalism

Assessing the quality of nationalism is difficult. Doing so requires judgment calls on the part of the author and indulgence on the part of the reader. The categorical distinctions offered in the following pages are made in the spirit of a thought experiment and are intended to be taken as such.

TABLE 3.4: Orientation of nationalism

Country	Character of nationalism: Orientation to outside influence in general (smooth versus prickly)	Orientation of nationalism to the promoters of democracy in particular (favorable versus unfavorable)
Albania	Smooth	Favorable (NA)
Algeria	Prickly	Unfavorable (NA)
Argentina	Prickly	Unfavorable (−56)
Bangladesh	Smooth	Favorable (+12)
Bosnia	Smooth	Favorable (NA)
Chile	Prickly	Favorable (+20)
China	Prickly	Unfavorable (−23)
Egypt	Prickly	Unfavorable (−57)
India	Prickly	Favorable (+31)
Indonesia	Smooth	Unfavorable (−37)
Iran	Prickly	Unfavorable (NA)
Jordan	Prickly	Unfavorable (−58)
S. Korea	Prickly	Favorable (+20)
Kyrgyzstan	Smooth	Favorable (NA)
Macedonia	Prickly	Favorable (NA)
Mexico	Prickly	Favorable (+15)
Moldova	Smooth	Favorable (NA)
Nigeria	Smooth	Favorable (+43)
Pakistan	Prickly	Unfavorable (−53)
Peru	Smooth	Favorable (+30)
Philippines	Smooth	Favorable (NA)
Saudi Arabia	Prickly	Unfavorable (NA)
Singapore	Prickly	Favorable (NA)
South Africa	Smooth	Favorable (+31)
Tanzania	Prickly	Favorable (+7)
Turkey	Prickly	Unfavorable (−74)
Uganda	Smooth	Favorable (+45)
Venezuela	Smooth	Favorable (+16)
Vietnam	Prickly	Unfavorable (NA)
Zimbabwe	Smooth	Favorable (NA)

Table 3.4 contains information on the orientation of nationalism in the countries under examination. The left-hand column offers a guess on whether the nationalism of the country is best characterized as "prickly" (that is, resistant to outside influence) or "smooth" (that is, receptive to outside influence). The only data used here are impressions drawn from secondary sources and personal experience in the field.

The right-hand column offers a judgment on whether the country's nationalism is generally favorable or unfavorable to the northwest. Here I draw on several sources. One is data from the Pew Global Attitudes Project (Pew Foundation 2007). A recent Pew survey, which was conducted in 46 countries and territories, asked people for their opinions on a range of issues. One question asked whether respondents have a favorable or unfavorable view of the United States. Because the United States is by far the biggest contributor to democracy promotion around the world, and because the United States is the largest country in the northwest, attitudes toward it may be used as a rough proxy for orientations toward the suppliers of democracy assistance. It is important to note that anti-American attitudes – perhaps all the more in the first decade of the 21st century – are *not* a sign of an antidemocratic culture (Moon 2003). (The elements of culture that *are* important for democracy, tolerance, and a spirit of equality, were previously discussed). Anti-American attitudes may serve, however, as a good indicator of cultural resistance to the democracy-promotion programs of Americans and other Westerners. The Pew surveys have data on attitudes toward the United States for 18 of the 30 countries under examination. In the right-hand column in Table 3.4, the number in parentheses indicates the percentage of respondents who reported a "favorable view" minus the percentage that reported an "unfavorable view" of the United States in the survey released in June 2007. I consider countries with positive numbers (which indicate more favorable than unfavorable views) to have a favorable orientation toward outside democracy-promoters and those with negative numbers (which indicate more unfavorable than favorable views) to have an unfavorable orientation.

For the 12 countries for which the Pew surveys do not provide data, I rely on other sources. One is the WVS. In the most recent wave of surveys, the WVS has added the question of whether "cultural invasion by the West" is a "very serious," "serious," "somewhat serious," "less serious," or "not serious" problem. The only countries for which data are currently reported are Egypt, Iran, Jordan, Saudi Arabia, Iraq, and Morocco. Of these six, the last two are not included in our analysis here because of a shortage of data for them on the other WVS items considered in previous sections of this chapter. Data are not plentiful, but what we have are helpful. They reinforce what the Pew surveys show for Egypt and Jordan and offer information that Pew lacks for Iran and Saudi Arabia. In Egypt, 64 percent considered Western cultural invasion a "very serious" threat whereas another 19 percent considered it a "serious" threat. In Jordan, an even more overwhelming 85 percent considered the threat "very serious" and another 7 percent rated it as "serious." These numbers are consistent with the overwhelmingly anti-American attitudes in these two countries that are reported by Pew. In Iran, for which Pew lacks data, 55 percent called the threat "very serious" and 15 percent "serious." In Saudi Arabia, the analogous figures were 67 and 15 percent. These unequivocal findings allow us readily to conclude that Iranian and Saudi Arabian nationalism are unfavorably disposed toward would-be promoters of democracy from the northwest corner of the world.

In using these data provided by Pew, as with the WVS data, caution is in order. What we have here are snapshots that do not account for possible fluidity in respondents' attitudes. Still, they provide us with useful data for making assessments, time-bound though they may be.

For the remaining ten countries I rely upon impressionistic data and inferences drawn from regional patterns. Albania may safely be considered favorable to outside democracy-promotion efforts. It is one of the last places in Europe President Bush could visit during his second term in office and still expect to be warmly received, as he was in June 2007. The U.S. bombardment of Serbia on behalf of ethnic Albanians in Kosovo in the late 1990s left Albanian public opinion, which was enamored with the West even before the attack on Serbia, even more hospitable to Western involvement than it was earlier. Algerian nationalism, if it conforms to the Middle Eastern and North African pattern, is as unfavorable to the West as Albanian nationalism is favorable. Nationalism in Bosnia is hard to characterize, because there are really three distinct nationalisms in the country (Bosniac-Muslim, Croatian, and Serbian). The Bosniacs and the Croats, who together make up three-quarters of Bosnia's population, are generally pro-Western, so Bosnia's nationalism may be considered favorable. Moldova is also a divided society, but its nationalism is generally pro-Western, and bullying by Russia has solidified this tendency. Kyrgyzstan is a harder call. Its nationalism is ambiguous and fluid, although on balance it may be considered pro-Western. Southeast Asia presents a mix. Nationalism in the Philippines and Singapore tends to be receptive to Western influence, whereas Vietnamese nationalism is hostile. If Zimbabwe conforms to the African regional pattern, its people welcome Western influence. In the Pew surveys, sub-Saharan Africa is by far the most pro-American region on Earth. Even the Muslim-majority countries of Senegal and Mali are overwhelmingly pro-American, as is Zimbabwe's large southern neighbor, South Africa.

TABLE 3.5: Cultural disposition to external democratizers, assessed by the character of nationalism and the orientation of nationalism toward suppliers of democracy assistance

| | | CHARACTER OF NATIONALISM | |
		Smooth	Prickly
ORIENTATION OF NATIONALISM TOWARD SUPPLIERS OF DEMOCRACY ASSISTANCE	Favorable	Albania, Bangladesh, Bosnia, Kyrgyzstan, Moldova, Nigeria, Peru, Philippines, South Africa, Uganda, Venezuela, Zimbabwe (1)	Chile, India, S. Korea, Macedonia, Mexico, Singapore, Tanzania (2)
	Unfavorable	Indonesia (3)	Algeria, Argentina, China, Egypt, Iran, Jordan, Pakistan, Saudi Arabia, Turkey, Vietnam (4)

Table 3.5 puts together the two major dimensions of nationalism under examination. Countries in quadrant 1 present the least problematic environment for democracy-promoters. This cell of the table houses countries whose nationalism is generally not hostile to outsiders and is generally friendly to the part of the world that provides democracy assistance. Local actors in these countries may benefit from outside help. Their credibility with their countrymen may be compromised little or not at all by association with outsiders. Albanian, Peruvian, South African, and Zimbabwean democrats may welcome the aid and put it to good use without violating national sentiment. At the other end of the spectrum lie the countries in quadrant 4. Here, one finds both prickly nationalism and suspicion of the countries from which most democracy-promoters hail. Some Chinese, Egyptian, and Pakistani democrats might welcome outside assistance, but many of most savvy activists will shun it, and for good reason. They will know that the aid may do their cause more harm than good. Quadrants 2 and 3 contain ambivalent cases. In quadrant 2 are countries whose nationalism is prickly, but not hostile to northwestern influence; in quadrant 3 is a country whose nationalism is smooth, but unfavorable

TABLE 3.6: General assessment of the prospects for external democracy promotion

		CULTURAL DISPOSITION TOWARD DEMOCRACY	
		More favorable	*Less favorable*
CULTURAL RECEPTIVITY TO DEMOCRACY PROMOTION	*More receptive*	Albania, Bosnia, Chile, S. Korea, Kyrgyzstan, Macedonia, Mexico, Moldova, Peru, Philippines, Singapore, South Africa, Tanzania, Venezuela, Zimbabwe (1)	Bangladesh, India, Indonesia, Nigeria, Uganda (2)
	Less receptive	Argentina, China, Pakistan, Vietnam (3)	Algeria, Egypt, Iran, Jordan, Saudi Arabia, Turkey (4)

to penetration by actors from the northwest. Tanzania is an example of the former; Indonesia is the sole case of the latter.

Countries in quadrant 1 will be the least resistant to democracy-promotion efforts from the outside; those in quadrant 4 will be the most resistant. Quadrants 2 and 3 are grey areas.

CULTURE AND EXTERNAL DEMOCRACY PROMOTION: OVERALL ASSESSMENT AND PRESCRIPTIONS

A General Assessment

We may summarize the findings by collapsing the information presented in Tables 3.3 and 3.5 into a single table. Table 3.6 provides this general scheme. Here, countries that fall into cells 1, 2, 3, 4, 5, and 7 in Table 3.3 are considered to have cultures that are generally favorable for democracy. Thus, the countries in cells 3, 5, and 7 in Table 3.3, whose combined ratings on tolerance and equality make them ambivalent in terms of over-all propensity to democracy, are lumped with the countries in cells 1, 2, and 4, which have more unequivocally favorable cultural orientations. All of these countries together are considered to have cultural orientations that are propitious for democracy. In Table 3.6, they appear in the left column (quadrants 1 and 3). Countries that are grouped in cells 6, 8, and 9 in Table 3.3 are considered to have an overall cultural disposition toward democracy that is unfavorable. They appear in the right column in Table 3.6 (quadrants 2 and 4). The classification shown in Table 3.6, by placing the ambivalent cases with the positive cases, provides a permissive, optimistic synthesis of the evidence on tolerance and equality.

The rows in Table 3.6 synthesize the information in Table 3.5. Countries are divided into those that are more and less favorable to democracy promotion by outsiders. The countries in quadrant 1 in Table 3.5 are shown in the top row in Table 3.6 (quadrants 1 and 2). So too are countries whose cultural orientation toward external democratizers is ambivalent – that is, those that are placed in quadrants 2 and 3 in Table 3.5 – put in the top row in Table 3.6. This means that both countries whose cultural orientations toward outside involvement are positive and those whose orientations are ambivalent are considered "more receptive" to external involvement in Table 3.6. This assessment again amounts to a sanguine summary of the evidence. Only countries that have both prickly nationalism and an unfavorable orientation toward the providers of democracy assistance – those in quadrant 4 in Table 3.5 – are considered to be culturally "less receptive" to democracy assistance in the summary in Table 3.6. Only they appear in the bottom row (quadrants 3 and 4) in Table 3.6.

The countries that appear in quadrant 1 in Table 3.6, by virtue of their cultural disposition to *democracy* and their cultural disposition to *democracy promotion*, are potentially good candidates for external promoters of democracy. These countries represent every major region of the developing world except the Middle East. There is no obvious concentration of countries in confessional terms. Two of the countries are predominantly Muslim (Albania and Kyrgyzstan) and two are roughly evenly divided between Muslims and Christians (Bosnia and Tanzania). Buddhism, Confucianism, and Christianity are all prominent in South Korea and Singapore. The rest of the countries are predominantly Christian, although some, such as the Philippines and Macedonia, have large Muslim minorities. The countries span a wide range of socioeconomic development, from wealthy South Korea and Chile to impoverished Tanzania and Zimbabwe.

The countries in the other portions of the table are not good candidates for democracy promotion. The danger with countries in quadrant 2 is that outsiders' efforts will be wasted. The countries may be receptive to outsiders, but cultural conditions might not be conducive to democratization, leaving democracy-promoters empty-handed. Of course, culture is only one of many possible determinants of democratization. The impressive records of India (ever since independence) and Indonesia (in the post-Suharto era) show that the matters discussed in this chapter are only one – and perhaps not the most important – part of why open government rises or falls. But, external democracy-promoters should, in any event, be aware that they may face cultural barriers to democratization, even if the promoters of democracy themselves are well received.

The countries in quadrant 3 present a different hazard. Their cultures may be auspicious for democracy, but also resistant to outsiders. Here, wasting resources is less of a danger than is damaging democratization by associating it with alien forces.

Quadrant 4 contains the countries that may be resistant to both democracy *per se* and to external democracy-promoters. They present the least promising cases for external democracy promotion.

Prescriptions

The first prescriptive implication of the preceding analysis regards where to promote democracy and where not to. Some countries should be regarded as much better bets than others. Some should be ruled out entirely as candidates for external intervention. Although democracy promotion may proceed smoothly in the countries in quadrant 1 of Table 3.6, it probably will not do so in the countries elsewhere in the table. If outsiders choose nevertheless to try to promote democracy in any of these countries, they should maintain a low profile. Particularly in countries such as appear in quadrants 3 and 4, outsiders are likely to encounter hostile nationalism. The lower their profile and more modest their stated aims, the better.

Would-be external promoters of democracy have no business operating in the countries in quadrant 4. That is not to say that the cause of democracy is hopeless in these countries. In Turkey, for example, it is demonstrably anything but hopeless. But, foreigners need to tread lightly – or, better yet, not at all – in these places, where cultural change, which rarely happens quickly, is a prerequisite to effective promotion of democracy by external actors. Prior to such change, foreigners' efforts may be worse than useless.

All of the countries under consideration that fall in quadrant 4 are located in the Middle East and North Africa. In these countries, the spirit of equality, at least as measured in this chapter, is relatively low. What is more, majorities in each country have dim regard for the intentions of Western powers and especially the United States. Particularly important in this region is America's long-standing policy of unconditional support for Israel. Americans may hold dear their country's unstinting loyalty to Israel and be ready to bear any burden and pay any price to maintain it. But, they then should honestly face up to the devastating effects the policy has on the image of American intentions in the region and the possibility of contributing to democratization there.

The second prescriptive implication regards the wisdom of diversifying the sources of democracy assistance. The goal of diversification should not be burden-sharing among the promoters of democracy, which is not really necessary, because the northwest can well afford such efforts as it now sponsors and does not need financial help. Nor should the goal be to promote "diversity" for its own sake. The aims of diversification should rather be to involve donors who will not offend local nationalism and include actors who, because of their own experience, are especially savvy at reading and responding to conditions in the target country. Diversification may take one of three forms: 1) varying the national source of assistance; 2) internationalizing the source of assistance; and 3) de-statizing the source of assistance.

Varying the national source of democracy aid means countries from outside the northwest taking a larger role as providers of help. The present chapter has treated democracy assistance as a Western-initiated and Western-financed business, as the bulk of it does emanate from the West. But, it may originate from other quarters. Such aid may be particularly effective. Valerie Bunce and Sharon Wolchik (2006) have shown how aid from the early democratizers in Eastern Europe (such as the Czech Republic and Hungary) to initially less-successful democratizers in the same region (such as Slovakia and Serbia) helped sustain a "second wave" of democratization within post-communist Europe in the late 1990s. Activists in the latter countries benefited from the advice on political strategy proffered by their counterparts from neighboring countries who had recently faced – and won – a similar struggle. Some of these efforts were backed, at least indirectly, by Western funding. But, the aid, in fact and in appearance, had more of an East-to-East than a West-to-East character. And, the fact that the advice was devised by East Europeans made it shrewder – as well as more intelligible and palatable to its recipients – than it would have been coming from Western agencies.

Indeed, countries outside the northwest may have a substantial part to play. South-South aid may be of particular importance. Post-apartheid South Africa, with its substantial resources and recent history of successful, mass-driven democratization, has a special place in Africa. At least in the post-Mandela era, its government has refrained from supporting democratization abroad. In fact, the government of Thabo Mbeki has actually provided aid and comfort to the chaotic dictatorship of Robert Mugabe in Zimbabwe. The policy, however, may be attributable to the ethical and psychological shortcomings of President Mbeki, whose child-like veneration for Mugabe endured even as South Africa itself swelled with refugees from Mugabe's vicious autocracy. Should South African leaders choose to support democratization abroad in the post-Mbeki era, however, they would hold distinct advantages. They would enjoy prestige as fellow Africans and victors in a struggle against a racist dictatorship that, at least tacitly and intermittently, enjoyed the support of the government of the United States.

Whether the leaders of major Third World (and formerly Third World) democracies such as South Africa, India, South Korea, Indonesia, and Brazil will push for open government outside their own borders remains to be seen. Democracy may be too young and fragile in these countries (with the possible exception of India) for elites to consider promoting democracy abroad. Such caution may be well founded. But, the involvement of these countries would diversify, and possibly enrich, the wellsprings of democracy assistance. Even here, however, donors must be mindful of the prickliness and orientation of nationalism and the potential for cultural resistance to outside interference.

Internationalizing assistance is another way to soften the encounter with the cultures of target countries. All of the efforts discussed in this chapter are, in some sense, "international" in character. But, here, I refer explicitly to international organizations whose membership consists of governmental representatives from multiple countries. The UN and the Organization of American States (OAS) are examples. They normally rub local nationalism in the target country more gently than do, say, American agencies. The expansion of the UN's and the OAS's election-monitoring functions over the past two decades provides an example of successful internationalization of an important democracy-promotion task. It is important to remember, however, that people in the target countries are often wise to the real sources of national power that underlie international organizations. The UN and the OAS are effective, in part, because they are not (or are no longer) seen as tools of the U.S. government. The same cannot be said of, for example, the World Bank.

Destatizing the sources of assistance is the third means of diversification. Some leading democracy-promotion agencies, as noted above, are non-state entities. NDI and the Adenauer Foundation are examples. However, these agencies do rely largely on government contributions; they are supported by the taxpayers of the United States and Germany, respectively. They operate with little interference from the U.S. and German governments, but they are not, strictly speaking, independent. Actors in host countries associate them with the countries of their origin. The Soros Foundation's OSI is independent of government influence, which gives it credibility that state-funded organizations sometimes lack. Still, the status of its founder, George Soros, as a lord of global capitalism who made his billions as a currency speculator, influences the OSI's reputation. People in countries whose economies Soros has singed, such as Russia, Malaysia, Indonesia, and Thailand, do not necessarily regard Soros and the OSI as disinterested and benign.

Other organizations, however, are entirely detached from both governments and profit-making. They may enjoy special prestige. The student-initiated movement to divest from companies that did business in apartheid-era South Africa was a model of successful democracy promotion (Rodman 1994). The effort, which started in the United States and spread to Europe, was not only independent of national governments, it emerged in opposition to them, and particularly to the Reagan administration's policy of "constructive engagement," which in practice amounted to warm relations with South Africa's whites-only government. The movement did not even have boots on the ground in South Africa. Its activities were limited to changing the behavior of Western corporations whose investments sustained the South African economy. Its lack of a physical presence in the target of democracy assistance minimized the danger of offending local nationalism. The leaders of the movement, moreover, did not act alone. They followed media reports on how leaders of the main anti-apartheid organization in South Africa, the African National Congress (ANC), regarded the divestment movement. So, too, did they consult with the ANC. They followed the cues of the ANC's leader, Nelson Mandela, who strongly supported the American and European students' actions.

The anti-apartheid effort was a social movement, and movements are by nature fleeting. Non-state entities that have lasting organizational structures may also engage in democracy promotion. An example is the Carter Center, headquartered in Atlanta, which monitors elections and engages in other relevant activities abroad, especially in Latin America and the Middle East. The Carter Center typically does not offend local nationalism because of its complete independence from the U.S. government, and indeed its reputation as an antagonist of the administration of

George W. Bush. The founder of the center, former U.S. president Jimmy Carter, is known in Latin America as a human rights advocate and in the Middle East as a critic of the U.S. government's unconditional support for Israel. The Carter Center does not have a major global democracy-promotion program; its political activities are largely limited to election monitoring. But, if it or other such non-state organizations were to develop a major capacity for democracy promotion, they might fill important niches. One can readily imagine, for example, a Carter Center-sponsored democracy-promotion agency in Cairo, Amman, or Buenos Aires meeting with less suspicion than USAID programs do.

Despite the drawbacks of engaging in democracy promotion in many countries, it is important to acknowledge that democracy promotion has become a multibillion-dollar industry that employs thousands of people. Even if God Herself were to reveal this day definitive evidence that all democracy-promotion efforts did more harm than good, the officials at USAID, OSI, IRI, and the Ebert foundation would still be at work tomorrow – and the day after tomorrow and probably for a long time after that. Funds have been allocated, bureaucracies built, talented people employed, and an international community of experts formed. The democracy-promotion business has a spirited and entrenched institutional life of its own, and its size and complexity grows by the year. Still, mindfulness of cultural constraints should help would-be promoters of democracy at least to do no harm to the cause they hope to advance.

DANIEL CHIROT

4 Does Democracy Work in Deeply Divided Societies?

The sad fate of recent political reforms pushed on the Middle East and on some African countries should make all of us skeptical about the value of blanket recommendations to promote democracy as a universal solution to the problems of autocratic and corrupt regimes. As the cases of Iraq and Lebanon in the early 2000s have demonstrated, if ethno-religious communities that compete with each other place their own values, interests, and loyalties above those of a theoretical national welfare, then stable democracy is impossible. This is all the more so if such competition is viewed as being zero-sum, with gains by any community necessarily resulting in equal losses by the others.

THE PROBLEM OF DIVIDED BUT STRONG COMMUNAL, CULTURALLY BASED IDENTITIES

In a prescient comment made at a time when it seemed that deep religious conflicts were less important than they had been in the past, Milton Friedman wrote, "Fundamental differences in basic values can seldom if ever be resolved at the ballot box; ultimately they can only be decided, though not resolved, by conflict. The religious and civil wars of history are a bloody testament to this judgment" (Friedman 2002: 24). Friedman concludes from this that extending market relations into as many areas

---

I would like to thank the other authors in this volume and especially its editors for their excellent comments. I am also very grateful to Jason Brownlee for his close reading of my first draft and his perceptive critique and recommendations, and to Marko Papic for his useful bibliographic suggestions. Finally, I thank Sophie Namy whose excellent paper for my seminar provided me with insights into Sri Lankan and Indian history that helped me greatly.

of social life as possible and away from politics is the best way to avoid such conflicts. Coming from a noted economist, this is not surprising. It mirrors the Enlightenment's faith in commerce as a solvent best able to resolve the passions that lead to violence because economic relations are likely to be based on rational self-interest. Albert Hirschman's great work on this subject, *The Passions and the Interests* (1977: v) opens with Montesquieu's famous quote, "And it is men's good fortune that they are in a situation where, at the same time that their passions make them think mean thoughts, they nevertheless have an interest in not being nasty." Hirschman goes on to show that many Enlightenment thinkers came to believe that commerce, and more generally, economic activity was more rational, and, therefore, less likely to lead to bloodshed than religion, considerations of honor, prestige, or sheer lust for power.

It is terribly difficult, however, to separate the material interests of various communities from their loyalty to their members and their religious or other ideological values. In practice, these are so intertwined that untangling beliefs that are created to legitimate interests from interests that emerge from deep loyalties or beliefs is best left to theorists who take it on faith that one or the other of these provides the key independent variable to explain behavior. Fortunately, we do not need to do this. If competing communities' economic interests are highly correlated with different culturally based identities, they become much harder to reconcile than purely economic differences between groups, even if material differences are at the heart of actual disputes. In other words, merely encouraging commerce is not enough.

Why do Shia Muslims fight Sunni Muslims in Lebanon and Iraq? Is it because of deep religious differences that go back to seventh century power struggles between various Arab clans for control of their new empire, or in Lebanon is it, as Fouad Ajami has persuasively argued in *The Vanished Imam* (1986), really because Shia Muslims were long a marginalized, impoverished underclass looked down upon by both Christian and Sunni Arabs? Ajami is certainly right that it was economic deprivation, and its inevitable accompaniment, social contempt, that shaped Lebanese Shia anger and eventually their political rise to power. Yet, this growing power has come about through explicitly religious leaders, and in both Lebanon and Iraq, where the Shia were similarly marginalized for a long time, their political activism is legitimized by their faith and led by imams, not secular politicians. On the other hand, in the case of Iraq, we know that the majority of southern Iraqi Shia are descendents of Arabs who were Sunni until the nineteenth, and often the early twentieth century (Nakash 2002: 14–48)! How and why these Sunni Muslims converted to Shi'ism is a long, a complex story that has to do with the ways in which nomadic tribes were sedentarized in places where the small urban elites were already Shia, the commercial advantages obtained by Shia merchants in the holy pilgrimage cities of Najaf and Karbala, Ottoman and later British policies that went awry, and much else. The point is not to deny that Shia-Sunni differences date back to seventh century conflicts for political power in the Muslim Empire of that time, but to show that such simplified historical explanations that rely on age old ideological and theological differences have too little explanatory power to stand alone.

Vali Nasr makes it clear that Shia and Sunni conflicts combine very old historical elements with contemporary religious interpretations of Islam, memories of long ago political and economic differences with entirely modern ones, and practically inseparable ideological and material conflicts.

There are few places in the world where the confusion between religiously, ethnically, nationally, and economically motivated conflict is as obvious as in the Middle East. Are Druzes an ethnic community or a religious one? Is Walid Jumblat, their hereditary leader in Lebanon, primarily interested in defending Druze property rights and economic well being, or in preserving their obscure faith that is an offshoot of an eleventh century Shia sect that developed under the rule of the Egyptian Fatimids? Is it that the Lebanese Druzes are held together mostly by kinship ties that trump all other loyalties in an area with such a weak state and turbulent history that only alliances of extended families can offer basic protection of life and property? All of these are valid explanations, and which came first is probably an unsolvable historical puzzle.[1]

Similarly, whether or not to call Shia and Sunni Muslims different sects, different religions, or in places such as Lebanon and Iraq, different ethnic groups can best be left to those who insist on precise definitions rather than genuine understanding. They are all of these, mixed together and separated by belief, history, kinship, and competing interests.

There are many excellent definitions of ethnicity put forward by political theorists, but, in the end, it turns out that ethnicity, like nation, is

---

[1] Few American policy makers have much knowledge about the immense diversity of clans, tribes, sects, theologies, and ethnicities in the Middle East. Druzes, Alawites, Mandeans, Nusayris, Isma'ilis, and many other kinds of Muslim or semi-Muslim sects exist, without mentioning divergences between mainstream Shia and Sunni, Sufi orders, or the bewildering number of Christian or semi-Christian groups. For a brief, learned introduction to the main religious groups, see Hourani (2002: 172–188). On Druze history, see Firro (1992) and Swayd (2006).

a subjective sense that somehow, whether through assumed kinship or common beliefs and values, "we" all have enough in common to stick together against other communities (Smith 2001; Fenton 2003). Were the Croats, Serbs, and Bosnian Muslims in the Yugoslavia of the 1980s increasingly hostile to each other because of their ethnic differences? If so, what, other than religion, distinguished them as they spoke a common language, shared a common state, and were not different in any obvious physical way? Would Yugoslavia have had a civil war that broke it apart if its economy had thrived in the 1980s? Probably not, as much work has shown (Woodward 1995). Yet, as Takis Pappas (among others) has demonstrated in explaining the secret of Slobodan Milošević's rise to power, had there not been deeply held and relatively old (that is, dating to at least the nineteenth century, and perhaps earlier) ethnic and national mythologies about Serbia and Croatia that legitimized radically exclusionist behavior by their leaders, mere economic difficulties would not have created a civil war (Banac 1984; Judah 2000; Pappas 2005).

We could travel around the world and through time to come up with countless examples of deep divisions within states that were based on such a conflation of ideology, values, and material interests that reconciliation between communities proved impossible and conflict became inevitable. Americans, for example, tend to forget that in 1860 the differences between the South and the North were a mixture of all of these. Slavery was the key, of course, but poor Southern whites (except in Appalachian mountain regions) who had no slaves joined in willingly to defend their culture against Yankee outsiders. John Reed (1983) has explored the cultural differences that persist to this day between white Southerners and the rest of the United States, and he has gone so far as to claim that they are a distinct ethnicity with its own religious and social values that transcend pure material interest. This white Southern ethnic group, as it happens, came very close to forming its own nation, and it is only in retrospect and with a good bit of historical fudging that we Americans have come to think of the Civil War as just a big mistake that interrupted what had been and then again became a nation with shared values and interests. The South was, and in many respects remained well into the twentieth century (perhaps into the twenty-first), a different culture, partly for economic reasons, but also because of antiliberal values with respect to race and religion (Hartz 1955; Potter and Fehrenbacher 1976; Marx 1998; Black and Black 2002).

This reference to the American South brings us back to the main topic at hand, the difficulties of solving deep communal divisions with democracy. Although the American election of 1860 was not democratic by today's standards as women and nonwhites were excluded, it was, for its day, quite democratic, as the large majority of male whites were eligible to vote. The election that resulted in Lincoln's victory solved nothing and led directly to a bloody Civil War. This war might have occurred anyway, even without an election, but the election certainly did nothing to ease the conflict over slavery and what had become two different economies and cultures. The election of 1860 fit quite neatly into a remark about elections made by the political scientist Donald Horowitz (1985: 83–89). Elections in deeply divided societies are a kind of census that measures how many are on each side because people vote with their community and very few think of elections in terms other than a way of promoting their ethnic, religious, or regional group's interests, whatever these may be based on. Identity trumps direct material interest. Rich and poor Druzes, Shia Muslims, Serbs, or Southern whites in the United States have more often than not stuck together when faced by "outsiders," that is, those with different identities.

If economic class comes to be highly correlated with cultural identity, it becomes much harder to resolve differences with democratic or other forms of bargaining. That is what Milton Friedman meant by the remark cited at the beginning of this chapter. Furthermore, economic class does not trump kin or culturally based forms of identity, but rather the other way around. Cultures may result in part from old economic differences between communities or societies, and may at some point come from particular (to use Marxist terms) "modes of production," but once they become the basis of strong group identities, they take on a life of their own. This is why Lenin was so shocked by the betrayal of Western Europe's, especially Germany's, working class at the start of World War I, when socialist parties overwhelmingly chose to be loyal to their nations, not their class (Lenin 1939: Preface from 1917). This is also why Marxist attempts to deal with ethnic and nationalist differences tend to be reduced to simple assertions that all those strong non-class identities are simple examples of false consciousness, or can be explained away as really being based on economic class, whatever nonsense other analysts, and people themselves, may say (Balibar and Wallerstein 1991).

All this is by now quite well known, as are its implications for understanding why it is difficult to create what Fareed Zakaria has called liberal democracy. As the number of states with formal voting that can claim to be in some sense democracies has increased since the collapse of European communism in 1989–1991, so have the number of "illiberal" democracies, that is, those that do not respect constitutional norms, individual freedoms, or the property rights of those in the opposition, and that use elections to legitimize autocracy (1997). Many of these are formal democracies in which elections cannot solve communal conflicts, but rather tend to exacerbate them because they are so threatening to the losers who know that they risk losing everything. As Zakaria has put it in his well-known article that now seems astonishingly prescient:

> Once an ethnic group is in power, it tends to exclude other ethnic groups. Compromise seems impossible; one can bargain on material issues like housing, hospitals, and handouts, but how does one split the difference on a national religion? Political competition that is so divisive can rapidly degenerate into violence. Opposition movements, armed rebellions, and coups in Africa have often been directed against ethnically based regimes, many of which came to power through elections (1997: 36).

So, to cite a well-known Leninist text, although with the goal of promoting viable, stable, and liberal democracy rather than a Bolshevik revolution: what is to be done? Before addressing this question, it is useful to look more closely at a few representative cases.

WHEN DEMOCRATIC ELECTIONS EXACERBATE COMMUNAL CONFLICTS

What has happened in Côte d'Ivoire (the Ivory Coast) since the early 1990s is quite representative of African cases. Briefly, this was a country that became the most successful example of export led, agricultural development in Africa in the 1960s and 1970s. Cocoa, and to a lesser extent, coffee and other tropical crops (including lumber), provided the wealth that made Côte d'Ivoire the envy of its neighbors. But, this stimulated migration from its less successful neighbors, and a substantial internal migration from its Muslim and Savannah north into its forested and Christian/Animist south where the richest cocoa and coffee lands were being established in newly cleared forest lands, and where the capital city of Abidjan became one of West Africa's main commercial hubs. As long as the economy boomed, and the country was led by a reasonably benevolent dictator able to hand out benefits to regional elites throughout the country, political discontent and ethnic rivalries could be contained. The fact that the president was a southerner, as was most of the political elite, was generally accepted. Unfortunately, the economy began to stagnate in the 1980s and 1990s as cocoa prices fell and insufficient investment failed to diversify the economy. By 1990, the old way of doing business was facing extreme pressures at the very same time that Côte d'Ivoire's big power supporters, chiefly France, were starting to insist on democratization as a way of solving endemic corruption and waste. Also, the collapse of communism in Europe led to an international atmosphere that demanded more democracy. This is when the monopoly of power held by the old dictator and first president, Houphouët-Boigny, began to break down as ethnic discontent was increasing. Southern political leaders told southerners that they had been cheated by outsiders and were now threatened by "foreigners," whose voting power might put them at great risk. Northerners were told by their leaders that southern power (Houphouët was an Akan from the southeast) threatened their property rights. Southerners themselves were divided between the power holding Akan speakers and people in the southwest whose lands had been most subject to immigrant settlement. Houphouët was able to hold on until he died in 1993, but then tensions over forthcoming elections split the country apart. To remain in power, southern politicians essentially took away citizenship rights from northerners, calling all of them immigrants. This also led to gradual expropriations in the southwest of lands developed for decades by migrants from other parts of the country and from neighboring, mostly northern states. Eventually, this led to a series of violent elections, coups by northern military officers, and, in 2002, the division of the country into a rebel north and a south controlled by a minority politician from the southwest, Laurent Gbagbo, who held onto power by manipulating ethnic hatreds and relying increasingly on strong arm tactics by his ethnic militias. The solution that emerged in 2007, and might work, is a compromise between competing regional elites who will hold rigged elections, allowing Gbagbo to retain power, but sharing some benefits with those northerners willing to go along (Crook 1997; Boone 2003: 326; Chirot 2006).

The establishment of formal democracy in 1990 did not create Côte d'Ivoire's economic and social problems, but it certainly aggravated them. It did nothing whatsoever to resolve them. Ethnic communities had no trust in each other, and saw the potential victory of any single ethno-regional group as a disaster for others. Under such circumstances, establishing a genuinely transparent democracy could be counterproductive by making the tacit division of spoils between regional elites politically impossible.

In one form or another, this story could be told about much of Africa. It is not simply religion or ethnicity that is at stake, but also economic interests protected by communal membership. As Carles Boix has shown in his work, when some group controls a preponderance of the resources, those in control are fundamentally unwilling to let democratic elections change the situation, and those without the power to enforce their property rights are ultimately reduced to violence. Thus, the absence of stable property rights, combined with growing competition over scarce resources enhances any kind of communal conflict and makes it most unlikely that formal democratic mechanisms might mitigate conflict (Boix 2003, 2006).

In concluding remarks to a recent article, Boix also points to the fact that imposing democracy on a society without adequate institutional support is very difficult, requires a "heavy-handed" and prolonged occupation, and, therefore, broad support for a long time within the occupying country's own population. "Without generalized support, it ends up in failure – as shown by the partial reconstruction of the American South after the Civil War and its abandonment in the 1880s" (Boix 2006: 21).

Sri Lanka is another example of a country where democratic elections made ethnic tensions far worse and ultimately provoked a civil war. At the time of independence from Britain in 1948, Ceylon (as it was then called) seemed to be one of the most promising of the newly decolonized countries. It had a relatively high literacy rate and a well-educated, moderate elite, it had achieved independence peacefully, without creating much rancor, and it had a sound economy. The problem was that much of the Sinhalese Buddhist majority felt left out of power, not so much because the Tamil ethnic minority held more than its share of civil service jobs, but because the Anglophone, educated Sinhalese elite was disproportionately Christian and seemingly disdainful of Buddhist-Sinhalese tradition. Led by Buddhist monks and politicians who capitalized on this discontent, the Sinhalese population was mobilized to demand a more Buddhist, less English polity. This Sinhalese-Buddhist fundamentalism naturally alienated the Tamils who were dismissed as outsiders with no right to claim full Sri Lankan citizenship. Even though linguistic-religious exclusivity produced some violence, including the assassination by a Buddhist monk of the prime minister in 1959, elections continued to be held, and the Sinhalese majority increasingly pushed for the exclusion of Tamils from civil service jobs and university opportunities. Eventually, a radical separatist Tamil movement, the Tamil Tigers, took advantage of this by recruiting young, frustrated Tamils. Ruthlessly suppressing opposition to its draconian policies, the Tamil Tigers set up a virtually independent Tamil state in the north and parts of the east. Although successive Sri Lankan governments have tried to find compromise solutions to this problem, the radical Buddhist Sinhalese have never allowed this. So, in election after election, the balance of power held by these extremists has prevented a genuinely compromising policy. On the other side, the long civil war and high death toll, with well over 70,000 killed over the years, has solidified the power of the Tamil Tigers who will accept nothing short of complete separation. Continuing free elections in the majority of the country not controlled by the Tigers has resolved nothing (Tambiah 1992; Batholomeusz and De Silva 1998; Wilson 2000; Horowitz 2001; Namy 2006).

There are other similar cases where relatively free elections have repeatedly failed to produce regimes acceptable to all ethno-religious factions and instead turned into opportunities for the winners to pay off their ethnic supporters, but leave others dissatisfied. Nigeria has experienced this phenomenon from the time it became independent in 1960, and this has produced, since 1966, a series of military coups alternating with periods of relative democracy. It also resulted in one extremely bloody civil war in the late 1960s, and endemic local ethnic and religious violence that continues to kill thousands each year (Soyinka 1996; Rotberg 2004).

In those Latin American countries with substantial indigenous populations, for example Bolivia, past elections did little to address the demands of the poorer indigenous population, and with increasing democratization, ethnic tensions have increased as populist leaders have taken advantage of the widespread discontent to mobilize protest movements and make claims against the established elite. Whether this will result in ethnic and regional violent conflict in Bolivia is an open question right now, but the mere existence of democratic procedures is no guarantee that conflicts will be solved peacefully (Crabtree and Whitehead 2001; Eaton 2007).

Although discontent in East Pakistan (now Bangladesh) against West Pakistani domination long predated the civil war that led to separation in 1971, it was the attempt to hold free elections that proved a decisive breaking point. Because of East Pakistan's demographic weight, Bengali Pakistanis won a free election, but rather than be ruled by Bengalis, West Pakistan refused to accept the results. The outcome was an attempt by the Pakistani army to suppress East Pakistan, a revolt, hundreds of thousands of deaths, and the eventual separation of the two parts of Pakistan into separate states. Here, it was neither religion nor ethnicity alone, but the complex interaction between the development of a distinctive Bengali Islamic identity, linguistically based ethnic grievances in East Pakistan, and very different kinds of socioeconomic structures in East and West Pakistan that created growing political tensions. The attempt to hold together two very different Muslim societies made any democratic resolution difficult, but the ways in which political leaders exploited these differences before and after the election only made things worse. Again, the election was not the cause of long standing conflicts, but it was the event that turned a difficult situation into a murderous civil war (Sisson and Rose 1990; Uddin 2006).

In Yugoslavia, both Slobodan Milošević in Serbia and Franjo Tudjman in Croatia were elected in free elections, and both worked hard to exploit existing ethnic tensions. These were perfect examples of the triumph of nonliberal democracy at work, and it was chiefly their intransigence, supported by popular opinion, that led to the exceptionally brutal series of Yugoslav wars that killed hundreds of thousands in the 1990s (Hayden 1992).

One more example will suffice to show the range of possible catastrophes that democratic elections may produce. In late 1991, Algeria held its first free elections since independence. Discontent was high because its military dictatorship had failed to produce sufficient economic growth to employ a growing population, because its socialism had become so inefficient and corrupt, and because the entrenched elite seemed to care little for the well-being of the general population. In the first round of elections, it became obvious that a strongly Islamic movement would take power and overthrow the largely secular military elite, so the elections were cancelled, and this began a civil war that has killed over 100,000 people. This is not a case in which free elections produced a conflictual outcome, but in which elections revealed the unpopularity of the ruling elite, and it then moved to suppress democracy. The basis of organized discontent was not, in this case, ethnic, although there is considerable opposition to the regime among Algerian Berbers who feel marginalized by the Arab majority. Instead, it became religious and Algeria remains a cauldron of potential violence (Malley 1996; Martinez 2000).

This is not to say that dictatorships, or the kinds of fraudulent elections conducted in much of the world, are a solution, either, because there are many more cases in which political elites from one ethnicity, religion, or region have steered benefits very disproportionately toward their group, and made it almost impossible for other communities to redress the situation without violence. This has been the story in Rwanda and Burundi, in Sudan, Burma, Guatemala (where the violence was primarily a matter of class and ideology, but where indigenous Mayans suffered a disproportionately high number of deaths in the massacres of the 1970s and 1980s), the Congo, and other places. Even in Algeria, it is conceivable (but not very likely) that had free elections been allowed to proceed, there would have been no violence.

Holding elections and then violently suppressing the results, as happened in Algeria in 1992 and Bangladesh in 1971, combines the worst of all possible outcomes. Ethnic, religious, economic, and regional hostilities are mobilized, but then disappointed, and the result is likely to be lasting bitterness and civil war.

Clearly, democracy is not a panacea, and, in some important cases, it actually increases the potential for violence between competing ethnic, religious, and regional communities. To confound any neat conclusion, however, there are cases that demonstrate the exact opposite, where democratic institutions have made accommodation between competing ethno-religious and regional communities possible.

WHEN DEMOCRATIC ELECTIONS EASE COMMUNAL CONFLICTS

In 1969, there were deadly ethnic riots in Malaysia that threatened to ignite a civil war between a very large Chinese minority and a politically dominant Malay Muslim population. The Malays were a slim majority of the population. (Singapore, with its large ethnic Chinese majority, had been expelled from Malaysia in 1965 to guarantee the Malays' majority.) The Malaysian Chinese had a preponderant portion of the wealth. Yet, almost 40 years later, Malaysia is relatively, if imperfectly, democratic, holds regular elections, and remains peacefully ethnically diverse. The worst did not happen. The Malays kept their political power, but the dominant Malay political party struck a bargain with the dominant Chinese party to bolster its parliamentary majority against more extremist Muslims and discontented Malays. The Malay elite instituted a new economic policy that favored Malays, and university positions went mostly to the favored Malays. On the other hand, Chinese property was not confiscated. Because the government's economic policy was oriented toward market capitalism rather than socialist centralization, and because it was so favorable to outside investment, the economy boomed, and the Chinese as well as the Malays benefited.

In fact, the Chinese commercial elite, even under British rule, had been willing to collaborate with Malay leaders as they had been united in their opposition to the Communist insurgency that had been composed almost entirely of ethnic Chinese during the late 1940s and 1950s. This had enabled the British to win that guerrilla war and turn an independent Malaysia over to the leading, conservative Malay political movement in 1957. What therefore emerged was a workable alliance between a growing Malay middle class and business elite with their Chinese middle class and business counterparts, and this has guaranteed peace. Radical Muslim Malays and more radically inclined Chinese have been marginalized. Economic growth and the respect of property rights have eased Chinese fears, even though they are politically weaker than the Malays. The Chinese eventually were allowed to create private schools to educate those of their children who felt discriminated against by official pro-Malay policies, and the Chinese have prospered. The smaller Indian minority has also accepted this bargain that guarantees their survival and property at the cost of ceding political power to the Malays. Malaysia is not a society in which ethnic tensions have disappeared, and many poor Malays feel left out. Nevertheless, a bargain struck by elites of the main ethnic groups has held, and is legitimized by more or less free elections and parliamentary compromises (Horowitz 1985: 404–427, 582; Crouch 1996; Jomo 1997; Lee 2000).

This is a road that could have been followed by Sri Lanka, but was not. There, a more state-centered development strategy slowed economic growth, and instead of bargaining with each other, the more moderate Tamil and Sinhalese parties were taken over by their extremists.

India, an exceptionally diverse set of cultures, languages, religions, and regions, has held together in relative peace in large part because of its democracy. There has always been violence in some parts of India, much of it ethno-religious, but despite a bloody Sikh rebellion; continuing deadly violence between Muslims and Hindus in some (but hardly all) of India; uprisings and deadly ethnic clashes in the northeast; and a bloody civil war in Kashmir; in the end, most of the country has held together and not broken down into the kind of all consuming war and separation experienced by Yugoslavia, Pakistan, Sri Lanka, or African countries such as Sudan or Côte d'Ivoire. Given the enormous differences in wealth, religions, and ethnicity between various regions, how was this done? There was, to begin, a strong and united civil service inherited from British rule. After the bloody break with Pakistan and the associated killings and war at the time of independence in 1947–1948, India was led for a long time by the moderate Jawaharlal Nehru who insisted on maintaining democratic norms. Provinces were realigned so that in each ethno-religious majorities could have their government and substantial powers. Thus, it was possible for, say, southern Tamils to have careers and their own government without having to give in to the Hindu speaking northerners who dominated national politics. Because no ethnicity or religion has a clear majority and democratic federalism was maintained (except for a few short years under Nehru's authoritarian daughter, Indira Gandhi), democratic bargaining over interests prevailed. Political scientist Ashutosh Varshney has written:

> India has a dispersed, not a centrally focused ethnic configuration. Since independence no single identity or cleavage – religious, linguistic, caste – has had the power to override all other identities at the national level. . . . To come to power in Delhi, politicians must build bridges and coalitions across cleavages. In short, because of India's multicultural diversity, its politics is oriented towards ideological centrism (Varshney 2002: 73–74, 85).

Again, for all its imperfections, India is a clear example of a poor country beset by countless economic, social, ethnic, and religious conflicts that holds together democratically. Even during its long period of economic stagnation after independence, the political system survived and loyalty to the Indian nation solidified. Any attempt by a particular community to force the others to conform, or to accept exclusion from power, would have been disastrous. Those areas that have revolted have been precisely the ones where minorities felt it was impossible to have a say, either because they are too small to count, as in the far northeast, or because central rule has been excessively heavy handed, as in the majority Muslim parts of Kashmir. Meanwhile, Indian democracy has permitted lower classes to gain more influence, Hindu ultra-nationalists to compete for power peacefully, and most varieties of local separatists to be more or less accommodated into the political system and to pursue their claims without resorting to separatism, or at least to resolve disputes without breaking up India (Horowitz 1985: 672–676; Harris 2002; Rudolph and Rudolph 2002; Namy 2006).

There are, of course, many examples of democratic polities in the rich parts of the world that have defused ethnic conflict through democratic power sharing. These do not seem as dramatic because economic prosperity obviously makes it easier to spread out benefits, but it is worth mentioning some cases that demonstrate how democracy can mitigate ethnic conflict, and even contain it so that it remains peaceful. Canada and Switzerland, both highly federalized polities in which the regions have great power and can maintain their own languages and governments, are good examples. Arend Lijphart (1977) developed a whole theory of what he called "consociational democracies" to explain these successes. Unfortunately, some of his cases, most notably Lebanon, proved to be mirages, but others such as India, Switzerland, and Canada have worked relatively well. Majority or predominant ethno-religious groups have not generally attempted to impose themselves on minorities, or else over time have become more flexible about this, and thus allowed those with less power to share. Democratic norms have promoted negotiations over violent protest and federalism has allowed local majorities to hold regional power.

This can be contrasted with Northern Ireland, also an economically highly developed area, where Protestants for decades excluded Catholics from power and economic opportunity, until sectarian violence brought direct British rule and three decades of murderous conflict in the late twentieth century (McGarry and O'Leary 1995; Gallagher 2001).

It is possible that in the early twenty-first century Indonesia is setting out on the kind of democratic course that has worked in India. The outbreak of extreme ethnic, religious, and regional violence in many parts of that country in the late 1990s and early 2000s was largely caused by the nature of the repressive Suharto regime and the void it left as it collapsed. The ensuing uncertainty provoked struggles to redress old grievances, and a competition for power between various groups. Despite this, democratic reforms took hold and promise to promote a more peaceful outcome. Robert Hefner ascribes this success to the moderation of the mainstream, majority Islamic parties that learned from the horrible slaughter of their enemies in 1965–1966 and the subsequent repression of the Suharto years that neither violence nor sectarian intolerance are viable ways of holding their country together. Whether or not democracy lasts and holds together so many diverse groups in the future is far from clear, but it could happen if moderate Muslims continue to hold power in this, the largest of all Muslim countries in the world. So far, democratic elections have provided a soothing rather than a polarizing effect (Bertrand 2004; Hefner 2000, 2005).

But all this returns us to the question of how to achieve this? What can be done to make such a favorable outcome more likely? If, as we have seen, formal democracy with elections sometimes helps, but at other times makes the situation worse, what is the best way to promote peaceful outcomes?

MAKING DEMOCRACY: SOME DISCOURAGING HISTORICAL PRECEDENTS

It would be possible to code every country in the world, assign some value to the degree of ethnic or religious division, the extent to which each is democratic, and then measure how well or poorly this correlates with political violence, including civil war. This would be a useful exercise, but an incomplete one because it would miss the causal mechanisms that lead to political violence and the important, although sometimes subtle differences between very different kinds of democracy and the vastly different historical traditions in the many countries that have tried to adopt some kind of democracy.

Making working democracies is partly a matter of getting communities in conflict with each other to bargain, but also of having the right institutional framework widely accepted by all, or at least most of the contending groups.

When there were proposals to resolve Yugoslavia's ethno-religious differences in the early 1990s, one popular idea was to create "cantons" on the Swiss model, and a kind of confederation, or at most a loose federation of small units that could each be relatively homogeneous. Needless to say, even though they are not geographically very far apart, Switzerland, whose cantonal system developed over seven centuries before it evolved into the modern Swiss state, has had an entirely different history than Yugoslavia, and its model is probably totally useless elsewhere (Barber 1973; Steinberg 1996). Similarly, the "pillarization" adopted by the Dutch to smooth religious tensions between Catholics and Protestants, and later extended to include other groups, never really had much chance of working in Lebanon, which was set up to give the major communities proportional power, but never created much sense of genuine national unity, and so has led to repeated, violent disasters (Zijdervel 1998; El-Khazen 2000).

The problem with making generalizations about democracy is not only that there are such large differences between individual cases, but also that many of those who propose to spread democratic reforms around the world, particularly Americans, have forgotten the history of how democracy evolved in those Western countries where it originated, and particularly how it developed in the Anglo-American context or in a very different way in France. Great Britain, France, and the United States may be the three major power examples of democratic development, but the advocates of democratization in the twenty-first century rarely reflect on how these three countries actually became democratic.

English democracy was not decreed, but developed slowly out of a medieval compromise between local lords, the church, and the monarchy. Similar compromises were worked out throughout much of Western Europe, but in England, this peculiar power sharing agreement somehow survived as an archaic remnant of the medieval "Standestaat" (Woodward 1938; Bagehot and St John-Stevas 1966; Plumb 1973; Poggi 1978). That this institution cobbled together through centuries of frequently violent conflict should have left England with a parliamentary system capable of being adapted to the growing demands of the new middle classes in the nineteenth century, and then to those of the working classes in the twentieth, was something that would certainly have astonished the elites who crafted the Magna Carta in the thirteenth century and the politicians who, four-and-a-half centuries later, turned the Tudor/Stuart Parliaments into a political force capable of overthrowing the monarchy itself.

France had a different evolution. Its medieval parliamentary institutions were destroyed by the centralizing monarchy. This made its trajectory to democracy in the nineteenth and twentieth centuries much harder. Its democratic institutions repeatedly failed, and its last successful military coup was in 1958. This led to its Fifth Republic. The prior four republics were interspersed with two empires, two different kinds of monarchy, and one brief corporatist-fascist experiment (Agulhon 1995; Cobb 1998: 24–36).

The United States is still on its first republic (or second, if the Articles of Confederation are counted), but had a very nasty civil war before its unity was solidified. The original American colonies that formed the United States benefited from what was, by then, a long English tradition of regional self-government and parliamentary norms. Even so, repeated bargains between regions had to be struck to keep the system together. From the Constitutional Compromise of 1787, through the many attempts to conciliate growing Northern and Southern differences, to the electoral compromise of 1877 that allowed the South to maintain a system of racial exclusion and white domination for another 90 years, it was only by compromising its liberal principles that American democracy grew strong enough to finally resolve some of this regional cultural clash without provoking a new civil war (Marx 1998).

Anthony Marx's comparison of the United States and South Africa (with Brazil as the contrasting, different case) forcefully makes the point that white nationalism was solidified after wars between different white communities by marginalizing blacks and defining them as "others" who were not part of the nation. In a more recent work (2003) he extends this argument to the origins of French and English nationalism that united disparate regions and communities by defining the excluded, enemy "others" on religious grounds. English national unity was forged on anti-Catholicism in the sixteenth and seventeenth centuries, and French nationalism on anti-Protestantism. Thus, the comforting story of how the French, English, and Americans overcame communal divisions by being inclusively "civic" and democratic is belied by the historical reality, and all three had their share of internal wars and persecution of certain selected communities.

Unfortunately, this is deeply discouraging, because it suggests that to create unity from diversity requires excluding some and finding an enemy against whom to unite a majority. Only when that has been done and there is a strong sense of nation can democracy work because different communal interests then become secondary to an overriding national cause. Bargaining instead of civil war becomes relatively easy, and democratic elections can pick winners and losers peacefully. Because of shared national values, losers need no longer feel that they will be dispossessed. Indeed, there is ample evidence that all strong European nations emerged from warfare that united them against outsiders, and that democracy, where it emerged, did so through struggles that often turned violent. This has been one of Charles Tilly's consistent themes throughout his distinguished scholarly career (Tilly 1975, 2004).

Miguel Centeno has made an equally discouraging argument about Latin America. Latin America was actually much less militarized and had far fewer international wars than Western Europe, but this resulted in a lower degree of national integration, particularly in countries with large ethnic or indigenous populations, and consequently, a very high degree of internal repression. Thus, nationalism developed, but because it was generally not necessary to mobilize the peasant masses of the nation against external enemies as much as in Western Europe, integration between rich elites and the masses was never as complete. This may well be one of the reasons Latin American states are less united across class and ethnic lines than Western European ones and the United States, and this has made democracy far more fragile (Centeno 2002).

Where does this leave us, other than to urge states beset by ethnic, religious, or sectional conflicts to decide whom to persecute and exclude to unite, and then to get involved in desperate wars with their neighbors to integrate those who constitute "the nation." Is this the only way to establish the national unity that makes stable democracy possible? Does India need a Pakistan on its borders to unite it? Was Malaysian Prime Minister Mohamad Mahatir right to demonize Jews, Americans, and the West to unite his own disparate communities?

Fortunately, more optimistic conclusions can be drawn as long as we remain cautiously aware of how easily a blanket push for immediate democracy can cause more harm than good. Creating democracy may take more than one generation, but it need not take as long as from the Magna Carta to the establishment of universal suffrage in England – 700 years. It may not require the exclusion of different ethnic or religious groups, of civil wars, or the waging of wars against neighbors. But, it does require much more than holding elections and moralizing pressure from foreigners, a point nicely elucidated by Thomas Pangle in his philosophically oriented chapter in the present volume.

PEACEFUL AND LESS PEACEFUL STRATEGIES FOR INCORPORATING MINORITIES

The problem is that almost all modern states, including those that consider themselves to be legitimate nations, contain religious, ethnic, regional, or even in some cases economic groups whose loyalties are suspect. In many cases, these distinct groups go so far as to claim that they ought not be part of the state in which they reside because others who do not serve their interests dominate the state, or worse, persecute them. States that have not succeeded in creating a national consensus about whom they represent are in the most precarious situation, but even the most highly integrated, successful nations were far from being that in the past. The reality is that the nation-state is a project that is rarely if ever fully finished, not a primordial fact waiting to burst into existence (Geary 2002; Smith 1986; Weber 1976). Even some very old states that once claimed to be solidly nationalized such as Great Britain and Spain might still split up into different nations, whereas smaller, once seemingly homogeneous entities such as those in Scandinavia are now presented with a growing minority immigrant problem. Very few modern nations

TABLE 4.1: Strategies for dealing with minorities in a nation state

	Inclusion	Separation	Exclusion
Tolerant	Gradual and mostly consensual assimilation	Multiculturalism	Consensual emigration or separation
Intolerant	Forced assimilation	Segregation	Ethnic cleansing or genocide

that are deemed solid became that way without civil wars and international conflicts to decide where their boundaries would lie.

Establishing stable democracies in the modern world, where the role of states in providing education, securing property rights, offering jobs, and enforcing core values is crucial, the treatment of minority or less powerful communities is one of the major, often the single most important issue. No longer is a traditional imperial system, such as the one practiced by the Ottomans, feasible. Then, various ethno-religious groups could follow their own laws and practices as long as they did not interfere with central Ottoman Muslim rule; but this all broke down in increasing inter-communal warfare as the Ottoman Empire tried to create a modern, united nation-state capable of mobilizing its forces against its European enemies (Barkey and Von Hagen 1997; Keyder 1997; Mardin 1997).

What strategies have been followed to deal with minorities, and how successful have they been? There have been three broad ones, but each can be divided into two parts, relatively tolerant and relatively intolerant approaches. The three kinds of strategies are inclusion, separation, and exclusion. Table 4.1 lays these out (O'Leary 2001; Chirot and McCauley 2006: 159).

The curious thing about this chart is that many existing nation-states have used all of these strategies at one time or another to strengthen nationalist unity. In the United States, for example, assimilation of voluntary white immigrants was not always perfectly tolerant, but on the whole it was, and rarely became brutally intolerant. The same cannot be said of how African Americans or Native Americans were treated. Forced assimilation, segregation, and genocidal ethnic cleansing were all practiced at one time or another on some nonwhites. Abraham Lincoln at one time said that, "[P]hysical differences between the white and black race ... will forever forbid the two races living together upon terms of social and political equality." So, he concluded that emigration of freed slaves back to Africa was the best solution (Marx 1998: 59). That form of "tolerant exclusion" was the original idea behind the creation of Liberia, although it proved wildly impractical as a realistic solution. More recently, tolerant multiculturalism that recognizes the legitimacy of holding onto different languages and cultures has become more widely accepted in the United States, but it is still contested. It may be shocking to see multiculturalism and segregation put into the same category, but both make the claim that establishing a single, unitary culture is impossible, so different ethnic groups will remain separate in many ways. The tolerant version is presumably kinder, but some assumptions made by both strategies are similar.

Some of the ways in which nations have become more culturally homogeneous have already been discussed. England excluded Catholics from political participation, and even though eventually this rift was healed within England itself, it never was in British controlled Ireland. France went through a long series of forced, very brutal assimilations. This is what Ernest Renan meant about nations having to forget as much as they remembered about their past. He was thinking of the genocidal massacres that only slowly unified France, particularly the thirteenth century Albigensian Crusades, the sixteenth century Protestant-Catholic wars, and the bloody civil war that was the French Revolution (Anderson 1991: 199).

There could hardly be a better example of a forged sense of nationalism than how, after the American Civil War, a mythologized version of the romantic South gradually got most Americans to forget both the brutality and real nature of the war, and that it was fought by the South to preserve slavery, not some genteel way of life or constitutional "states' rights." Today, a number of the East and Central European nations, some claiming to be quite old, are solid nation-states because their large minorities were recently exterminated, expelled, or cut away after war. Poland is a good example, as are Greece, Romania (except for its Gypsy and Hungarian minorities), Hungary, and of course the little new former Yugoslav states. Turkey is yet another example. Its remaining minority problem with the Kurds, where forced intolerant assimilation has not really worked, was greatly simplified by the massacre of Armenians, the forced changes in boundaries, and the expulsion of almost all of its Greek Christians. The new nation-states of Slovakia and the Czech Republic separated peacefully, thus providing a recent, gentle example of tolerant separation, although Slovakia still has problems dealing with its Hungarian minority and both have Gypsy minorities that are far from assimilated. The Czech Republic, however, might not have been established so peacefully had its very large ethnic German minority not been forcibly and brutally expelled after World War II (Naimark 2001 discusses many of these ethnic cleansings).

In Latin America, there have been attempts to assimilate indigenous populations by forced acculturation. Some have been gentler, gradual assimilations, but there have also been numerous examples of virtual segregation and genocidal ethnic cleansings and massacres. Russia as an empire before 1917, in Soviet times, and now has used all of the possible strategies, from ethnic cleansing of various Caucasian people, deportations, consensual or forced assimilation, multiculturalism, and shedding of ethnically hostile provinces. (One of Naimark's cases [2001: 85–107] regards the treatment of Chechen and Ingush people by the Soviet Union.) Throughout the world, we can find numerous examples of all possible strategies, cases of extremely intolerant brutality, others of tolerant strategies, and many cases of both success and failure with each particular approach. What is important is to admit that turning heterogeneous populations into nations is a long and complex process. It may be accomplished relatively peacefully, but it has always and everywhere had the potential to become violently conflictual.

To create a working democracy, it is necessary to create a sense that, as Liah Greenfeld (1992) put it, the nation becomes the central political identity of all, or almost all within the state's borders. Swiss or Indian multiculturalism, Czech and Slovak peaceful separation, separation after a long period of repression, bloodshed, and civil war as between the Republic of Ireland and Great Britain, or tolerant assimilation, as in the United States with white immigrants can all work. So can forced assimilation, as happened with many ethnic and religious minorities in France; but, if the process is incomplete, it risks producing permanent ethnic conflict, as has happened with Kurds in Turkey (McDowall 1997: 418–444). Segregation works only as long as the segregated community is so totally marginalized as to become completely impotent, but it can work to unite a majority against the segregated minority as it did in the United States for almost a century following the Civil War. To finally achieve full democracy in the United States meant ending segregation and moving toward a version of tolerant assimilation. (Many Americans call this multiculturalism, but they are mislabeling what actually happened.) Genocide and ethnic cleansing can also work. Turkey may be a very imperfect democracy, but it is difficult to imagine any kind of a viable democracy, or even a Turkish state in anything close to its present borders, if the Armenians and Greeks had remained demographically significant communities in Anatolia and Istanbul. The relatively smooth transition to democracy in most of eastern and central Europe after 1989 would have been much harder had most of each state's major minorities not been massacred or expelled in the twentieth century.

As it is not my purpose to recommend new genocides or brutal attempts to assimilate recalcitrant communities to dominant national identities, the question at hand becomes: What viable tolerant strategy can be used to create the kind of harmony necessary for democracy to work? As this could be the subject of an entire book all by itself, the answer here must necessarily be brief.

HOW TO PROMOTE TOLERANT DEMOCRACY

The first rule is to remember that in many cases, ranging from medieval England to contemporary India, the elites of various communities based on region, ethnicity, or religion had to be reassured that they would not lose their property, local power, or opportunities to gain from being part of the state. That remains important today.

Playing by such rules almost necessarily diminishes the possibility of having full democracy. It has long been known that tolerant (Zakaria would say liberal) democracy has to protect minorities from majorities; however, it is at least, if not more, important to protect communal leaders, that is, the elites who are also seen as the protectors of their communities against other competing groups. It is those elites, particularly their younger and best educated members, who are the most likely to start revolts against the state on behalf of their perceivedly persecuted communities if they are dissatisfied. If they are not guaranteed security of opportunity, it will be very easy for such young elites to persuade many in their communities to oppose the state. Democratic elections cannot resolve this issue. Elites in each of the participating communities have to be given substantial reasons to participate in the political process that may eventually lead, but perhaps not right away, to democracy. Only then can democratic bargaining gain a foothold.

Civil society organizations, so highly touted as the basis of democracy from the time of Tocqueville until now, can help only if they are led by elites who accept the nation, and, therefore, are willing to gradually democratize because it does not threaten either their interests or their communities' future prospects. Then the leaders of these communities become willing to bargain with each other as representatives of their groups. If, at first, elites are not chosen democratically: no matter.

Democracy must be put off in favor of something like what the English and Americans first had, bargaining between elite representatives of various local and communal interests. Once they learned how to do this, democratic institutions had some chance of developing.

At all times, property rights need to be respected. That is more important than establishing democracy, because democracies in which the rights of various ethnicities, religions, or regions are not guaranteed have little or no chance of working.

This, however, raises a very difficult question. Tolerance is not simply a matter of bargaining between elites or respecting property rights. The United States had this well before it became tolerant of non-whites, and we know that deep prejudices can persist long after minorities are no longer a threat to the nation. Given the fact that intolerant exclusion can work, and that many of Europe's democracies built national solidarity by persecuting and, in many cases, destroying minorities, how is this to be avoided? The only solution is to eventually move beyond community toward acceptance of the primacy of individual rights. As long as Jews, Tutsis, Chinese, Armenians, Catholics, or any other group are treated as entities that are characterized by their own rules, customs, and group rights, but in which all the members of that community are essentially the same and only have rights through their group, tolerance remains a very fragile commodity. Adam Seligman shows in his paper in this volume that accepting different others is more than a matter of tolerance; individualizing rights involves privatizing differences in ways that could hardly exist in the pre-Enlightenment past.

India is very far from having achieved that level of generalized acceptance of individual over communal rights, and none of the Western European democracies really did until sometime in the twentieth century. Until that happens, it is possible to hold nations together through bargaining between elites and communities. But, instituting mass voting creates the opportunity for communal leaders to gain power by promoting prejudice and discrimination.

Therefore, during the long period in which democracy remains very imperfect (as it still is in India, for example, where local elites manipulate results to keep themselves in power, and where the appeal to caste and sectarian passions remains an ever present danger), some attention must be paid to instilling those Enlightenment notions that individual rights are important. This means eventually accepting the idea that no one should be characterized primarily by ascriptively assigned ethnicity, religion, or regional membership, or, at least, that those ascriptive qualities are of secondary importance. That is a multi-generational transformative project. It only happened recently in the West, and cannot be imposed on non-Western societies. Such notions must develop within each society, and come from their own intellectual elites. In the meantime, it would be well to recognize that progress can be made in creating more stable modern societies without necessarily insisting on what Westerners consider to be formal democracy, absolute respect for differences, or extensive individual rights. It is hard enough to maintain such values in long established liberal Western democracies, much less imposing them on others.

As national solidarity is being built, as elites are integrated into a functioning and secure system of bargaining for political power, and as greater respect for individual rights and greater tolerance become more widely accepted, economic growth is also vital. If every group feels it has more to gain by remaining loyal to the nation than by leaving it, or trying to seize power to exclude others, the long, tedious process of building liberal democracy is made far easier.

If all this sounds like a very tall order, it is. Premature democracy in divided societies is likely to cause more harm than good. Excluding local or other ethnically and religiously based elites as part of democratization is a prescription for disaster. Neglecting the reality of intolerance and the general lack of respect for individual rights in most societies turns the search for democracy into a vain exercise, but creating tolerance and respect for differences without the support of local elites is impossible. Democracy must develop as a set of alliances between elites, and only over time can its more basic values be instilled.

That is how some Western societies did it, and it is foolish to pretend that it was easy. This does not mean that non-Western societies cannot achieve some version of liberal democracy. Some have gone quite far in that direction, but with differences that unduly disturb Western observers (Bell 2006). Quick elections, imposition of institutions by outsiders who do not know the local situation, and preaching from afar are not the way to do this.

We can now answer the question posed at the start of this essay. Can democracy help resolve deep communal divisions? Yes, but much has to be done to establish the right institutions before full democracy can work. Ultimately, part of this work has to be a change of certain values and attitudes about ethnicity and religion, but, that is a final step that can neither be forced nor accomplished before the right institutions are in place and working well. In other words, some version of liberal democracy can be spread, and once it is in place, it can work wonders in mitigating ethnic and religious conflicts. But, establishing tolerant, lawful, functioning democracies requires patience, generations of hard work, and a willingness to accept very incomplete and different versions of that democracy for a long preparatory period.

5 Democracy, Civil Society, and the Problem of Tolerance

INTRODUCTION

Whereas democracy may or may not be "exportable," it is pretty clear that the civil society of any particular country or society most probably is not. This is especially the case if we take civil society to mean something beyond those institutional mechanisms that Robert Dahl (1972) identified with polyarchy. These institutional arrangements of: (1) elected officials; (2) free and fair elections; (3) inclusive suffrage; (4) the right to run for office; (5) freedom of expression; (6) alternative information; and (7) associational autonomy; may well be fundamental building blocks of democracy and, as such, universally realizable. The concept of civil society, however, would seem to point to something a bit more elusive and just possibly a bit more country specific and particularistic and, therefore, difficult to "export" in the same manner. How so?

All societies at all times face three fundamental challenges. These include the need to: (a) organize their division of labor; (b) to expand trust beyond the primordial unit of family (however conceived), that is, to generalize the terms of trust beyond the narrowest of circles; and (c) to provide some sense of meaning to both individual lives and collective endeavors (Eisenstadt 1995). All social institutions can be understood ultimately in terms of their reference to one or more of these three sets of challenges. What the notion of civil society adds to different sets of institutional solutions to these challenges is something overwhelmingly local in character. It is something that may be identified with, to use the terms of the eighteenth-century Scottish moralists, the "vanity and approbation" of that particular society; that is to say, with the unique way each and every society addresses the three sets of challenges just noted.

The organization of civil society has thus to do with the realm of values and beliefs. As such, it will always carry with it particularistic, local, and specific characteristics. It will be in some sense different in each and every locale and so its content will not be fully generalizable. For, if the term "civil society" is to mean anything, it must mean something specific. Although the division of labor may well be developing on a global scale, it is clear that the generalization of trust and the terms of meaning in different societies are different and likely to remain that way for the foreseeable future. Indeed, many papers in this collection stress precisely the particularistic, local character of those challenges facing democratization in different parts of the world. Most especially, the paper of Daniel Chirot goes a long way toward showing just how circumscribed and ethnically defined communities (of trust and meaning) present a continual challenge to the generalization of the formal aspects of democratic decision making. Local cultures count, and they count most in the formation of elites who are, after all, the carriers of ideological programs including those of democratization.

In this paper, then, I will query if the local cultures, which provide the basis of our own ideas of democratic civility, are really universal. I will argue that rather than a discussion of the concept of civil society, it may be more useful to understand the fundamental problems of democratization as the problem of living with, or, more classically, of tolerating difference. Tolerance of difference – classically of religious difference, but also of racial and ethnic differences – is in fact the first condition for the emergence of any form of civil life. I shall moreover claim that our own Western European and North Atlantic notions of tolerance rest on very particular foundations, not shared in many parts of the world, and that we would do well to understand our own prejudices and the particularistic assumptions that we bring to the idea of civil society before attempting to promote its virtues throughout the world. This is especially important because in many contemporary forums the idea of civil society continues to be presented as a panacea to all of society's ills. There thus may be many ways of tolerating difference, not all of them circumscribed by our own ideas of civil society.

A BRIEF HISTORY OF THE IDEA OF CIVIL SOCIETY

In the years since the revolutions of 1989, the idea of civil society has come to mean many different and contradictory things to many different people. It has been espoused by liberals and conservatives, religious elites and staunch supporters of the secular order, by parties of the left and of the right, by opponents and proponents of globalization, disestablishmentarianism, and just about everything else. To begin our own inquiry, I suggest an ever so brief and hence necessarily partial historical review of the term's use, and some of the problems inherent in that use. Following this review, I will go on to look at one particular problem inherent to democratic forms of organizing social life, and one that the idea of civil society does not seemingly address in an adequate manner. I will conclude the final section of my paper by exploring the somewhat outdated idea of tolerance as an alternative concept to that of civil society and one that we should perhaps reconsider in our discussions of democratic regimes.

The idea of civil society became a popular political slogan in the late 1980s. Its contemporary origin is in the critique of both state socialist and advanced capitalist regimes (Seligman 1992). Although popular in Eastern Europe during this period as a critique of state socialism, after the period of transition in the early 1990s, it was used less and less, because it is more effective as a tool for criticism than for construction. After the fall of communism, the need to develop a language of democracy, political parties, and the rule of law took precedence over the language of civil society. At about the same time, the term entered the mainstream of Western political discourse, with everyone using it as they saw fit. Indeed, the very ambiguity of the term accounts for its continuing use and popular adaptation. It means many different things to different people; from democracy to individual rights, to community (hence conservative, libertarian, and democratic-rights advocates all use the term). In addition, non-governmental organizations (NGOs) see themselves as models of civil society – understanding the term to mean that space that exists between the family and the state (which in some definitions includes the market and in some excludes it). This was, in fact, the "classic" modernist definition of civil society used by the German thinker G.W. Hegel. It was Karl Marx, we may recall, who pointed out that whereas this structural position (between family and state) did indeed characterize what is termed civil society, what in fact defined the dynamics of civil society, in the final analysis, was the class basis of its participants. Thus, for him and his followers, civil society reflected class society. Although much of the richness of social life was perhaps lost in this reduction of civil society to class interests, much nevertheless remains true, as we can witness by the politics of both advanced and developing nations. NGOs, moreover, are, in most of the world, not free from the state. In Western Europe, most NGOs limit state support to 30% of their budget (still a hefty percentage).

In non-Western countries no such limits apply. NGOs are, of course, un-elected, responsible to no public body, and pursue very explicit national and international agendas, sometimes with budgets equaling those of small states. So whereas they may be a form of civil society, they are of a very particular ilk.

Given this background, especially in terms of our concern here with "exporting democracy," we should recall one significant historical fact about the origins of the early modern use of the concept. Civil society, as a concept in modern political thinking, emerged with great saliency in Scotland in the early and mid parts of the eighteenth century as part of the search for a new model of society in the decades following the Act of Union with the English Crown in 1707. The failure of the Jacobean revolts (against union with England) and the Scots' defeat at the battle of Culloden ended all attempts of the Scots to reconstitute a polity based on tribal, that is, on primordial units. It became clear that in the rapidly emerging commercial society of the eighteenth century this was no longer a feasible model. Another model of society was needed that was not tribal and not totally subservient to a distant State (certainly one seen as oppressive, as was the English Crown). The concept of civil society emerged as an alternative, where the basis of sociability was seen to rest in a shared capacity towards moral sentiments and natural sympathy among people seen to share in a public good. Ultimately, however, the concept of civil society as a philosophical and politically coherent idea was challenged; philosophically by David Hume, and politically by Karl Marx. We may add that it was also, in a sense, transcended sociologically by the developing struggles over full citizenship and inclusion of the working classes within the national societies of the nineteenth-century European nation states.

Yet, the concern with the idea of civil society – if only as a slogan – does not seem to pass. There continue to be conferences all over the world on civil society and religion, civil society and the state, civil society and poverty, democracy, Chinese culture, women's liberation, etc. One reason for this is that the nation-state, with its unique conceptions of citizenship that once clearly demarcated the realm of political action is itself changing. Global politics (of immigration, transnational business and social movements, ecological concerns, anti-globalization policies and parties, etc.) and global markets have all reframed the terms in which the eighteenth-century ideas of civil society were politically institutionalized (universal suffrage and liberal citizenship within the confines of the nation state, and more recently, a rights-based political discourse).

Civil society continues to provide a direction, if not yet a clear concept, of thinking of politics outside the framework of nation-state institutions. It is in this sense that it should engage us here, especially given that so much of politics in many parts of the world seem to draw more on tribal heritages than civic ones.

THE PROBLEM OF DIFFERENCE AND DEMOCRATIC REGIMES

I suggest that the continuing interest in the term reflects the problem of its emergence – only now on a global scale. This problem at its heart is the problem of difference: of how to constitute a polity among strangers, among those not united by bonds of kinship, affect, or a shared sacred tradition. If we return to my earlier parsing of the fundamental problems of our shared human endeavor, the problem is of constructing society with those who do not share our own terms of meaning and who are not part of our extended kinship group (however conceived). They share with us in the division of labor, but that is all. In many ways, this was *the* political problem of the modern era and in many ways it has not left us. In some ways this problem of difference is best represented in the pervasiveness of the "Jewish Question" throughout the politics of nineteenth-century Europe and the naïve belief that formal citizenship – when granted – would suffice to integrate the Jews into the European social and political order. The horrors of the last century did much to disabuse us all of that belief. Yet today, we can well ask if European democracies are not, once again, struggling with this problem of difference, or "otherhood," in the context of their Muslim citizens and residents – with results that are still unclear. So the problem of civil society, of constituting a shared ground of sympathy and moral approbation (essentially of trust) among individuals who do not share ascriptive or sacred bonds or the bonds of a shared structure of meaning remains a critical problem; in the communities of Western Europe, to some extent in the United States, and certainly beyond.

In many ways I would go so far as to say that this problem – of difference – stands at the root of democratic politics, which are, after all, predicated on a politics of interests – that is, on a politics of different individuals and groups pursuing their particular interests (within an agreed upon set of "rules of the game," of course). Democracy in fact tends to highlight difference, to stress what makes us different, at least as far as our interests are concerned.

To allow the pursuit of such a politics without threatening the very existence of the polity some overall unity or shared moral purpose must be posited. It is thus not surprising that democratic polities have often tended to be ones with very sharp boundaries and relatively clear definitions of membership. We can see evidence of this in ancient Greece, in Renaissance city-states, European nation-states, and in the contemporary United States. In all cases, democratic regimes present themselves to us as having very sharp boundaries; that is, as having clear articulations of who is inside and who outside, who is a member and who not – as well as very clear definitions of the terms of membership. The recent French ruling on the head-scarf is a very clear, contemporary illustration of this attitude. It is notable that within their boundaries democratic societies have always assumed a rather high level of identification of the citizen with the polis; a great degree of internalization of what sociologist Edward Shils (1975: 3–16) once called the "central value system" of society. This has been expressed in what are often termed "republican" versions of citizenship – that tradition studied so well by historians such as Quinten Skinner (1990) and J.G.A. Pocock (1975) and indebted, in no small measure, to the heritage of the Italian city states.

I don't know if these characteristics of democratic regimes – the high degree of identification with regime combined with clearly defined, rigorously patrolled boundaries – are indeed necessary conditions for the maintenance of democracy. It may be that they are. External regulation and authoritative coordination from above, as in authoritarian regimes, are replaced with internal regulation and voluntary cooperation from below in democratic ones. To effect this, one must, therefore, rigorously control who is allowed membership into the collective and, perhaps more emportantly, ensure a high degree of commitment to collective goals and desiderata.

Democratic regimes thus exist in an abiding tension between a politics of interest – pushing its citizens to focus on what divides them; and a politics of consent – pushing citizens to affirm what unites them. This tension, I hasten to add, is not a characteristic of all political and social systems, at least not to the same extent. Totalitarian systems, fascist regimes, communist societies, theocracies, and, on the other side of the coin, empires, do not betray the same tensions. The former can abide much less amounts of difference. Empires, on the other hand, can countenance a much greater degree of difference than can democracies. Even within democracies there are various differences between what have been termed liberal and republican versions, where the former allow a much greater institutional recognition of difference than the latter. Needless to say, the founding fathers of the United States recognized this tension and worked out mechanisms to accommodate it. The famous wall of separation between Church and State in the United States – that most religious of countries – is predicated precisely on the founders' recognition that it is better that people's politics be divided by their different material interests (which would then play out in the political sphere of the legislature) than by their religious differences (which could have potentially ruinous effects on social and political life). If current practice in places like the Balkans, the Middle East, the Indian subcontinent, and parts of the Republican Party in the United States are any guide, people like James Madison were stupendously correct in their assessment.

Problems of dealing with the constitutive difference between citizens in the public sphere are, of course, not unique to the United States. Nor is the "liberal" or perhaps liberal-individualist solution unique to that social formation, but, in fact, defines modern societies in one form or another, although with important variations. Recall, for example, the classical enlightenment response to "the Jewish Question," given by Count Stanislav de Clermont-Tonnerre in 1789: "We must refuse everything to the Jew as a nation and accord everything to the Jew as an individual." This became perhaps the paradigm statement of attitudes toward the other – his and her constitution solely as individual entities rather than as members of corporate groups. Article I of the Declaration of the Rights of Man and of the Citizen (August 26, 1789) of the French National Assembly states: "All men are born and remain free and equal in rights: *social distinctions can not be found but on common utility.*" This is a total reconfiguration of the meaning of identity along the lines of utility functions rather than what may be termed constituted selves.

In both Europe and the United States, however, a fundamental problem remains. Rights do not provide recognition, and recognition – as political philosophers from Adam Ferguson to G.W.H. Hegel and down to our own contemporaries have reminded us – is the core of modern politics (Taylor 1992). For thinkers such as Adam Ferguson and Adam Smith, it was the core of the idea of civil society as well. Yet, today, the models of this recognition are much more collective than those conceived by the social visionaries of eighteenth century: Edinburgh and Glasgow. Indeed new and old forms of group-based identity continue to arise, all making vocal and public demands for recognition. This is, in fact, the social significance of such holidays as Kwanza, or of a Boston Rabbi lighting a Chanukah menorah on Boston Common, or a French Rabbi on the Champs de Mars for that matter. All betray the demand for recognition, for a recovering of one's identity, and demanding public recognition for it. Not surprisingly, these demands are most often framed religiously.

This is as true in Europe as in the United States. The controversial French ruling over the head scarf and the debates over the preamble to the European constitution are but a few among myriad cases attesting to this facet of contemporary politics. In Lodi, northern Italy, for example, on October 15, 2000, the local Catholic inhabitants desecrated a site upon which a mosque was to be built by pouring pig urine all around it (*La Republica* 2000). The idea was that by rendering the site impure they would be able to stop the mosque from being built. A month later, in Rouato, the Mayor issued a municipal ordinance (almost immediately overturned in court) forbidding non-Christians from approaching within 15 meters of a Church, other examples can of course be cited (*Il Giorno* 2000). In Flanders, last year, a local government outlawed the wearing of full face covering in public, citing security considerations (www.flandersnews.com). The severe anti-Muslim sentiment expressed in parts of Europe, not only by skinheads, neo-Nazis, and supporters of Le Pen, but also by much more respectable figures are frightening examples of this same dynamic. One need not look to such writers as the late Ms. Fallaci because even such respected scholars as Jacques Ellul (2004) have contributed to these developments – as can be verified in his posthumously published work, entitled *Islam et judeo-christianisme*. Although this book appeared with a preface by the very distinguished French philosopher Alain Besancon, it reads somewhat like a medieval anti-Semitic tract, except here it is the Muslims and their "God" (whatever that means) who are presented as without love and so beyond the pale of shared humanness. The problem of recognition (and lack thereof) is thus no minor issue at the fringes of the political arena – but is at the very center of our social life making demands that cannot be met by the privatization of that for which we demand recognition.

This problem of recognition is in fact of much broader dimensions and touches on yet another set of meanings identified with the terms of civil society. I refer here to the identification of civil society with a new type of "modular man" that was famously propounded by the late Ernest Gellner (1994), one of the most respected anthropologists of the twentieth century. Gellner was an expert on Islam and a scholar overwhelmingly involved with the transitions to democracy of the post-communist societies of Central and Eastern Europe following the revolutions of 1989. In one of his last works, he attempted to argue that civil society was to be identified with a certain type of personality structure – in a manner not unlike the modernization studies of the 1950s and 1960s. Gellner (1994: 100) attempted to correlate civil society with individuals who were capable of entering into "effective association and institutions without these being total, many-stranded, underwritten by ritual and made stable through being linked to a whole inside set of relationships . . . tied together and so immobilized." He saw these individuals as uncommitted to any set of prescribed roles and relations or sets of practice, sharing in convictions that could change and entering into "highly specific, unsanctified, instrumental and revocable links or bonds." In short, he identified civil society with modern, liberal, secular social agents. Indeed, his desideratum bears an uncanny resemblance to the Article 1 of the Declaration of the Rights of Man and Citizen quoted above: *the evisceration of all non-utilitarian or non-functional social distinctions.*

However, not only does such an identification beg the question of how such individuals come to be, it also writes off the majority of mankind as somehow beyond the pale of civil society. This is then a rather particularistic vision and ethnocentric in its scope despite its universalistic pretensions. Given the not so distant European history, it is a rather short-sighted and I think highly suspect vision as well. It certainly limits our ability to deal with current realities, replete as they are with the return to particularistic, group identities and religious commitments. It even limits our ability to deal with the situation in Europe today where the demographic crises and increasing immigration of individuals who do not share such modular identities is currently challenging the very bases of the European culture as well as its social and political landscape. It does, however, force us to move beyond the rhetoric of civil society if we are to find a language adequate to deal with precisely that problem of difference and otherness that stands – I am suggesting – at the core of what we understand as the problem of civil society. To do so, I would like us to re-engage with an equally hoary term, rooted in pre-modern times, but one that I think will offer a more direct means of dealing with difference. By this I mean precisely those forms of constitutive differences that the concept of civil society does not seem to address. I refer to the concept of tolerance. The recourse to this term is, I assert, imposed upon us by the increasing divergence of subcultures within societies and the failure to achieve that homogeneity of populace that was the dream (in fact the ideology rather than the reality) of the European nation-state. The type of mutual recourse to 'vanity and approbation' that the Scottish moralists set at the heart of civil society can only be effective given a set of – what Charles Taylor (1985: 18–24) termed – "strong evaluations" that are overwhelmingly shared among the populace. It is this common culture that is, however, the focus of so much political tension in today's world, whether over Islam in Europe or Spanish language use in the United States – not to mention those areas where such conflict has taken the form of political violence.

In light of these realities, I would like to resurrect the debate over the concept of tolerance, explore some of its strengths and weaknesses and see just how far it may take us in providing what can perhaps be called a necessary precondition to any real sense of a civil society or democratic civility.

CONSTITUTIVE DIFFERENCE AND TOLERANCE

Tolerance, as Bernard Williams (1996: 18–28) once remarked, is an "impossible virtue." It is impossible because it involves accepting, abiding or accommodating views that one rejects. It calls us to live in cognitive dissonance and presents contradiction as a sought after goal. We are obliged to "bear" what in fact we find unbearable. Of course, if we did not find this, that, or the other word or deed objectionable there would be no call to tolerate them. The whole issue of tolerance only arises when some act or speech is deemed objectionable. Viewed from one perspective then, tolerance is a virtue so demanding as to be "impossible" for realization, perhaps even logically untenable, involving us in the laws of contradiction.

Yet, from another perspective, tolerance is a virtue far from sufficient. It is deemed too vapid, too thin, and far from adequate to the construction of a civil order or civil society of mutual appreciation and recognition. Tolerance with its historical associations of suffering the presence of what is detestable (in the eyes of God and mankind) is, in this reading, too feeble a thing to promote. Pluralism and the celebration of difference and otherness, this is what is called for rather than the insipid call to tolerance.

Complicating this picture even further is that whether we view tolerance as either impossible or insipid, argument can be made that in neither case does it take us very far. For most would agree that there are actions (and perhaps words as well, although that is much debated at present) that are beyond any moral compass and should not be tolerated. Many of the horrors of the twentieth century encompassing genocide and other crimes against humanity would fall under this rubric. And so, if certain sets of acts clearly are beyond what can be tolerated, we are left with the need to define the boundary of what can and cannot be tolerated. It is far from clear what criteria would be used to define such a boundary. Such a task seems then to push the problem of tolerance up one analytic level, but not to resolve it.

Despite these problems and the logistical conundrums they propose, I will make the argument for tolerance, as indeed a minimalist position, although for all that one not easy to attain (although not impossible either). In addition, I assert that what passes for tolerance (let alone more robust virtues) in contemporary modern societies is often not tolerance at all, but rather some mixture of indifference, RealPolitik, and the denial of difference (that is, the denial that there is really something else, other, different, and thus perhaps threatening that I must engage with in a tolerant manner).

The denial of difference comes in many forms, most often as what may be termed the aesthetization of difference (differences are a matter of tastes, not morals, and as there is no accounting for tastes, no real tolerance of difference is called for, rather a recognition of each individual's "right" to their own opinion). The aesthetization of difference is often accompanied by a trivialization of difference. Here, the differences or the arenas of difference are not deemed important enough to merit a principled tolerance. Another's poor taste in neckties is not something that demands of me a tolerant attitude, even though I find them both offensive and in bad taste. Precisely because they are a matter of taste (aesthetics) and of no great significance (trivial), tolerance does not effectively enter the picture.

These moves of making difference a matter of aesthetics or trivializing it are, of course, ways to avoid having to engage with difference. By trivializing what is different, one makes a claim to the essential similarity or sameness of the non-trivial aspects of selfhood and shared meaning. What makes us the same (as Jews, Episcopalians, Americans, or radical feminists) is much more essential to our definitions of who we are than what divides us (your horrendous taste in bathroom fixtures). This is a form of denying difference rather than engaging with it. We do it all the time; it is of the very stuff of our social life.

In a certain sense such denial of difference (relegating it to the aesthetic or trivial) is itself a form of indifference towards what is other and different. By framing our difference from Alter's position or action in terms of tastes or the trivial we are not forced to engage with it and can maintain an attitude of indifference. I may find your religious beliefs foolish and your sexual appetites objectionable, but neither are illegal nor hurtful to others. They do not affect me in my relations to you (as, say, members of the same university department) and so, in the long run, are a matter of indifference to me.

As we push this argument one step further we come to realize, of course, that indifference, at least in liberal-individualist societies, is not simply a psychological state or a form of social etiquette. It is in fact ensconced as a fundamental aspect of the social order, in the form of our legal and principled separation of public and private spheres. For what is deemed private is removed from public scrutiny and ceases to become a subject for tolerant or intolerant attitudes on the part of others in society. Defining a realm of privacy is tantamount to defining a realm of principled indifference where issues of tolerance are not to be broached and are indeed rendered irrelevant. Not surprisingly, the freedom of conscience – which was in fact the freedom of religion – went hand-in-hand with its privatization. We must also note that, according to Jose Casanova (1994), the privatization of religion together with a politics of rights rather than a politics of the good and a secularized public sphere are all in some sense the hallmarks of a liberal vision of modernity (although this is less so in more republican versions of the Enlightenment project). Moreover, and according to popular wisdom, if only those intractable and fundamentalist Jews, Christians, Muslims, Hindus, or Sikhs could accept these principles, which are only reasonable and so accessible to all, we would have solved the problem of tolerance, and the sooner the better. And of course here precisely is the rub. For accepting these principles essentially means accepting as well a certain liberal, post-Protestant vision of selfhood and society that is not shared across the globe and across human civilizations. We are, as can be seen, back to Ernest Gellner's notion of multi-spherical selves, of modular man and, in fact, the intolerance of such modular models, to all those not cast in their mold.

More to the point, these different liberal attitudes, that although seen uncritically to be of a tolerant nature, are in fact less than tolerant in that they disengage with difference rather than practice the "impossible" virtue. They are perhaps in fact more than anything a way to elide the whole problem of tolerance in modern society rather than realize it. Critically, they would not necessarily be effective in societies that did not share liberal individualist assumptions on self and society and it is in fact far from certain that they will continue to work in those that do. For what is understood as tolerance in modern Western European and North Atlantic societies has much to do with the liberal synthesis as it has evolved in these societies (with all their differences) over the past 200 years.

Foremost in their construction was, as just noted, the public/private distinction. For if not really indifference, the liberal distinction between public and private realms, is among other things, a distinction in realms and types of toleration – certain beliefs and/or practices are deemed private and so beyond the realm of what even enter a calculus of tolerance. Here then, not quite indifference *simpliciter*, but more a principled indifference. For one has no **right** to intervene in private matters, or even to judge them. In this reading, all conflicting views are reduced to an almost aesthetic realm of different matters of taste (or as the current popular imagery has it of life-styles – as they say so tellingly in the United States "different strokes for different folks"). As is clear from the preceding, I question if this is tolerance at all. For if liberalism is neutral towards different conceptions of the good, can we then say it is tolerant of them? Principled indifference is not the same as tolerance.

Moreover, many would argue that tolerance as a practice flows from autonomy as a virtue or a good, which is fine, except that at this point the supposedly liberal indifference to ideas of the good becomes untenable. As Bernard Williams (1996: 25) has stated: "only a substantive view of goods such as autonomy can yield the value expressed by the practice of toleration." Moreover and more crucially, the positing of a good always involves us in that familiar situation of a "conflict of goods," which liberalism cannot really avoid, even though this is one of its central premises.

Although saving liberal individualism from its inherent contradictions is clearly an important task, I propose at this point to reformulate the problem, to step back a bit from our own rather individualist readings of tolerance, and look at the problem through somewhat different lenses, those of more traditional societies. It may be useful to recall here that in medieval cannon law, tolerance was practiced towards two groups of people – Jews and prostitutes – and I wish to emphasize the group aspect. Both were groups who were indeed tolerated, and for whom tolerance was seen as a second best solution. Better would be to do away with them, but the consequences would have been too detrimental to society. Ridding society of prostitutes was seen as an invitation to greater adultery, sodomy, and other sins of the flesh, and, of course, ridding society of Jews would have meant doing away with the one group whose recognition of Jesus as Christ in the second coming was a major element in the eschatological scenario. Hence both groups had to be tolerated. Hence, too, the very negative associations we have with the word tolerance, whose cultural baggage includes some very horrible episodes in the historical relations between Jews and Christians (Seligman 2004).

I wish to stress that tolerance is very much about groups and about group identities. Tolerance, as understood and practiced, was a matter of attitudes and behavior towards corporate groups and thus towards individuals as members of those groups, rather than towards individuals in their unique individuality. Given the terms of membership and identity in pre-modern and in religiously organized societies this is, of course, not surprising. Recall that "rights" were, in this world, not anything accorded to individuals, but to corporate groups. Such were the categories of medieval law and society and it is only sensible that such were the terms of tolerance in these societies. Although there is nothing startling here, it should give us pause for thought, for what I want to claim is that tolerance – and intolerance for that matter – does inherently have to do with groups and with individuals as existing within groups, rather than with individuals as autonomous, self-regulating moral agents, endowed with individual rights and acting as such on the public stage. This is the problem with Ernest Gellner's identification of civil society with a very particular type of personality – that of the Kantian, self-regulating, autonomous moral self. Unfortunately, most of humanity, today as in the past, believes in heteronomy rather than autonomy and see themselves as constituted by membership in ascriptive groups rather than as self-defining moral agents. It is therefore groups and group identities that must be admitted into our contemporary political thinking. And, if we are to find a way to generalize trust beyond the primordial family unit, it will have to take these identities into consideration and not limit itself to our individual utilities within the division of labor – as much of contemporary theorizing seems to do.

My point is thus not that pre-modern societies were *more* tolerant than modern ones, or *less* tolerant, in any quantitative sense, but rather their form of social organization was one that made the whole problem of tolerance relevant. Modern societies have elided the whole problem of tolerance rather than solved it. Where and when this works, fine. Where it doesn't, however, one cannot simply add "modernity" to the mix, like salt in a vegetable soup. Moreover, and this is a good deal more to the point, modern identities are themselves changing and the type of individual selves that were long seen as necessary concomitant to the nation-state – and which Gellner identified with civil society – are also changing, as is the nation-state itself. Subnational and transnational identities are growing apace. Religious, ethnic, and ethno-religious identities are making new claims on individuals' sense of self and society. Given these developments, the quintessentially modern moves, which obviated the problems of tolerance and intolerance, no longer quite hold. For these reasons we must mine other sources and perspective. Here, however, let us work out some of the analytic aspects of this issue not fully addressed before.

First, I think it is important to point out that tolerance is a very circumscribed virtue. It is not the solution to all evils, it is not a panacea. Nor is it without boundaries. Clearly some types of behavior are intolerable – although, as we said, it is not absolutely clear how one would go about defining what is beyond that pale. Certain religious and philosophical categories come to mind – ideas of natural law or, in the Jewish context, the Noahide commandments present some useful general orientation (Stone 1991). However, within these limits there is certainly great room for disagreement, for disgust, for rejection of much of what one considers as wrong, misguided, immoral, reprehensible, and hence for the need to tolerate what one believes to be wrong and that which makes one uncomfortable.

Certainly one cannot be expected to tolerate a clearly defined threat to one's identity. When that threat is directed at one from outside, let us say through the barrel of a rifle, one cannot be tolerant, and such a case presents us with no serious analytic problem. But, what if what is considered a "threat" comes from a different direction, from inside. Let us take the example of the West Roxbury Numismatic Society. Having met for decades discussing, analyzing, and trading coins – all of a sudden a few of our members begin to bring in stamps, refusing to even look at a coin, and proceeding to take up meeting space and time with matters philatelic: must we tolerate them? Do they not equally present a threat to who we are: the West Roxbury Numismatic Association? For sure, we do not have to exterminate our budding stamp collectors, only politely tell them to leave and perhaps join the Philatelic Society that meets down the street. We may tolerate their existence in the greater Boston area, but not as part of our identity, of who we are.

The relatively simple point I am trying to make with this example is that groups have boundaries. They cannot exist without boundaries. One cannot make claims to any type of identity without that identity being defined – which in some sense involves it being bound and circumscribed as well. To ask a group to tolerate what threatens that identity is to ask of the group to dismantle itself, to make itself cease to be, and, if anything is a model of intolerance, it would be this eradication of existence. Tolerance then is a virtue that has everything to do with boundaries and with margins. It does not have to do with all-out threats to who we are – whether those threats come from outside or from inside, whether they are physical or symbolic in nature. Rather, tolerance has to do with behaviors and/or beliefs that exist on "the margins" of the group's identity. Again, we may think of Jews and prostitutes in medieval Canon law as presenting good examples of precisely this type of marginality – along with lepers, sometimes Muslims, beggars, strangers (Bejcyz 1997). All existed on the borders or margins of society. Not beyond and not fully within (Nirenberg 1996).

If we follow this logic to its conclusion we reach a very interesting finding: the thicker the boundaries, the greater number of individuals, behaviors, and attitudes will reside on that boundary; the thinner that boundary, the fewer. Hence, the thicker the boundary, the more issues of tolerance and intolerance are raised and become relevant, as the greater the chances one will come into contact with behaviors and beliefs that one finds objectionable (without them necessarily threatening one's identity – although perhaps causing one to make endless calculations as to the existence or non-existence of such a threat). And, of course, it is once again clear why tolerance was such an important theme in societies with strong group identities – they are societies with very thick boundaries, very wide corporate identities, and group definitions that necessitate such tolerance however often and tragically they may be defined by its empirical absence or failure.

Within the public sphere of liberal, individualist societies, however, boundaries are parsed into razor thin edges and individuals interact not as members of groups, but as bearers of rights (citizen rights, social rights, human rights, and so on). Group identities have been, in the public sphere, replaced by individual identities and the problem of tolerance of difference has been replaced by the legal recognition and entitlements of rights. This is what I mean when I say that modernity has elided the problem of tolerance, obviated the necessity to be tolerant, rather than make people tolerant. It has replaced tolerance with rights. In so doing, it has also undermined the very foundations of any conception of a civil society, if that term is to have any meaning beyond the formal rights of the citizen.

This is what I referred to earlier when I said that the eighteenth-century debates over civil society were transcended in the nineteenth, and later, twentieth-century struggles over citizenship rights. The victory of rights was, however, at the cost of precisely that aspect of the problem – mutual recognition and approbation – that the idea of civil society had attempted to address.

Critically this development, of the liberal-individual self, has more than political dimensions. It is also the basis of social and economic life in most Western liberal societies and is a critical aspect of globalization. This is the difference between what Ernest Gellner (1988:44) termed "multi-stranded" and "single-stranded" relations. In the first "a man buying something from a village neighbor in a tribal community is dealing not only with a seller, but also with a kinsman, collaborator, ally or rival, potential supplier of a bride for his son, fellow juryman, ritual participant, fellow defender of the village, fellow council member." This situation is very different from the "single-stranded" relations we enter into when purchasing a commodity, wherein our calculations are, on the whole, orientated around purchasing the best possible commodity for the least price. And, if you recall, it was the single-stranded relations that he emphasises in his view of the modular human being who was the repository of civil society virtues. This self, however, partakes in a vision of selfhood that, I claim, leaves a good deal of humanity beyond the pale.

In contrast, tolerance is all about the type of relations that exist on these thick boundary lines of identity – identity that must by definition be a group identity of sorts. Much of the economic and political thrust of the modern world order is of course about replacing group identities with individual ones, replacing tolerance with rights, and replacing a relatively small number of multi-stranded relationships with an almost infinite number of single-stranded ones. In the process, tolerance goes from being a community-centered act to an individual, almost psychological attribute or personal characteristic (and this would play into Gellner's argument).

CONCLUSION

Of course, there is nothing wrong (practically or morally) with "solving" the problem of intolerance by removing the social conditions that make tolerance necessary. On the contrary, when it is possible, it seems to work well. But, my feeling is that the conditions that defined the "high-modernity" of the Western European and North Atlantic nation-state – and that allowed this particular solution, or rather elision of the problem – are currently changing. A return to group-based identities and to religious commitments in many parts of the world, the growth of transnational identities predicated on religion, ethnicity, and nationhood not dependent on Statehood are all calling into question the type of individual identities that stood at the core of the revolutionary idea of citizenship. Examples of this abound, one has only to look at the growing worldwide split between Shi'ite and Sunni Muslims (a distinction, which on the Indian subcontinent, was unmarked and unnoticed two generations ago) to see its potentially destructive consequences. Indeed, today in Britain, at least some Shi'ite Muslims, from Pakistani background, who feel themselves increasingly alienated from British society and, of course, have no living connection to Pakistan are turning to Iran as a new Zion – as a geographical locus of religious and political identities, as, indeed, the former becomes increasingly understood in terms of the latter.[1]

What we witness today is in fact a huge withdrawal of different groups into themselves, a closing of ranks against the outside world and a reticence to interact with those who are truly other or different. The growth of human rights as, what Michael Ignatieff (2001) called a form of "idolatry," that is, as a "trump" in every countervailing argument will not in itself counteract this development, which, in turn, will leave rights themselves as nothing but formal enactments of positive law, bereft of the very legitimizing aura that made of them beacons of freedom in the past 200 years.

The maintenance of pluralistic forms of society and a tolerance of constitutive difference may paradoxically turn on our ability to re-engage with other, older traditions and eschew the "trump" of individual rights. This is no doubt a strange and counterintuitive call, which some may see as conservative, if not reactionary, in its implications. In truth, however, it is a call, not to return to the Christian sources of rights, but rather to bring about a total reconceptualization of the categories within which we *think* the problems of the self and the other and so too the cognate problems of political order, individual rights, and collective responsibilities. What is called for is not a simple return to Christian sources, but rather a re-engagement with all sacred traditions, including those well beyond the Christian – to go beyond the current impasse of post-Christian (i.e., secular) political categories. Such an engagement may in fact bring us to very new ways of understanding how a secular constitutional order

---

[1] This is a personal communication from members of the British Pakistani community. I am unaware of research done on this, although there may indeed be such research.

supporting a liberal politics could come together with a heteronomous morality, in a manner not rooted in the workings of individual autonomy and Kantian self-regulation. This, as I see it, is the only real way of beginning to address the problems identified originally with the idea of civil society.

INSTITUTIONS AND PROCESSES

6 Electoral Engineering in New Democracies

Can Preferred Electoral Outcomes Be Engineered?

Competitive elections are the lifeblood of democracy. Indeed, the subfield of democratization remains strongly influenced by the theoretical formulations of Robert Dahl and Joseph Schumpeter, which define democracy largely in terms of competitive contests for votes to occupy public office (Dahl 1971, 1989, 1998; Schumpeter 1976). Even scholars wary of the so-called "electoralist fallacy" equating elections with democracy (Schmitter and Karl 1991; O'Donnell 1994, 1998) do not imagine that democratization can take place without instituting competitive elections at some point. Consequently, competitive elections are a centerpiece of democratization efforts and are seen by many as an end in and of themselves – as showcased in the American-led campaign in Iraq.

Despite this essential connection between elections and democratization, the introduction of elections also poses significant risks to prominent domestic and foreign political players. As Carles Boix notes, elections represent regular opportunities for society to rewrite the rules of the game and consequently threaten those who benefit from the status quo (Boix 2003). Competitive elections not only pose a threat to entrenched elites, but also may threaten Western interests and undermine political stability in general. Thus, the idea of electoral engineering entails using electoral rules to fashion elections that will produce those benefits associated with democracy, whereas reducing the degree of possible negative consequences that may arise from their introduction (Reynolds 2005). Although there is a mountain of scholarly work on the myriad effects of electoral systems, scholars have devoted considerably less attention to other forms of electoral engineering. In this essay, I attempt to survey a broader range of rules and other electoral decisions to provide a more comprehensive evaluation of the extent to which domestic and international actors can use institutional devices to craft specific outcomes.

This chapter will examine the various ways that electoral rules and other decisions and actions involving elections can be used to accomplish this task. To what degree can those interested in introducing competitive elections hope to engineer preferred outcomes? Which goals are most amenable to engineering and which are largely outside the purview of the electoral engineer? In answer to these questions, I make five main arguments, all of which highlight the genuine but limited ability of electoral engineers to fashion preferred outcomes using electoral rules. First, electoral engineering is possible and electoral rules have a significant effect on political outcomes. Indeed, because electoral rules are not neutral in their effects, politicians can either adopt rules with an eye to facilitating certain outcomes or ignore the accumulated experience regarding electoral system effects and hope that whatever system emerges will result in positive outcomes. Clearly the former approach is preferable. Second, despite the utility of electoral engineering, it is not a cure-all for all the problems associated with introducing elections in previously authoritarian systems. It must be acknowledged that there are real limitations to this enterprise and there are certain problems that are quite resistant to remediation through manipulation of electoral rules, timing of elections, or international monitoring and foreign aid. Third, electoral rules are rather blunt instruments that are best used to promote universal effects on all parties rather than to influence the electoral fortunes of particular political actors. Fourth, electoral rules often have not had the same effects in new democracies that they tend to have in established democracies. Thus, electoral engineers may have misguided or exaggerated expectations of their abilities to fashion particular outcomes using electoral rules, particularly in the first few elections held after a democratic transition. Finally, electoral engineers face a dilemma in that certain steps taken to achieve one goal may actually undermine efforts to achieve other important goals. Therefore, electoral engineers need to carefully consider all of the ramifications of their decisions and take a holistic approach to their craft.

This paper will be divided into five sections. First, I define and briefly discuss the process of electoral engineering and the various instruments that domestic and international political actors can use to influence electoral outcomes. Second, I offer a normative discussion of what ought to be the goals of electoral engineering. Third, I examine the means at the disposal of political actors to meet these goals and provide some examples that shed light on the degree of success attainable for each goal. In the fourth section, I discuss the issue of competing goals and how rules must be fashioned so that the pursuit of one goal does not inadvertently undermine other goals. I end with some conclusions and tentative policy recommendations.

I. DEFINING ELECTORAL ENGINEERING

For the purposes of this paper, electoral engineering will refer to the use and manipulation of various features related to the conduct of elections to influence and shape electoral and political outcomes. There are many specific rules and other decisions related to the conduct of elections that can be manipulated to craft alternative political outcomes, but I will concentrate on four major areas: electoral systems, secondary electoral rules, the timing of elections, and international influence through election monitoring and election-related foreign aid.

Electoral Systems

Although electoral systems sometimes refer to all of the rules pertaining to an election, I conceive of electoral systems more narrowly as the rules governing the translation of votes into seats. For every election, decisions must be made on how to distribute public offices based on the votes cast. These rules have profound implications because they reward certain types of parties or candidates, whereas penalizing others, sometimes so severely as to render them incapable of political survival. Giovanni Sartori captured the perceived power of these rules to fashion specific political and electoral outcomes when he famously argued that electoral systems were "the most specific manipulative instrument of politics" (Sartori 1968). Whereas there are many different ways that one can translate votes into seats, most states and thus most scholars have concentrated on two broad classes: proportional representation (PR) and single-member district (SMD) elections. The former refers to a class of electoral systems that use multi-member districts and party lists to elect slates of candidates from competing parties, whereas the latter refers to elections that rely on competition among individual candidates for a single seat in a given district.

Secondary Election Rules

There are various other electoral rules unrelated to the translation of votes into seats that can also be used to influence political outcomes that

I will refer to as secondary electoral rules. The most important of these are: 1) registration rules, which govern the formation of political parties and their official registration as electoral agents; and 2) nomination rules, which govern how individuals become candidates for election either as members of parties or independents. Sometimes these rules disallow certain types of parties (e.g., ethnic, religious, or regional parties) by simply forbidding their formation. Other registration and nomination rules are more subtle. For example, high signature requirements or candidate deposits can be used to deter the emergence of small, uncompetitive parties and/or independent candidates and a registration requirement that necessitates that registered parties must have a presence in all or most regions of the country severely limits the emergence of ethnic and other regionally-based parties (Birnir 2004).

Election Timing

The timing of elections matters. In particular, if there are multiple arenas of electoral competition (national and regional or presidential and legislative) the sequence and proximity of these elections has been shown to have important effects. In presidential democracies, scholars have argued that concurrent presidential and legislative elections have significant effects on the party system (Shugart 1995; Samuels 2004); whereas others have argued the sequence of national and regional elections can have important consequences for the territorial integrity of multi-ethnic states (Linz and Stepan 1996).

International Influence

Finally, there are actions taken by external actors such as international organizations and foreign states that can have important effects on electoral and political outcomes. In particular, I will focus on two arenas of international intervention in a country's electoral process: election monitoring and election-related foreign aid. Election monitoring refers to the process of certifying that a specific election was "free and fair," in that proper democratic procedures and international norms for free elections were followed during the campaign and on Election Day (Carothers 1997; Elklit and Svensson 1997). Election-related foreign aid refers to various development programs sponsored by international organizations and foreign governments that are designed to promote competitive electoral politics such as programs devoted to building political parties, promoting a free press, and supporting civil society organizations.

As stated earlier, by going beyond the effects of electoral systems per se, I hope to offer a relatively comprehensive evaluation of the prospects and limitations of engineering elections in new democracies using all the tools available.

II. THE GOALS OF ELECTORAL ENGINEERING: MINIMIZING THE RISKS WHILE MAINTAINING THE BENEFITS OF COMPETITIVE ELECTIONS

Before getting into the opportunities and constraints of electoral engineering one must outline the goals that would-be electoral engineers should strive to achieve.[1] I do so by considering the benefits and, more importantly, the risks that accompany the introduction of competitive elections. I argue that the major goals of electoral engineering should be instructed by an attempt to minimize the risks of competitive elections, but maintain their inherent benefits.

The expected benefits of free and fair elections derive from their equation with democracy. Elections are expected to provide the best opportunities for genuine representation of social interests within policy-making, particularly for groups previously repressed or marginalized by an authoritarian regime. They are also presumed to make government more accountable to the voting public and consequently to make governments more legitimate given these increased avenues by which citizens are able to have a say in their own governance. Ultimately, democratic governments should perform better than non-democratic ones because constitutional restraints and public scrutiny keep the former from abusing power and regular elections force them to respond promptly to problems and citizens' demands (Dahl 1998; Schmitter 2004; Halperin et al. 2005).

Although elections may prove capable of providing the above benefits to greater or lesser degrees even in new democracies, new elections can also lead to detrimental outcomes. I offer the following list of five potential drawbacks of competitive elections. The list is not exhaustive and the individual items are not mutually exclusive. Instead, it is an attempt to capture the main hazards that scholars have identified with the introduction of new elections.

---

[1] Of course, the list of goals for electoral engineers could be infinite. The list I propose is not meant to be exhaustive, but merely illustrative of the major goals most commonly mentioned by scholars and politicians.

Elections as a Mechanism of Authoritarian Control

Scholars have acknowledged that elections (even competitive ones) sometimes act as much as a means by which elites control and channel public demands as they are a means by which societal interests have access to political decision-making (Trounstine 2006). Recent developments in places like post-communist Eurasia and Latin America that have witnessed the deterioration of press freedoms and competitiveness of elections have renewed the focus on this problematic aspect of elections. Indeed, the growth in the number of regimes that allow for some semblance of competitive elections, but are severely lacking in certain key aspects of genuinely free and fair elections has prompted scholars to introduce a new regime type – competitive authoritarianism – to capture the growing trend (Diamond 2002; Levitsky and Way 2002; Schedler 2002).

As Schedler argues, authoritarian incumbents have a variety of resources at their disposal to intervene in the electoral process so that they are virtually guaranteed to retain their power. Most notably, officeholders can monopolize and control press coverage of the campaign; use financial and other resources of office to buy votes through patronage; manipulate the nomination procedures so that threatening opposition parties and candidates never appear on the ballot; and use coercive and tax agencies of the state to harass the opposition. If all else fails, those in power can change election results after the fact through various means of electoral fraud (Schedler 2002).

Such manipulation of multiparty elections is tempting for non-democratic elites because of the legitimacy that elections bestow on the regime both domestically and internationally. "Managed" elections offer elites the prospect of manufacturing the semblance of democracy but not facing the uncertainty that genuinely free and fair elections impose (Levitsky and Way 2002). Of course, as will be discussed next, even manipulated elections pose their own risks to those conducting them and may be a vehicle for increased democratization, thus providing domestic and international proponents of democratization their own opportunities for engineering alternative outcomes (Levitsky and Way 2002; McFaul 2005, 2005).

Undemocratic Winners

In a much-cited 1997 article, Fareed Zakaria provocatively quoted Richard Holbroke on the eve of elections in Bosnia: "'Suppose the election was declared free and fair' ... and those elected 'are racists, fascists, separatists, who are publicly opposed to [peace and reintegration]. That is the dilemma'" (Zakaria 1997). The dilemma of undemocratic winners in competitive elections is manifest in various ways. O'Donnell popularized the concept of "delegative democracy" to connote the problem of the concentration of (executive) power, that is, the tendency of democratically elected chief executives usurping all power in between elections and running roughshod over legislative and judicial organs of power in part based on the justification that they were directly elected by the people (O'Donnell 1994, 1998).

Yet, another problem arises in contexts where anti-democratic and/or anti-Western forces enjoy high levels of genuine support within the populace. Popular elections, even those devoid of manipulation, may lead to genuine electoral victories of nationalist parties that successfully seek votes by promising to further the interests of a single group or the country at large at the expense of other groups or countries.[2] The success of Hamas in recent Palestinian elections is but one example of such a scenario.

ELECTIONS AND ETHNIC CONFLICT

Closely related to the problem of undemocratic winners is the proposition that, under certain circumstances, competitive elections can actually exacerbate rather than help to alleviate ethnic conflict. Part of the explanation behind this dilemma lies in the problem just discussed regarding undemocratic winners – extreme nationalist parties may emerge and effectively contest free and fair elections. However, the link between competitive elections and interethnic conflict deserves particular attention because it goes beyond the prospect of a few unsavory contenders for office. As Mansfield and Snyder demonstrate in their chapter for this volume, democratic elections held in underdeveloped and unstructured political systems provide both the will and means for politicians to use extreme nationalism as a mobilizing tactic to gain advantage in the electoral arena. In short, they have shown that democratic elections can actually promote the emergence of nationalist politicians and parties that

---

[2] For examples of this problem in relation to ethnic and nationalist parties see Horowitz 1985. For examples of this problem in terms of anti-Western parties see Windsor 2003. Stepan argues that those wary of elections in Islamic countries warn against the "Islamic election trap," which refers to the prospect of competitive elections bringing to power Islamic parties that are hostile to both Western interests and democracy itself (Stepan 2004).

would not exist otherwise because playing the nationalist card is often a very sound strategy for those who want to win elections, particularly in new democracies with weak democratic institutions and media systems (see also Snyder 2000 and Mansfield and Snyder 2005). Wilkinson has pushed the argument one step further by implicating the electoral process itself in ethnic violence, showing that riots between Hindus and Muslims in India increased at the local (town) level when elections were held and were more frequent and deadly the more competitive elections were (Wilkinson 2004: chapter 2). It should be noted, however, that whereas Wilkinson sees competitive elections as a source of ethnic violence at the local level, he also argues that at the state level more electoral competition (in the form of state governments sufficiently beholden to a voting bloc of minority citizens) forces state governments to intervene more quickly to quell these same ethnic riots and thus lessen their harm (Wilkinson 2004: chapter 5).

Exclusion: Women and Ethnic Minorities

Elections are supposed to empower the population and make it easier for various social groups to have a hand in the policy process. However, a persistent problem in all democracies is the disjuncture between the ethnic, gender, and economic composition of national legislatures and the mass public. National legislatures worldwide tend to be bodies relatively lacking in women, ethnic minorities, and those from lower economic classes and this discrepancy is greater in new democracies in the developing world than in established democracies in the West (see the Parline website of the Inter-Parliamentary Union (IPU), www.ipu.org). Most observers see this as a problem because they see a connection between descriptive representation (the fact that an elected representative shares key demographic characteristics such as ethnicity or gender with constituents) and substantive representation (the ability of representatives to pursue policies that are in line with the interests of particular social groups) (Mansbridge 1999; Bratton and Ray 2002).

The inability of women and/or ethnic minorities to gain election to the national legislature in significant numbers can have a number of detrimental implications for the health of a democracy. First, there is a powerful symbolic effect. Legitimacy is compromised because key social groups do not feel as though they are fully integrated in the democratic process. Second, particularly for ethnic minorities, failure to gain legislative representation may prompt anti-system political activity to the point of secession, which could threaten the very survival of the state. Third, the quality of public policy may be compromised because voices of socially and economically vulnerable groups are not present in legislative debate. For these reasons and many others, I argue that electoral engineering should include steps to guard against the exclusion of women and minorities from the legislature.[3]

Dysfunctional or Unstable Party Systems

Finally, democratic elections can often produce rather chaotic, unstable, or dysfunctional party systems that, in turn, severely handicap effective governance. The problems that may arise within a party system, particularly one in a new democracy, are manifold, but I will concentrate on two key components of the party system. First, there is the number of political parties. The number of parties is a key concern because it has important implications for representation and effective governance. Problems can arise from a party system with too many parties or too few. If too many parties populate a party system chaos can ensue, specifically in the formation of governing coalitions within parliament (King et al. 1990). Fragile governing coalitions that cannot maintain a legislative majority for any significant duration can bring democratic policy-making to a halt through frequent votes of no confidence in parliamentary systems and gridlock in presidential systems (Mainwaring and Shugart 1997). If too few parties exist, important social interests do not feel adequately represented and may opt to pursue politics outside of electoral or even democratic channels.

Second, party system institutionalization – the degree to which parties are the central player in electoral politics and inter- and intra-party politics are regularized – should be a prime concern (Mainwaring 1999). A party system that is not institutionalized has a high rate of volatility such that each election basically witnesses a new slate of parties competing for office. High electoral volatility damages democracy by undermining ties between parties and key social groups and political stability in general (Mainwaring 1999; Madrid 2005; Mainwaring and Zucco 2007). Moreover, non-institutionalized party systems tend to have a high number of independents and a high number of party defections within the legislature (Moser 2001). Both independents and transient legislative party affiliations undermine the representational function and hamper the ability

---

[3] As Fish notes in his chapter for this volume, recent scholarship examining the effect on culture has picked up on this theme, demonstrating that exclusion of women may be the key cultural feature that hinders democratization in Islamic countries (Fish 2002; Norris and Inglehart 2002).

to form and maintain majority coalitions in the legislature (Rose, Munro, and White 2001).

Given these ramifications, I argue that electoral engineers should try to craft electoral systems that they think will promote the appropriate number of parties given the political context and build strong political parties with staying power and robust linkages to key social constituencies.

III. ELECTORAL ENGINEERING: PROSPECTS AND LIMITATIONS

Given the magnitude of the dilemmas for democratic governance and political stability in general presented by undesirable winners, manipulated elections, and ethnic conflict, it may be surprising to those unfamiliar with the scholarly literature on electoral systems to discover that the most well developed areas of electoral engineering involve our latter two issue areas: exclusion and, in particular, the party system. This results perhaps from the fact that it is easiest to draw concrete causal connections between electoral systems and the number and type of political parties and the number of women or ethnic minorities elected to the national legislature (Riker 1982). Basically, the connections between electoral rules and these outcomes are the most straight-forward and, dare I say, these are, perhaps, the easiest tasks to tackle using electoral systems. Another reason may be that the study of electoral systems has its roots in established Western democracies, where the number of parties and descriptive representation were issues of great importance partly because problems of electoral manipulation or ethnic conflict were not as endemic as they are in third wave democracies.

Regardless, as will be shown, would-be electoral engineers have much firmer recommendations based on much more empirical evidence when it comes to fashioning the number of parties using electoral systems than combating manipulation by sitting incumbents or avoiding civil war. However, even in the much-studied realm of the party system and (to a lesser extent) descriptive representation, there is great reason to question whether the experience of Western democracies can be extrapolated to new democracies. In this section, I offer an overview of what I see as the principal instruments available for avoiding or managing the five negative outcomes that can arise with the introduction of competitive elections just outlined and the strengths and weaknesses of these measures.

Electoral Engineering and Undesirable Winners

Electoral rules and the timing of elections do have significant effects on who wins and loses electoral contests. Politicians know this and, thus, closely monitor and often fiercely battle over the choice of electoral systems (Remington and Smith 1996; Cox 1997; Boix 1999). Likewise, if electoral schedules are not fixed, incumbent and opposition politicians alike attempt to time elections to their benefit. Thus, it is not unreasonable to imagine that one could fashion particular partisan outcomes by manipulating electoral rules and the timing of elections.[4]

Despite the genuine impact of electoral rules and timing on the electoral fortunes of particular electoral actors, I argue that electoral engineering is not conducive to pursuing narrow partisan or ideological ends. This is so for several main reasons. First, the underlying reasons why certain types of parties tend to benefit under certain electoral systems are *not* partisan or ideological by nature (Moraski and Loewenburg 1999). In other words, plurality elections favor large parties and PR systems encourage smaller parties regardless of their ideology. Of course, for a given party in a given election, one may be able to identify characteristics that are susceptible to electoral system influence (such as size or geographic concentration) and, for ideological or partisan reasons, could fashion an electoral system that marginalizes that party. However, there are two problems with this approach. First, in marginalizing one party or type of party deemed undesirable one may also be undermining the success of preferred parties. This is precisely what happened in the first post-Taliban elections in Afghanistan. Allies of President Hamid Karzai pushed for the adoption of a single non-transferable vote (SNTV) system in part to fragment the opposition. This was accomplished, but the system also fragmented the pro-Karzai vote, which significantly undermined legislative support for President Karzai's reform program (Reynolds 2007). Second, electoral conditions can change and the same rules that benefited a particular party or ideological trend in one election may benefit the other side in future elections. Thus, electoral rules designed to benefit certain parties or ideological trends can backfire and scholars have shown that

---

[4] Russian President Boris Yeltsin was particularly energetic in his attempts to use election timing to his own electoral benefit and that of his allies. He refrained from holding early elections immediately after the fall of Communism in 1991 out of fear that the Communist Party of the Russian Federation as successor to the Soviet Communist party would have too many organizational advantages. At the end of his career, he resigned the presidency and called an early presidential election to take advantage of his chosen successor's (Vladimir Putin) popularity at the time.

political institutions like electoral systems have a certain "stickiness" – that is, persistence over time – that prevents elites from changing the rules on a whim to correct past mistakes.[5] (Just ask critics of the Electoral College in the United States!)

Second, there are normative obstacles to ideological and partisan electoral engineering. At its core, a democratic election is a process not an outcome and, to be perceived as legitimate, elections must allow major political forces to compete and take their legislative seats if won freely and fairly. These normative demands of democratic elections restrain those interested in democracy promotion from entertaining many measures designed to marginalize specific political parties lest they be equated with their anti-democratic adversaries who manipulate elections to their own ends. For example, outlawing certain types of parties, even those deemed anti-democratic, will be difficult for those committed to building democracy because these same mechanisms often are used by undemocratic forces to marginalize legitimate opposition groups.[6] Moreover, international agencies, foreign governments, and NGOs engaged in democracy promotion have clear ideological and party preferences, but must be very careful how they promote these interests so that they are not open to similar criticism (Anglin 1998). This, of course, puts democracy advocates at somewhat of a disadvantage in relation to undemocratic actors who are less concerned with the niceties of the electoral process and thus have many more levers at their disposal.[7]

Finally, it should be noted that it is nearly impossible to use electoral rules to marginalize parties with widespread popular support in free and fair elections. Proportional representation can encourage smaller parties and thus lessen the *over-representation* of a large party in the legislature. Plurality elections can only penalize parties incapable of winning district races. If a party that is ultra-nationalist, anti-democratic, or anti-Western has a significant support base capable of overcoming most

---

[5] Russia is a good example of this. After the first post-communist election, President Yeltsin and his liberal allies were dissatisfied with the results produced by the mixed electoral system that they themselves devised and attempted to change it. However, Yeltsin met with stiff resistance from the legislature and eventually backed down on virtually all of his plans for reform (see Remington and Smith 1996; McFaul 2001; Moser and Thames 2001).

[6] Outlawing parties based on ethnic, religious, or racial identities is often practiced by pseudo-democratic regimes with the expressed intent of maintaining ethnic harmony. Of course, in many instances this is simply cover for authoritarian measures to sideline legitimate ethnic or religious parties (see Moser, forthcoming).

[7] Windsor (2003), for example, argues that in regions like the Middle East, the United States must be willing to accept electoral results that run contrary to short-term U.S. interests to demonstrate that it is truly committed to democratization in the region.

electoral thresholds under any given electoral system there is very little that can be done to thwart its electoral success short of measures that would compromise the democratic process itself.

Election Monitoring, Foreign Aid, and Electoral Manipulation

Trends in third-wave democracies since the turn of the century offer two rather contradictory views regarding the prevalence of electoral manipulation and the ability to counteract it through electoral engineering. On the one hand, electoral manipulation seems to be growing as a mechanism by which authoritarian regimes use elections to legitimate their rule while avoiding any real threat to their power from the political opposition. In Latin America, post-communist Eurasia, and Africa, hybrid regimes that allow semi-competitive but tightly controlled elections are seemingly on the rise and appear rather robust in many cases (Levitsky and Way 2002). On the other hand, there also have been noteworthy cases in which states that were manipulating elections (e.g., Mexico, Ukraine, Georgia) were forced by a mobilized civil society to offer cleaner elections that resulted in more democracy in general (Howard and Roessler 2006). Moreover, some observers argue that electoral engineering in the form of international intervention played an important role in conjunction with other factors in calling forth this renewed democratization (Bunce and Wolchik 2006; Kuzio 2006).

International activity, particularly election monitoring, seems to be the most useful instrument of electoral engineering available for countering electoral manipulation. Very little systematic research has been done on whether electoral systems have an impact on the propensity of incumbents to manipulate elections.

Carothers offers a number of positive contributions made by international election observers. Most notably, such observation can detect, publicize, and thus deter electoral fraud. At the very least, through their very presence, international election observers make it more difficult for incumbents to steal elections with blatant acts of fraud. Furthermore, international election observation can bolster transitional electoral processes by encouraging skeptical citizens and reluctant opposition politicians to participate. Finally, the practice of international observation reinforces the notion that free elections are an international norm and can raise the quality of elections by improving standards of electoral administration (Carothers 1997: 19–20; McFaul 2005). Broader democracy promotion programs that encourage the growth of civil society and support freedom of the press further bolster the ability of domestic forces to resist state coercion and mobilize to demand an end to fraudulent elections and an increase in democratic freedoms as demonstrated by the chapter by Seligson and his co-authors, which shows that democracy promotion programs have a discernible positive impact on democratic consolidation (Seligson, Finkel, and Pérez-Liñán, this volume). In combination, election monitoring, which helps establish a norm of free elections and can publicize transgressions against that norm, and democracy promotion programs, which empower domestic groups to mobilize against the state, provide a potentially powerful bulwark against the attempts by authoritarian elites to use elections as a legitimizing tool that actually forestalls democratization.

Despite these genuine benefits, there are also very real limits on the ability of international actors to constrain electoral malfeasance. Some of these are natural limits that international actors face when confronting determined domestic actors with resource advantages and a home-court advantage (Way 2005). It should first be noted that there are so many opportunities and forms of electoral misconduct that it is virtually impossible to completely eliminate the practice even under the best conditions. However, other obstacles are self-imposed by poor practices. Carothers and others have noted that election observers have hurt their cause by concentrating much too heavily on processes occurring on Election Day when most manipulation (e.g., unfair application of registration laws, unequal access to media, unfair use of state resources for campaign expenses, and harassment of opposition parties) occurs well before the polls open (Carothers 1997; Anglin 1998). Moreover, a set of consistent standards by which to judge the relative quality of elections has been elusive (Elklit and Svensson 1997). Finally, a lack of professionalism has led to some observers being manipulated by locals for their own political ends and others using their reports to further their own partisan or ideological agendas, undermining democracy promotion in the process (Carothers 1997; Anglin 1998).

However, the greatest threat to the efficacy of Western democracy promotion programs may be a backlash from authoritarian regimes themselves, driven in large part by their perceived success of these programs. Authoritarian leaders in Eurasia, Asia, Latin America, and the Middle East have taken a number of steps to remove what they see as a significant threat by outlawing, restricting, or otherwise sidelining the activities of international NGOs. Whereas bastions of authoritarianism like the Middle East have long utilized and perfected various measures to counter the effectiveness of international NGOs, countries that were previously more open to international organizations have quickly moved to shut their doors to such influence, particularly if they have witnessed significant political change in a neighboring state that they have attributed to international influence. The concerted effort by authoritarian governments in Russia and Belarus to thwart the effectiveness of international NGOs and "orange technologies" in the wake of Ukraine's Orange Revolution is but one telling example (Gershman and Allen 2006).

Electoral Systems and Ethnic Conflict

The debate over the relationship between electoral systems and interethnic conflict has spawned two competing perspectives. Scholars led by Arend Lijphart have recommended PR as a method of cooptation of ethnic minorities within a broader system of consociationalism (see Lijphart 1977 and Lijphart 1985). A rival school of thought headed by Donald Horowitz (1985 and 1991) has countered that consociational systems lock in ethnic divisions and that electoral systems in divided societies need to provide incentives for voters to pool their votes behind moderate, multi-ethnic coalitions. Reilly (2002) has argued that preference voting systems, such as the alternative vote (AV) and single transferable vote (STV) may provide the centripetal incentives necessary to push voters and elites into coalitions that reach across ethnic divisions.

There are several problems with both sides of this debate. First, unlike other facets of the electoral system literature, the dependent variable – interethnic conflict – is broad and unwieldy, making it very difficult to systematically isolate the effect of electoral systems from other obvious factors influencing this outcome. In other words, it is very hard to tell whether the electoral systems advocated actually provide the results advertised. Second, the empirical evidence that has been offered appears ambiguous at best. Reilly notes that similar electoral institutions (preference voting systems) produced significantly different results in five countries that experimented with them. He concluded that a number of conditions need to be fulfilled for preference voting systems to have their intended effects, including (among other things): the existence of a core group of moderates, extended experience under the system, ethnically diverse electoral districts, and voters willing to cross ethnic lines when distributing their preferences (Reilly, 2002: 166–169). Similarly, consociationalism has a rather mixed record in defusing interethnic conflict. Moreover, Norris (2002) found that although PR may indeed increase minority representation in many cases, she did not find that PR promoted a higher sense of legitimacy of the political system among ethnic minorities. Thus, as critics of consociationalism argue, increased representation may not necessarily lower ethnic conflict. Finally, as I will show next, one can expect similar contextual constraints on even the more limited claims that PR provides increased representation for all ethnic minorities.

Electoral Systems and Descriptive Representation

Electoral engineering is most associated with two sets of outcomes: descriptive representation of women and minorities and basic characteristics of the party system. Much theoretical and empirical work has been done to show that certain types of electoral systems offer historically marginalized social groups greater opportunities for representation. Most agree that PR is a key ingredient in improving the prospects for representation for both women and ethnic minorities (see, especially, Lijphart 1991, 2004; Norris 2004).

Scholars have offered a myriad of interrelated features associated with PR systems to account for the system's greater propensity to produce female legislators.[8] Matland and Studlar (1996) have integrated these elements of PR elections into a contagion model to explain the higher representation of women in PR elections. They contend that increases in women's representation are initiated by smaller parties committed to the promotion of women. This commitment to female representation is then emulated by larger parties competing for similar constituencies until the process reverberates along the whole ideological spectrum.[9]

The ability of ethnic minorities to win legislative seats is usually seen as a consequence of electoral systems and the size and geographic concentration of minority populations (Reilly and Reynolds 1999: 48–51). The argument that PR systems foster the representation of ethnic minorities has typically rested on the idea that they encourage the emergence

---

[8] PR is thought to favor female candidates because: 1) it is less candidate-centered than SMD elections; 2) allows for the emergence of smaller parties (which may be more "women-friendly"); 3) promotes greater legislative turnover and thus more opportunities for women; and 4) PR party lists provide more incentives for gender-balancing than single-member district contests (Engstrom 1987; Norris 1987, 1993; Rule 1987, 1994; Matland and Studlar 1996).

[9] Such contagion is not exclusive to PR systems, but is more extensive and spread more quickly in PR systems for several reasons. The multiple parties often produced under PR systems provide greater opportunities for the emergence of "women-friendly" parties, which tend to be smaller parties that would be shut out of competition in two-party systems usually produced in SMD elections. Secondly, the centralized control over nominations makes it easier for parties under PR systems to react to stimuli for increasing female representation. Finally, electoral threats from parties promoting women are more serious in PR elections because of lower disproportionality between votes and seats. In SMDs, the priority is finishing first so as to capture the seat. The margin of victory does not matter. Thus, in safe districts even substantial defections toward a third party promoting a female candidate does not necessarily challenge the major parties' share of seats. In PR systems with large district magnitudes, even small shifts in the proportion of votes may take away seats from the major parties (Matland and Studlar 1996: 712–713).

of ethnic parties. PR systems do this by lowering the electoral threshold necessary to gain representation, which increases the number of parties thus making smaller ethnic parties more viable (Norris 2004: 208–213).[10] Although generally viewed as inferior to PR systems, SMD elections also can be conducive to minority representation under certain conditions. The election of ethnic minorities in SMD systems tends to be based on geographic concentration and the ability of a minority group to constitute a critical mass within a given electoral district. In so-called minority-majority districts, opportunities exist for the emergence of ethnic parties, which can displace one of the major parties within their "home regions" (e.g., the Bloc Quebecois in Quebec), whereas major parties feel pressure to nominate more minority candidates as seen in the United States (Lublin 1997; Canon 1997; Tate 2003). Thus, geographic concentration of minorities can overcome the bias against small (ethnic) parties and minority candidates under plurality systems (Barkan 1995). However, given that PR systems are expected to promote minority representation under a greater number of circumstances than SMD elections, its preferred status remains intact even when acknowledging the prospect of minority representation under other systems (Lijphart 2004).

There is significant empirical evidence that PR systems increase the representation of women and minorities, particularly the former. On average, countries employing party-list PR had more than double the proportion of female legislators (20%) of countries using SMD elections (9%) (Rule 1994: 18). Moreover, women's representation grew at a dramatically higher rate in countries with PR elections than in countries with SMD elections (Matland and Studlar 1996: 709). The empirical evidence is less striking for minority representation, but this has not seemed to erode the scholarly support for PR as a central mechanism for promoting this goal.[11]

Despite the scholarly consensus on the merits of PR for the representation of marginalized groups, research on new democracies demonstrates that electoral engineering is not a panacea in this arena because the effects of electoral systems that are regularly seen in established democracies

---

[10] This can be seen particularly in ethnically divided societies with PR systems that have very high district magnitudes and very low legal thresholds, which provide few obstacles to election for even the smallest parties. Perhaps the best example of how PR systems can promote the election of minority ethnic groups through ethnic parties is Israel, which had seven parties representing specific ethnic or religious constituencies out of a total of twelve parties winning seats in the 2006 parliamentary elections to the Knesset.

[11] The dearth of empirical investigation of the sources of minority representation results mostly from to difficulty of collecting data on the ethnic identity of individual legislators (see Norris 2002: 211–213).

may not automatically hold for developing countries. Matland has shown that there is no systematic relationship between PR and the election of women in less developed countries. He argues that there may be a minimum threshold of political development that needs to be surpassed before women can effectively organize and use institutions such as the electoral system to further their interests. Prior to reaching this threshold, factors that commonly affect women's representation in industrialized democracies do not seem to have an effect in less developed nations (Matland 1998). Other scholars, such as Reynolds (1999) and Norris and Inglehart (2001), have noted the significance of cultural attitudes on women's representation, suggesting cultural constraints on female social advancement may override the incentives of electoral systems favorable to women's representation. Indeed, Norris and Inglehart (2001) found that electoral systems did not have a statistically significant effect on women's representation once other control variables were introduced; however, cultural variables retained a statistically significant effect. Comparison of women's representation in mixed electoral systems offers further evidence that the promotion of women's representation under PR systems is not a universal phenomenon. The difference between the PR and SMD tiers of mixed systems in consolidated democracies was always substantial and statistically significant; on average, more than twice the percentage of women were elected in PR tiers than in SMD tiers, whereas the difference between the two tiers was usually not statistically significant in post-communist states (Moser 2001).[12] However, other studies have shown no difference between new and established democracies in terms of the positive impact that PR has on women's representation (Kentworthy and Malami 1999; Yoon 2004; Kostadinova 2007).

In the case of ethnic minority representation, the primary complicating factor in using electoral systems to engineer increased representation of minorities is that effects are highly conditional on characteristics of individual ethnic groups. Again, research on mixed electoral systems highlights this phenomenon. In a study of four mixed systems

---

[12] Moreover, post-communist states present one case (Russia 1995) in which the relationship runs counter to expectations. In Russia's 1995 parliamentary election women gained office in significantly greater proportions in the SMD tier than in the PR tier. There was a statistically significant *negative* relationship between PR and the proportion of women elected to parliament. This negative relationship between PR and women's representation is actually present in Russia for all three post-communist elections once one accounts for the anomalous case of the Women of Russia bloc, which gained a significant number of PR seats and virtually no plurality seats in 1993, but faded from the electoral scene after that initial election (Moser 2001).

(New Zealand, Russia, Ukraine, and Lithuania), it was found that, in the aggregate, ethnic minorities did not achieve greater representation in the PR tier over the SMD tier (Moser and Scheiner 2007). Moreover, electoral system effects were found to be highly contingent on the demographic characteristics of ethnic groups. In other words, certain types of ethnic groups had an advantage under PR elections, others gained more representation in plurality elections, and still others saw no difference between electoral systems. Highly assimilated ethnic minorities witnessed no significant difference in their ability to gain election under PR versus SMD electoral arrangements. As one might expect, large, geographically dispersed ethnic minorities achieved greater representation in PR elections, but small, geographically concentrated minorities were actually better represented in the SMD tier. Those groups that were both large and geographically concentrated (e.g., Russians in Ukraine) saw little difference between PR and plurality elections because they could achieve significant representation under both types of systems (Moser and Scheiner 2007; Moser 2008). Therefore, contrary to much of the existing literature (particularly work associated with Lijphart's consociational approach), PR may not be the most appropriate electoral system in all countries facing severe ethnic divisions. In fact, certain ethnic groups may be at a disadvantage by a PR system.

A final consideration that must be kept in mind is whether the election of members of marginalized social groups actually results in increased symbolic legitimacy of the regime and substantive representation through public policy deemed positive by the groups in question. It is too early to tell whether increased descriptive representation of a socially marginalized group such as women in Afghanistan will result in better public policy for them. However, there is a growing literature on the legislative and symbolic impact of descriptive representation in established democracies in the U.S. and Europe and third wave democracies in Latin America. This research offers a mixed picture. Some studies find little evidence of greater legitimacy stemming from increased numbers of female legislators (Dolan 2006; Lawless 2004), whereas other studies find greater symbolic effects (Fox and Lawless 2005; Campbell and Wolbrecht 2006). Similarly, some studies argue that women have a substantial impact on the type of legislative policies produced (Caiazza 2004; Schwindt-Bayer 2006), whereas others have found that gender has little impact on legislative behavior (Tolbert and Steuernagel 2001). Finally, some studies have found that successful efforts to include more members of marginalized groups have resulted in a backlash from voters and parties of the majority in both the electoral and legislative arenas (Haider-Markel 2007). Such a backlash could at least partially offset gains in substantive representation.

Electoral Systems and the Party System

Two of the most hallowed theories of political science are Duverger's Law, which argues that plurality electoral systems tend to produce two large parties, and its corollary, Duverger's Hypothesis, which argues that PR systems tend to produce multiparty systems (Riker 1987). The effects of plurality elections are realized through two interrelated processes: a mechanical effect and a psychological effect. The mechanical effect refers to the fact that plurality systems tend to produce a large amount of disproportionality between votes and seats, rewarding large parties with an overabundance of seats compared to votes, whereas short-changing small parties. The psychological effect arises when voters and elites anticipate the disproportionate rewards of the system and shift their support from small parties to large parties. Although all electoral systems experience these effects, scholars have agreed that the plurality system represents the "strongest" electoral system, that is, the system offering the most constraining influence on the number of parties (Sartori, 1986; Taagepera and Shugart 1989; Lijphart 1994; Cox 1997). The intuitive power of the theory as well as the cumulative evidence in support of this claim have led many to presume that plurality elections will produce two-party systems under virtually any circumstances (see, for example, Lijphart 1991).

However, like electoral system effects on women's representation, there is growing evidence that plurality elections may not have the same constraining effect on the number of parties in new democracies as it has consistently shown in consolidated ones. Papua New Guinea is the most dramatic exception to Duverger's Law among pure plurality systems. Papua New Guinea used a pure plurality system in several elections since its independence in 1975.[13] These plurality contests were marked by severe party fractionalization in which more than a dozen candidates typically contested a single seat and victors often won seats with less than 20% of the vote (Reilly 1997: 5–6).

However, the popularity of mixed electoral systems, particularly in the post-communist world, offers a glimpse of the effects of plurality elections

---

[13] The AV system was used in competitive elections prior to independence and were once again introduced to some degree in 1997 (Reilly 1997).

TABLE 6.1: Effective number of elective parties (ENEP) for plurality and PR tiers in selected mixed systems

Country/Election	Average ENEP per district in plurality tier	Average ENEP per district in PR tier
Consolidated democracies		
Germany 1998	2.71	3.18
Italy 1994	3.04	5.88
Italy 1996	2.43	5.80
Japan 1996	2.95	4.00
Japan 2000	2.94	4.80
New Zealand 1996	3.29	4.03
New Zealand 1999	3.11	3.71
Post-communist states		
Lithuania 2000	5.80	5.56
Russia 1993	5.48	6.60
Russia 1995	6.61	9.46
Russia 1999	5.57	5.60
Ukraine 1998	5.99	6.36

in a broader array of states with poorly developed political parties.[14] The experiences of these states resemble the extreme party fractionalization under plurality rules of Papua New Guinea. Table 6.1 presents the effective number of electoral parties for selected countries with mixed systems that employ a plurality rule to determine seats in their SMD tier.[15]

There are two striking patterns in Table 6.1. First, post-communist states have significantly more candidate proliferation in their plurality

[14] Mixed electoral systems offer some advantages and a few hazards when used to examine the effects of their separate components. The advantage lies in the potential for controlled comparison of different electoral systems in a single electoral environment. I have argued elsewhere that mixed systems offer an excellent laboratory to study the effects of PR versus plurality systems while controlling for all other potential causal factors by holding them constant (Moser 2001). The principal risk lies in cross-contamination between tiers. Given the mutual influence that PR and plurality tiers may have on one another, one may expect that contamination from the PR tier has led to the overproduction of viable candidates in the plurality tier of these systems (see Herron and Nishikawa 2001). Despite the problems of cross-contamination, a comparison of mixed systems is instructive of the potential effects of "pure" systems had they been used, albeit imperfectly so. If some mixed systems display a substantial constraint on the number of parties in their plurality tiers, whereas others do not, one may argue that underlying political conditions do not support strategic behavior and could be expected to produce similar fragmentation if a pure plurality system were used (Moser and Scheiner 2004).

[15] Lithuania uses a two-round run-off election in its SMD tier.

tiers than the consolidated democracies. The Effective Number of Electoral Parties (ENEP) index runs between 2.5 and 3.0 in the plurality tier of mixed systems in consolidated democracies, which is actually quite similar to the experience of the pure plurality systems of Great Britain, New Zealand, Canada, and India. But, there is severe party fragmentation in all of the post-communist states. On average, there are nearly six viable candidates running in plurality contests in Lithuania, Russia, and Ukraine, which approximate the extreme case of party fragmentation found in Papua New Guinea. Second, the gap in party fragmentation between the PR and plurality tiers is telling. In the consolidated democracies, there tends to be a substantial gap, which suggests that the plurality tier constrained the number of parties vis-à-vis the PR tier as the literature would expect. The Italian case is particularly striking. Party elites coordinated their nominations so that a rather fragmented set of choices in the PR tier was winnowed down to something approximating two-party competition in plurality races. The drop in the effective number of parties from the 1994 election to 1996 suggests adaptation over time (see Reed 2001). Admittedly, post-communist states also tend to have a lower ENEP measure in their plurality tiers (although Lithuania is an exception), but the gap is not as substantial, particularly when noting the severe party fragmentation existing in the system to begin with.

It is conceivable that pure plurality systems could produce much less party fractionalization in the post-communist states described here than the plurality tiers of their current mixed electoral systems. Although contamination effects from the PR tier may account for some of the candidate proliferation in these countries (see Ferrara et al. 2005), I argue that the more likely culprit is a lack of the conditions necessary for strategic behavior to take place. Like Papua New Guinea, the field of candidates in a typical post-communist plurality race is so crowded that any single candidate can reasonably expect to be competitive by marshaling support from a small subset of the electorate. Consequently, for new democracies one must question whether elites could engineer two-party systems through the introduction of plurality electoral systems if they so desired.[16] The main point to be taken away from this research is the limitations inherent in electoral engineering. Engineering specific outcomes using electoral systems is very context-sensitive, even for outcomes such as the

---

[16] Recent cross-national analyses of pure electoral systems further confirm these findings. Clark and Golder (2006) find that PR elections with higher district magnitudes increase the number of parties in established democracies, but not necessarily in new democracies.

number of parties that are commonly assumed to be directly and strongly influenced by electoral rules.

IV. NAVIGATING COMPETING GOALS

As a final cautionary note, electoral engineers must be mindful that electoral rules often involve tradeoffs. Any step taken to induce a positive outcome in one arena may have detrimental effects in other areas. One can see this dynamic in the interplay between women's representation and minority representation. Although PR electoral systems are likely to be more conducive to the representation of both women and ethnic minorities, they promote the inclusion of traditionally marginalized groups in very different ways. Women tend to achieve increased representation through gender balancing within party lists of major parties, whereas ethnic minorities rely more on mobilization through ethnic parties outside the mainstream party structure (see Htun 2004). These two strategies often come into conflict because balancing is optimized through larger parties, whereas mobilization through niche parties is achieved through a party system that contains smaller parties. Thus, a PR system that is designed to enhance the prospects for representation of ethnic minorities by allowing small parties may accomplish this task at the expense of representation for women and vice versa (Moser and Holmsten 2008). Recent work on the gender composition of ethnic parties shows that these parties tend to elect significantly fewer women than non-ethnic parties, providing empirical support for fears voiced by feminist theorists such as Sarah Okin who fear that efforts to protect minority rights may actually harm the interests of women (Okin 1999; Moser and Holmsten 2008). Thus, even when electoral engineers can successfully achieve a desired outcome they must be mindful of externalities – the negative side effect of their actions in other arenas and on other actors.

One way out of this conundrum is to "bundle" electoral rules that promote the election of specific groups. For example, countries with low legal thresholds (and thus the propensity to produce many small parties) should consider also using gender quotas with mandate requirements that require the nomination of women in a certain proportion of top spots on all party lists. This will ensure that women are not excluded from the small number of winnable seats found at the top of such small parties (Jones 2004). Conversely, in ethnically divided countries with relatively high legal thresholds and/or gender quotas to promote the election of women some special provisions should also be made for the election of ethnic minorities such as a special, lower legal threshold for parties representing minority groups or reserved seats. This would allow minorities increased representation through ethnic parties, but maintain rules for the rest of the party system that enhance the prospects for women's representation and a less fragmented party system (Moser and Holmsten 2008).

CONCLUSIONS

This paper has offered a broad overview of the prospects and problems of using electoral rules to shape electoral and political outcomes in new democracies. Unfortunately, my conclusions do not lend themselves to a coherent set of policy recommendations. Instead, I will offer some general musings. First, in general, we should lower our expectations regarding our capacity to shape outcomes with electoral institutions. Certain problems, such as undesirable winners that have widespread popular support, simply cannot be engineered away without sacrificing core democratic elements of the election itself. Moreover, electoral systems' effects are not as predictable as commonly presumed and sometimes do not come out as planned, particularly in new democracies. Third, there is not a single, best electoral arrangement capable of resolving all the ills that the introduction of new elections might bring about. This is so because electoral systems involve compromises and tradeoffs – steps taken to improve one situation may cause problems in other arenas. Furthermore, the effects of electoral systems are often contingent upon the context in which they are operating. Thus, the same electoral system may have very different effects under different conditions. Finally, the best approach to electoral engineering may be a multifaceted one that includes several different combinations of rules. Combinations of different rules that offer competing incentives, such as mixed electoral systems or PR systems with electoral thresholds and "individualized" rules that target particular social groups, offer the best chance to achieve the greatest variety of "goods" usually desired from democratic elections.

JOHN M. CAREY

7 Does It Matter How a Constitution Is Created?

CONSTITUTIONAL MOMENTS

The world is witnessing a boom in constitution writing. A comprehensive study of the birth and death of national constitutions counts 736 written and promulgated from 1789–2005, or about three-and-a-half per year (Elkins, Ginsburg, and Melton 2006). Another worldwide study of constitutional adoption tallies nearly 200 new national charters just from 1975–2005, or closer to seven per year (Widner 2006). Some of these constitutions endure for long periods, their provisions widely respected in practice, and they come to embody in parchment the formal rules of political competition and policymaking in their respective states. Most have shorter, less distinguished tenures.

Constitutional moments are diverse. Some new constitutions are born in the wake of war, some coincide with the establishment of democracy or its collapse, some with the redefinition of national boundaries or the foundation of new states. Others accompany less radical changes and are adopted according to procedures established by a prior constitution. The actors involved and the procedures that characterize constitutional moments also vary. Some new charters are drawn up by small groups, perhaps advisers to a chief executive, whereas others are drafted by national assemblies or conferences including hundreds of participants. Participants are democratically elected in some cases, but not others. Many new constitutions must be ratified by popular vote to take effect, but not all.

The modern surge in constitutional moments presents the questions: Does it matter how constitutions are drafted and adopted? What are the ideals toward which constitutions might contribute? What characteristics of the drafting and promulgation process might matter to whether those ideals are realized? And how, if at all, could we know?

155

This essay begins to address these questions, although with the caveat at the outset that the answers are tentative. I begin considering a menu of ideals by which the success of constitutions might be gauged and possible links between those ideals and the nature of constitutional moments. Drawing from that base, the next section states some hypotheses about how characteristics of constitutional moments might affect the realization of constitutional ideals, then discusses challenges to testing the hypotheses empirically, and reviews some recent and ongoing research that promises advances in data and methods. The next section describes the (mostly) original dataset examined here, based on sixty-seven constitutional moments that took place between 1990 and 2005. Next, I present some patterns evident in these data that shed some light on some of the hypotheses, and follow with a discussion about what one might conclude from the patterns, as well as the considerable limitations on inference associated with the data assembled here. I conclude by summarizing the results and considering their implications for what democracy promoters might accomplish during constitutional moments, and how.

IDEALS AND PROCESSES

Scholarship on constitutions articulates a range of ideals to which they might aspire, in some cases implying propositions about how the process by which the charter is designed affects realization of these ideals.

Democracy

Democracy may be the most prominent among constitutional ideals. It is mentioned explicitly in at least sixty-two of the sixty-six recent charters considered later in this essay, and in 76% of all constitutions going back to 1789 (Comparative Constitutions Project 2007). Modern democracy promoters are adamant that the process of crafting constitutions ought to be inclusive so that constitutions might be embraced by the broadest possible range of citizens, and that constitutions themselves – even if not the specific governments they empower – ought to reflect a popular consensus. A recent review summarizes studies by the International Institute for Democracy and Electoral Assistance with "participatory processes [of constitution building] seem to have empowered the people" (Samuels 2006: 669). According to the Commonwealth Human Rights Initiative (1999), "Constitution-making should be a process that constructively engages the largest majority of the population. This is necessary to ensure that the end product is seen as legitimate, and owned by all the people."

The emphasis on inclusiveness as critical to the success of constitutional moments is echoed in much of the academic literature. Burton, Gunther, and Higley (1992) put a premium on consensus among political elites at the moment new political pacts are established as essential to their effectiveness and longevity. Gunther (1992) regards the Spanish transition as archetypal in this regard, pointing to the partisan inclusiveness of the parliament that ratified the new charter, and the willingness of the large parties to include representatives of small parties and regional interests on the critical subcommittee that drafted it (57–58). By contrast, in a requiem and post-mortem on Canada's 1982 Constitution Act, the impetus for which came primarily from national-level leaders, Banting and Simeon (1983) point to misgivings on the part of provincial-level politicians and parties as critical roadblocks.

The theme running throughout these accounts is that inclusiveness fosters shared expectations among political leaders regarding how subsequent decisions will be made and on the limits on power of governments to be created under the new constitution. North, Summerhill, and Weingast (2000) argue that differences in how widespread were shared beliefs about constraints on power account for the relative stability of the constitutional agreement struck in 1787 in Philadelphia as well as the transience of dozens of Latin American constitutions adopted throughout the nineteenth century.

Temperance
Another set of related constitutional ideals prioritizes limiting the power of office-holders, lowering the stakes of politics, and encouraging moderation and measured deliberation (Przeworski 1991; Weingast 1997; Rasch and Congleton 2006). With respect to the design of constitutions, the central theme here is division of power, such that no political actor can unilaterally make decisions and enforce them (Madison 1788).

Formal models illustrate that increasing the number of institutional actors who must agree to a policy change, or analogously, increasing the vote threshold for approving a new proposal, will both shrink the rate of changes and force those that are adopted toward the center of the policy space (Tsebelis 1995, 1999; Tsebelis and Money 1997). Constitutions that encourage this effect by establishing checks and balances are applauded on the utilitarian grounds that social welfare is maximized by minimizing the aggregated distances between citizens' preferences and the policies their governments adopt (Colomer 2001), and on the liberal grounds that built-in vetoes impede government abuse of individual rights (Riker 1982).

Durability

Another widely acknowledged goal of constitutions is durability. It might appear obvious that, if constitutions have any salutary effects, then durability is desirable on the grounds that something worth having is worth maintaining. On the other hand, most constitutions establish rules limiting the actions available to public officials, and the claim by any set of constitutional engineers to constrain subsequent generations is open to dispute (Holmes 1988). In the end, most observers concur that the appropriate balance between constitutional stability and transience is hard to identify.[1]

So if constitutions should be neither fleeting, nor set in stone, how long-lived should they be? Almost certainly, more so than they are in practice. The most comprehensive study of the duration of national constitutions puts the mean lifespan at sixteen years and the median at eight, substantially shorter even than the 'generational' terms in which the normative debate over pre-commitment is generally framed, suggesting that constitutional mortality is a bigger problem than obsolescence (Elkins, Ginsburg, and Melton 2006).[2]

Constitutional longevity may be desirable not just for its own sake, but because it makes possible other effects of constitutions. A primary job of constitutions is to resolve intractable coordination problems – for example, how political actors with diverse interests might contest for political authority on a regular basis without mutual destruction. Coordination equilibria require stable mutual expectations among actors, which,

---

[1] Even Thomas Jefferson, frequently cited as an advocate of a revolution every generation or so, is measured on the subject: "I am certainly not an advocate for frequent and untried changes in laws and constitutions. I think moderate imperfections had better be borne with; because, when once known, we accommodate ourselves to them and find practical means of correcting their ill effects. But I know also that laws and institutions must go hand in hand with the progress of the human mind. As that becomes more developed, more enlightened, as new discoveries are made, new truths disclosed and manners and opinions change with the change of circumstances, institutions must advance also and keep pace with the times" (Letter to Samuel Kercheval 1816, volume 15: 40).

[2] The recent adoption of the constitutions examined later in this paper limits the amount of light they could shed on durability, but Elkins, Ginsburg, and Melton's (2006) comprehensive statistical analysis indicates that constitutions adopted via more democratic procedures endure longer than those adopted in less democratic constitutional moments.

in turn, develop over time. Along these same lines, a potential second order benefit of durability accrues to citizens under democratic constitutions insofar as over time, converging expectations on the electoral viability of candidates and parties electoral competition, clarifying reputations and making it easier for voters to use ballots to punish bad performance and reward virtue (Carrol, Cox, and Pachon 2006; Tavits and Annus 2006).

HYPOTHESES

Does the way a constitution is adopted matter to whether it realizes the ideals reviewed in the previous section? In the arguments promoting each ideal, one can find claims that greater inclusiveness in constitutional moments should promote realization of the ideal itself. With respect to level of democracy, a recent International Peace Academy (2005: 2) report suggests that "a participatory process...results in a constitution that better represents the interests of population." And the Commonwealth Human Rights Initiative (1999) advocates "[focusing] on the participatory aspects of the process, with an aim towards finding strategies for deepening democracy." A persistent theme in the democracy promotion literature can be summed up as:

H1:   More inclusive constitutional moments → more democratic politics.

How might the nature of constitution-making affect whether constitutions encourage temperance? If constitutional design is about defining the scope and boundaries on state authority, and decision-making in constitutional moments is analogous to that portrayed by spatial models of policymaking, then including more actors in the process of constitutional drafting and promulgation ought to reduce their scope of agreement – that is, the powers they agree to delegate to the government – yielding constitutions with greater formal constraints on authority.[3] In short, the academic literature suggests that the number and diversity of actors at the table during constitutional moments may affect whether constitutions

---

[3] Not all actors exercise equal influence, of course, and recent research on Venezuela suggests that the balance of power between an incumbent government and its opponents, measured by vote and seat distributions in elections preceding constitutional moments, determines whether constitutions limit executive power, thus encouraging compromise, or amplify it (Corrales 2006). Electoral returns provide purchase on the relative power of each type of actor, but only when constitutional moments occur in contexts that are already reasonably democratic.

encourage political sobriety, the manifestations of which include limited government authority and policy moderation.[4]

H2:   More inclusive constitutional moments → more constraints on government authority.

One might infer further that, if inclusiveness in constitutional moments enhances the legitimacy of constitutions, enhancing a sense of popular ownership, whereas reducing the stakes of politics, that inclusiveness should contribute to constitutional durability.

H3:   More inclusive constitutional moments → stronger, and thus more durable, constitutions.

At least one line of reasoning, however, suggests caution along these lines. Russell Hardin (1989) challenges the emphasis that advocates of inclusiveness place on widespread agreement to and support of new constitutions, arguing that even recalcitrant political actors will acquiesce to a constitutional order once they recognize that:

- a critical mass of *other* actors recognizes a given set of rules, and
- there are insufficient resources to communicate an alternative set of rules around which mutual expectations might build.

The empirical implications of this argument are that, during constitutional moments themselves, universal "ownership" of a new constitution is unnecessary, and that more important is whether the constitutional moment delivers a clear signal that the new charter articulates a *fait accompli* – the only constitutional game in town.

EMPIRICAL CHALLENGES

How might one determine whether any of these propositions are on target? One strategy would be to identify a range of constitutional moments

---

[4] Beyond the number of actors involved in drafting constitutions, the nature of their interaction might affect outcomes. Rasch and Congleton (2006) suggest that when the rules for changing constitutions mandate cooling off periods, stability increases. Contrasting the Philadelphia Convention of 1787, which deliberated behind closed doors, and the French Constituent Assembly of 1789–1991, which recorded and published all its votes, Elster (1995) argues that private negotiations encourage genuine deliberation whereas fully transparent bargaining encourages grandstanding, intransigence, and, ultimately, less stable constitutions. Other characteristics of constitutional moments, such as the nature of media coverage and whether popular consultation procedures are built in, might also affect the degree to which constitutional designers are shielded from public pressure. The CWCR (2007) project is assembling extensive data on these matters.

across countries and over time, document their key characteristics (e.g. inclusiveness) as well as outcomes of interest (e.g. subsequent levels of democracy, constitutional stability), and draw inferences about the importance of constitutional moments from any patterns revealed in the data. This paper makes an effort along these lines, but acknowledges at the outset that this approach confronts at least two serious obstacles.

First is the challenge of creating and coding variables that accurately reflect concepts such as inclusiveness, level of democracy, constitutional strength, or the clarity of the signal regarding which among many potential constitutional options will be the focal solution. Second is that drawing inferences about the effects of constitutional moments according to their characteristics depends on the dubious assumption that constitutional moments are randomly assigned across cases (Widner 2007). To put a finer point on it, one might suspect that the inclusiveness of constitutional moments matters to subsequent democracy, but also that other factors such as wealth, ethnic heterogeneity, or recent political violence matter. If more inclusive and less inclusive constitutional moments are distributed across cases in a manner entirely unrelated to wealth, ethnic heterogeneity, and recent violence, then one can safely draw conclusions from patterns the data might reveal. But, if any of these prior factors affects the level of inclusiveness, it will mitigate one's ability to estimate the independent effect of inclusiveness. Worse still, if factors that cannot be, or are not, observed affect the inclusiveness of constitutional moments, such conclusions may be biased. If, for example, in contexts marked by recent civil war, defeated actors tend to be denied participation in constitutional deliberations, then one might mistakenly attribute to inclusive constitutional moments the salutary effects of more peaceful political contexts.

At least two major research projects are already quite advanced in assembling extensive datasets on the design of constitutions, their durability, and the processes by which they are produced. The *Comparative Constitutions Project*, directed by Zachary Elkins and Tom Ginsburg at the University of Illinois, identifies every constitutional 'birth' and major overhaul worldwide since 1789 and codes the content of hundreds of aspects of the documents themselves. The *Constitution Writing and Conflict Resolution* (CWCR) project, directed by Jennifer Widner at Princeton University, focuses on all new constitutions worldwide since 1975 and collects detailed information on the conditions and processes under which they are drafted and adopted, as well as outcomes such as subsequent levels of political violence. Data collection on both projects demands extraordinary amounts of careful and systematic work, and these efforts promise to yield vast improvements in the precision with which we can characterize both constitutional moments and the content of constitutions themselves (Comparative Constitutions Project 2007; Constitution Writing and Conflict Resolution 2007).

Preliminary analyses from the CWCR project highlights the challenge that nonrandom assignment, or endogeneity, presents for statistical inference about how constitutional moments affect regime performance (Widner 2007). The more circumscribed data presented here are useful mainly for providing rough description of some elements of constitutional moments, and some patterns with regard to constitutional ideals, but this paper does not attempt to test statistical models.

DATA

This chapter draws from the Comparative Constitutions Project dataset to identify a set of constitutional moments worldwide from 1990–2005 and as a starting point for measuring their inclusiveness.[5] The central characteristic of constitutional moments I set out to measure is inclusiveness, which is measured by a rough count of the number of institutional actors involved, by the characteristics of those institutional actors, and by various aspects of public participation through referenda. For outcomes, I rely on measures of democracy and of constraints on executive decision-making subsequent to adoption of new constitutions, and on changes to new constitutions within the first five years after adoption.

MEASURES OF INCLUSIVENESS

Institutional Actors

As measures of inclusiveness, this chapter relies primarily on the number and nature of veto players enfranchised during the constitutional moment. Veto players can be individual (e.g. a president or monarch)

---

[5] The master Comparative Constitutions Project database documents the adoption of any amendments to existing charters as well as constitutional replacements. Because some amendment processes fundamentally change the nature of a regime, whereas some new constitutions mark only nominal changes, the matter of how to identify a constitutional moment is not trivial. For the purposes of this paper, I include only constitutional replacements, although acknowledging that this decision, as with many others, entails a fairly blunt approach to the data.

or collective (e.g. a parliament or constituent assembly, a military junta, a former guerrilla movement enfranchised to participate in a constitutional moment). Central to much of the discussion on inclusiveness above is that key political actors can hold out for the inclusion or exclusion of specific elements in constitutional design – for example, guaranteed representation in specific government institutions, limitations on executive power, a form of territorial organization, or specific individual rights.

Measuring this facet of inclusiveness requires identifying veto players, which is no simple matter across widely diverse constitutional moments. My approach is to count Institutional Actors, which are any collective or individual actors with a formal role in drafting or approving a new constitution.[6] I count the citizens as an Institutional Actor in cases that include ratification by referendum. The starting point for identifying Institutional Actors was the PROMULG variable (V36) in the Comparative Constitutions Project (2007) dataset, drawn from the constitutional texts themselves, when promulgation processes are described therein. I then verified and supplemented this variable through careful reading of *Keesing's* (1990–2007) for the period surrounding the constitutional moment.

Not all Institutional Actors can make equal claims to democratic legitimacy, of course. Some gained their Institutional Actor status by force, some by divine right, others as appointees of a government, whereas still others were chosen in open and competitive elections. Institutional Actors of the last sort might be regarded as "most inclusive," so I distinguish constitutional moments in which democratically elected Institutional Actors participate with the dummy variable Elected Institutional Actor. For each constitutional moment, I examined all participating Institutional Actors, determined whether any was elected, and if so, when. Then I coded Elected Institutional Actor=1 if the electoral environment

---

[6] In keeping with this book's focus on constraints on *exporting* democracy, my initial instinct was to make separate counts of domestic and foreign institutional actors. But their *de facto* influence aside, formal involvement by foreign governments is extremely rare, allowing very little leverage on this matter. Based on the cases of constitutional renewal from 1990–2005 drawn from the Comparative Constitutions Project data, only Andorra in 1993 enfranchised foreign governments in its constitutional moment. The data being collected by the CWCR (2007) project will be simultaneously more comprehensive and more fine-grained, and may shed considerable light on the influence – whether formal or informal – of foreign governments, and other international institutions, during constitutional moments.

in the country during the year the Institutional Actor was elected was open and participatory; Elected Institutional Actor=0 otherwise.[7]

I also sought to distinguish Institutional Actors that were both democratic *and* collective from all others, on the grounds that assemblies are potentially the most inclusive political actors, owing to their ability to represent societal diversity, and because they might include multiple effective veto players (e.g. parties or coalitions with blocking power). The dummy variable Elected Assembly=1 if an assembly that was an Institutional Actor was selected in an open and participatory electoral environment; 0 otherwise.

It is important to acknowledge that these attempts to identify, count, and describe Institutional Actors provide only a crude reflection of how many actors, and which ones, wield effective influence on constitutional design in each case. For example, constitutional moments that outline a sequence of decisions, from drafting to deliberation to ratification, might fail to reflect the dominance of actors upstream – or those downstream – in the process. Widner (2007) notes that preliminary agreements made behind closed doors among leaders of key groups constrained choices subsequently available to South Africa's elected constituent assembly. To the extent this informal pact dictated terms, one might conclude that South Africa's formal Institutional Actors, the assembly and constitutional court, had little discretion over the constitution. Yet, in other cases, downstream Institutional Actors have ignored constraints imposed by upstream actors. The Philadelphia Convention of 1787 was famously charged with revising the Articles of Confederation rather than drafting an entirely new charter. More recently, Latin American assemblies initially empowered to make specific reforms have proclaimed themselves sovereign and declared for themselves a clean slate.

In short, Institutional Actor, Elected Institutional Actor, and Elected Assembly are admittedly unrefined measures of inclusiveness. They are based on the intuition that a constitutional moment in which an elected assembly drafts a document that must be approved by a council of representatives from subnational governments and signed by a king (Institutional Actor=3, Elected Institutional Actor=1, Elected Assembly=1) is more inclusive than one drafted by a military junta and approved by

---

[7] I rely on the PARCOMP (Competitiveness of Participation) variable from the *Polity IV* dataset to whether a country's electoral environment qualifies as open in a given year. PARCOMP ranges from 0–5, and reflects "the extent to which alternative preferences for policy and leadership can be pursued in the political arena" (Marshall and Jaggers 2007: 30). My threshold for coding an institutional actor as elected is PARCOMP>2.

referendum (Institutional Actor=2, Elected Institutional Actor=0, Elected Assembly=0). There is ample room for improvement in measuring inclusiveness. For now, I merely aim to find out whether these measures provide any purchase on distinguishing among constitutional moments.

Referenda

An alternative indicator of constitutional moment inclusiveness is whether citizens are directly involved via referendum. Constitutional moments are about evenly split on this count. Drawing from the Comparative Constitutions Project (2007) and Keesing's (1990–2007), I created a dummy variable Referendum to distinguish constitutional moments that involved referenda from those that did not. Noting that not all elections are equally free and participatory, however, I created a second dummy drawn from the *Keesing's* reports, for cases involving referenda, and scored as follows:

> Referendum Fair = 0, if there were credible reports of systematic voting irregularities from neutral sources (e.g. international electoral monitoring agencies or journalists);
>
> = 1, if there were reports of systematic irregularities from domestic political actors opposed to the referendum outcome, or else electoral boycotts on grounds of anticipated irregularities; and
>
> = 2, if there are no reports of systematic irregularities.

For most referenda, I was also able to locate data (e.g. from Keesing's 1990–2007; Nohlen, Krennerich, and Thibaut 1999; Nohlen 2005; African Elections Database 2007; Election Results Archive 2007) on levels of popular support and on overall turnout in referenda as other indicators of citizen participation and support during constitutional moments.

MEASURES OF CONSTITUTIONAL PERFORMANCE

Democracy

I follow the practice, now standard in broadly cross-national comparative research, of relying on the *Polity IV* index of democracy, which runs from -10 to 10 and is available now for most countries worldwide up through 2004 (Marshall and Jaggers 2007). I measure *Polity* scores three years after the promulgation (POLITY+3) of a new constitution, to allow time for effects of the new regime on politics to register. I also calculate the difference between *Polity* scores three years after promulgation and three years prior to promulgation (POLITYDIFF), to measure the marginal effect of a new constitution on level of democracy.

TABLE 7.1: Descriptive statistics

Variable	Observations	Mean	Std. Dev.	Min	Max
Polity +3 years	48	1.3	6.3	−10	9
Polity Difference (+3 minus −3)	48	2.6	7.5	−19	16
Executive Constraint (from *Polity IV*)	48	4.4	2.0	1	7
Referendum Support	24	85%	13%	52%	99%
Referendum Turnout	21	67%	19%	31%	97%

Constraints on Government Authority

To gauge the effectiveness of constitutions in binding officeholders, I rely on the Executive Constraints variable from the Polity IV dataset, three years after promulgation of a constitution (XCONST+3). This variable is a component of Polity IV's overall democracy index, but it specifically aims to reflect "the extent of institutionalized constraints on the decision-making powers of chief executives [by legislatures, parties, judiciaries]...The concern is therefore with the checks and balances." (Marshall and Jaggers 2007: 23). XCONST+3 ranges from 1 (unlimited executive authority) to 7 (executive parity with or subordination to other institutional actors).

Durability

The data on constitutional durability are drawn from a distinct source. The main dataset used elsewhere in the paper was built from an initial set of constitutional renewals from 1990–2005 identified by the Comparative Constitutions Project (2007). These data did not include information on subsequent constitutional stability, and their recent vintage allowed limited leverage in identifying constitutional changes or collapses. Subsequently, however, the CWCR project generously supplied information from its database, spanning 1975–2005, that allowed me to construct a variable, AMEND5, which equals 1 if a constitution was amended within the first five years after its promulgation; 0 otherwise.

Descriptive Statistics

The various variables assembled for this paper are described in Tables 7.1 and 7.2. For some years, POLITY+3, POLITYDIFF, and XCONST+3 cannot be calculated – recently promulgated constitutions for which *Polity*

TABLE 7.2: Categorical variable frequencies

Variable	0	1	2	3
Institutional Actors	–	17	30	14
Elected Institutional Actors	32	29	–	–
Elected Assembly	38	19	–	–
Referendum	36	29	–	–
Referendum Fair	8	5	5	–
Variables below drawn from Constitution Writing and Conflict Resolution database, used in examination of constitutional durability				
Amend5	150	44	–	–
Institutional Actor	–	113	68	6
Elected Institutional Actors	116	78	–	–
Institutional Actors Elected by PR	153	41	–	–

scores three years hence are not available, for example, or earlier cases in which data are missing in a given year. I have data for 48 observations on each of these variables. The post-constitutional countries lean toward the democratic side of the *Polity* scale three years out, and new constitutions were associated with movement toward democracy (an average of 2.6 points on the 21-point scale), although in both cases there is a lot of variance around the average.

Referenda occurred in twenty-nine of the sixty-five constitutional moments for which I could determine the process, and I obtained data on results (i.e. approval, twenty-four cases, or 83%; and turnout, twenty-one cases, or 72%) for most of those. The data include only cases where new constitutions were actually promulgated, so the distribution of support is skewed to the right (52%–99%), with a mean value, 87%, that suggests overwhelming approval. Turnout is more varied, although still distributed toward the upper end of the scale.

The top half of Table 7.2 describes the categorical variables from the Comparative Constitutions Project-based data used in assessing Hypotheses 1 and 2. Of the sixty-one cases for which I was able to determine institutional actor, about half involved two, with the rest about evenly split between one and three. There is no prototypical format in any of these categories. Cases with a single institutional actor are most frequently parliaments or constituent assemblies – although not always democratically elected – but also monarchs (the King of Saudi Arabia, the Sultan of Oman) and a Nigerian military junta. Multiple institutional actor cases often include referenda, but not all, and constitutional initiatives come from diverse sources, including parliaments, presidents, constituent assemblies, national conferences, councils of ministers, etc. Elected institutional actor shows that the cases are about evenly split on whether any institutional actor was elected in a democratic context. Democratic assemblies are a little more rare, participating in about a third of the constitutional moments for which I could code Elected Assembly.

The bottom half of Table 7.2 describes the variables derived from the CWCR data used to assess constitutional durability. The greater number of observations reflects the longer time period included in CWCR. Institutional actor and elected institutional actor are analogous to those constructed using the Comparative Constitutions Project-based data used elsewhere in this chapter.[8] The CWCR data allowed for construction of Institutional actor elected by PR, to identify whether any institutional actor was elected by proportional representation, which is generally regarded as a highly inclusive method of election owing to its low barriers to entry for minority groups.

The data here do not allow for inference based on conventional statistical models. In light of the limited number of cases, the substantial measurement challenges, and the potential for endogeneity, it would be unenlightening (and reckless) at this point to regress POLITY+3 on institutional actor, per capita GDP, etc., and then presume to learn much from the estimates. Instead, I merely present graphs illustrating some bivariate patterns (and non-patterns), leaving it to subsequent analysis based on more comprehensive data to confirm or reject the causal implications.

PATTERNS IN THE DATA

The first box-plot in Figure 7.1 shows that constitutional moments involving more institutional actors are associated with greater levels of democracy three years out. The median POLITY+3 for single-institutional actor constitutional moments is 1 (and the mean is below zero), whereas the

---

[8] IA is skewed toward fewer institutional actors than in the Comparative Constitutions Project-based data, perhaps because including reforms beyond wholesale constitutional renewals leads the CWCR data to include more amendments approved by sitting parliaments, or perhaps because IAs on the order of those identified by my search of secondary sources in augmenting the Comparative Constitutions Project-based data are undercounted. In any case, this chapter does not compare CWCR-based data to Comparative Constitutions Project-based data, and, as long as each data collection process was internally consistent, any patterns they reveal are instructive.

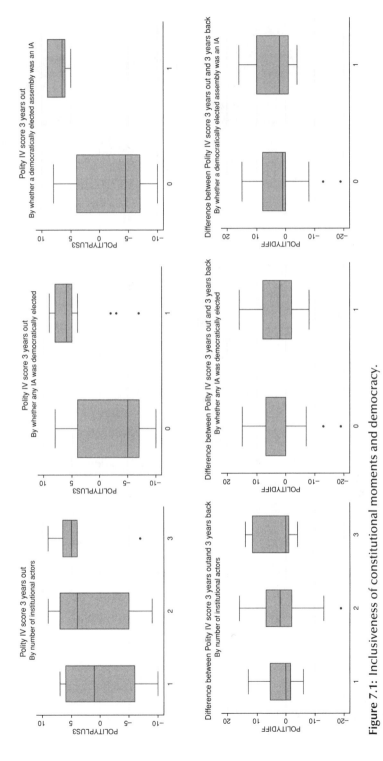

Figure 7.1: Inclusiveness of constitutional moments and democracy.

median when two institutional actors are involved is 4, and with Institutional Actor=3, it is 5. The box-plot immediately below, however, shows a less clear pattern in democratic improvement by institutional actor, suggesting the effect may result from more institutional actors being involved in constitutional moments where democracy is already strong. The median single-institutional actor case, as well as the median case where Institutional Actor=3, made no democratic improvement upon the promulgation of a new constitution, whereas there is a median gain of one point when Institutional Actor=2. The mean scores are a bit more encouraging for the multiple-institutional actor scenario, with an average POLITYDIFF=1.9 when Institutional Actor=1, 1.8 when Institutional Actor=2, and a substantial 3.9 when Institutional Actor=3.

Of the remaining box-plots in Figure 7.1, the top two illustrate the differences in subsequent democracy levels between cases with at least one freely elected institutional actor and those without, and even more starkly between cases with a freely elected assembly and those without. It is to be expected, of course, as shown up top, that in an environment where institutional actors are democratically elected, subsequent politics continues along democratic lines. The corresponding box-plots below exhibit less stark differences, but the patterns are in the expected direction. When no institutional actor is democratically elected, the median 'improvement' in democracy, from three years pre-promulgation to three years post-promulgation, is zero, and the mean value is 1.4. By contrast, when at least one institutional actor is democratically elected, the corresponding values are 2 and 3.5 – in both cases suggesting that democratic participation in constitutional moments is associated with subsequent increases in democratic politics more generally. When there is no democratic assembly among institutional actors, the median POLITYDIFF=1 and the mean is 1.5; whereas cases with an Elected Assembly have median improvements of 2 points, and mean of a substantial 4.1.

What about referenda? Their mere existence does not appear to have any positive effect on democracy, judging by the two box-plots on the left side of Figure 7.2. Three years out, cases without referenda were slightly more democratic and had made marginally more progress toward democracy than those with referenda, although the differences are negligible. The box-plots on the right side show that democracy, and progress toward democracy, are weaker where referenda are marred by irregularities and stronger where the referendum playing field is level. There is no surprise, of course, that environments that cannot produce fair referenda yield little in terms of democracy. In any case, I have values of

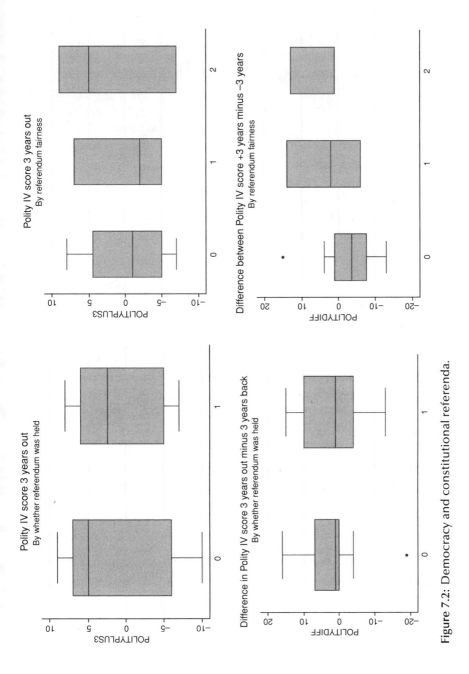

Figure 7.2: Democracy and constitutional referenda.

171

Referendum Fair for relatively few cases, so do not make much of that pattern.

Figure 7.3 contrasts patterns of Referendum Support and Referendum Turnout. The top left scatter-plot shows a weak positive relationship between percentage approval for a new constitution in a referendum and the level of democracy three years out. The plot immediately below shows a stronger correlation between percentage approval and progress toward democracy. The scatter-plot on the top right shows a clear negative correlation between referendum turnout and democracy three years out, whereas the plot immediately below shows a weaker negative pattern with democratic progress.

Turning from democracy overall to the effectiveness of constitutions in placing constraints on executive decision-making, the top left box-plot in Figure 7.4 shows a positive correlation between institutional actor and XCONST+3, with a median value around 3 when Institutional Actor=1 (mean 3.7), but 5 when Institutional Actor=2 or 3 (mean 4.7 and 4.5, respectively). The next two plots (middle-of-page) show that constraints on executives are far stronger when at least one institutional actor is elected (top), and most strikingly, when a freely elected assembly participates in constitutional design. The top plot on the right shows no evidence that referenda, in-and-of themselves, are associated with greater or lesser constraints on executives, although the last plot suggests somewhat greater constraints in environments where constitutional referenda were more fair.

Finally, turning to the CWCR-based data on constitutional durability, Figure 7.5 illustrates the proportion of new constitutions that were altered within the first five years after promulgation, by values of institutional actor, elected institutional actor, and institutional actor Elected by PR.[9] The top panel illustrates that constitutional stability increases (i.e. the proportion of constitutions altered is lower) with the number of institutional actor enfranchised in constitutional moments. There is little difference in frequency of alterations according to whether any institutional actor was freely elected, per the second panel, but the bottom panel shows that constitutional moments involving the most inclusive elected assemblies (Institutional Actor Elected by PR=1) are amended only about half as frequently as when no proportionally elected institutional actor participates.

---

[9] Keep in mind the Amend5 variable represents constitutional changes, so it captures an element of instability, but does not directly reflect constitutional collapses or abrogations. Comprehensive information on such events should become available as the Comparative Constitutions Project and CWCR projects progress.

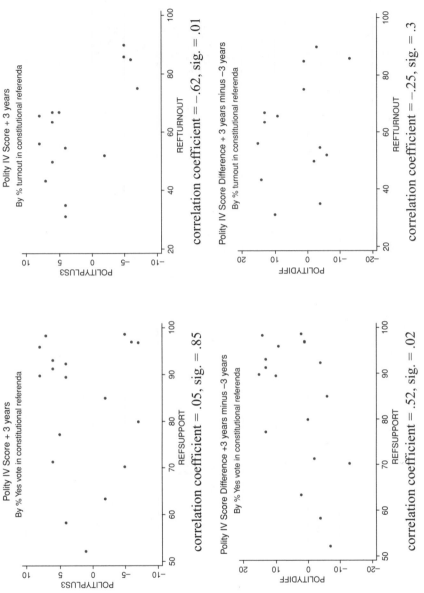

Figure 7.3: Democracy and voter support in referenda.

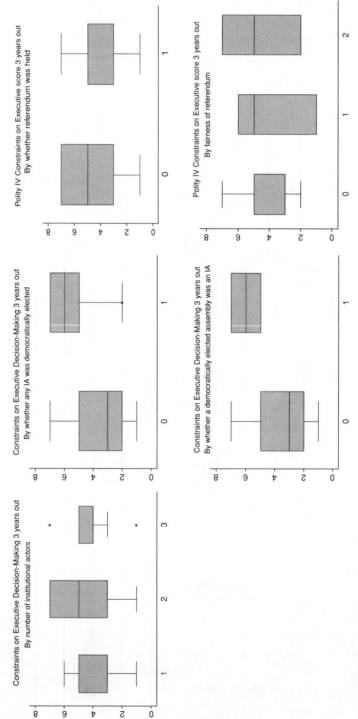

Figure 7.4: Constraints on Executives.

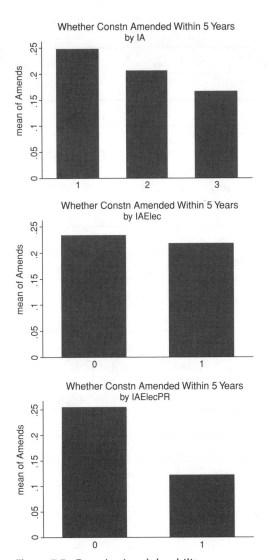

Figure 7.5: Constitutional durability.

CONCLUSION

For all its limitations, this series of bivariate comparisons lends preliminary support to each of the three hypotheses advanced earlier in this
chapter: that is, that the inclusiveness of constitutional moments contributes to higher levels of subsequent democracy, greater constraints on
government authority, and constitutional stability. The clearest patterns
emerging from the data have to do with the number of actors – and

particularly, the number of democratically elected actors – involved in the drafting and promulgation process. Where more institutional actors participate, subsequent democracy is stronger, although *improvements* in democracy and downstream constraints on executives are only marginally greater than with fewer institutional actors. When at least one democratic actor is democratically elected, subsequent politics is far more democratic than when none is, as one would expect, and there are modest but regular improvements in democracy. This pattern is repeated with respect to elected assemblies.

With respect to H2, the correlation between free election of Institutional Actors and subsequent constraints on executives is conspicuous. Constitutional moments in which elected assemblies participated almost always produced subsequent regimes in which executives were subject to effective constraints by other institutions. Similarly, regarding H3, the correlations between the number of institutional actors and constitutional stability, and that between participation by an institutional actor elected by PR and constitutional stability, are striking. It may be that more inclusive constitutional moments instill a widespread sense of ownership in, and commitment to, new constitutions among citizens. Alternatively, perhaps constitutional moments involving multiple institutional actors, or inclusive multi-member institutional actors, tend to write into their new charters provisions that make subsequent alterations more difficult. The mechanics of these relationships warrant scholarly attention, but even acknowledging limitations in both measurement and the ability to draw inferences about causality, the patterns in the data regarding institutional actors suggest support for the hypotheses that more inclusive constitutional moments contribute to democracy, government restraint, and constitutional stability.

Whether referenda contribute to any of these constitutional ideals is less clear. To the extent that the mere occurrence of a referendum clearly signals the adoption of a constitution, one might expect referenda to foster coordination around the new set of rules. Yet in themselves, referenda are not associated with any clear pattern of democracy, democratization, or executive restraint. Fair referenda fare [ouch] better than rigged ones on all these counts, but the number of observations is low and potential for spurious correlation is high. The data suggest that explicit support, in the form of 'Yes' votes is a more reliable indicator of high quality public participation in constitutional moments than is voter turnout, perhaps because implausibly high turnout figures are often reported in tainted referenda.

Does this exercise suggest any advice democracy promoters (or exporters) might offer during constitutional moments? Although referenda, per se, do not appear to guarantee that constitutional ideals will be realized, *fair* referenda are associated with progress, particularly when citizens broadly support the charter on which they vote. Yet, it is doubtful that entreaties to "Write a great constitution and hold a clean referendum on it" would make much difference. Democracy exporters might provide electoral assistance to improve the quality of referenda on the margin, and where constitutional moments involve referenda, every effort should be made along these lines. The more important implication of the evidence presented here, however, is that the content of constitutions depends on who sits at the table to hammer out their provisions. Inclusiveness among institutional actors involved in drafting and negotiating the content of constitutions correlates with greater democracy, more progress toward democracy, and greater constitutional stability. If democracy exporters can take any lesson from this survey of recent constitutions, it is to urge the enfranchisement of multiple institutional actors – and internally inclusive ones – in the formal procedures that define constitutional moments.

8 Building Democratic Armies

> The principal foundations on which the power of all governments is based (whether they be new, long-established or mixed) are good laws and good armies.
>
> Machiavelli, *The Prince* (1995: 38)

A secure environment in which the public need not fear physical violence is an indispensable prerequisite of democracy building. Having a reliable and competent police force is obviously a crucial part of providing public safety. Ultimately, however, the most critical institution a democratizing state must establish that will allow the police to do their work in the first place is the regular armed forces. Where there is widespread violence and/or armed conflict, the police ordinarily lack the capacity to normalize the situation and only a conventional army can bring about a stable environment. This seems to be a straightforward proposition, but democratization and democracy-promotion scholars seldom acknowledge that the projects of democratization cannot proceed without basic, street-level public safety.

Hundreds of books have been written on virtually every conceivable aspect of democratization, but the question of how democratic armies – that is to say, *armies supportive of democratic governance* (not of one or another political party) – might be molded in post-authoritarian states has received surprisingly little attention. This is a curious omission because – as has become all too clear in Iraq – it is virtually impossible to get on with the various political, social, and economic projects of democracy-building without establishing physical security. Nancy Bermeo noted, in 1992, that

I am grateful for the comments of the contributors, particularly Nancy Bermeo and Daniel Chirot.

"surprisingly little attention in the transition literature" had been given to the study of the military; since then matters have changed little (1992: 198). The few scholars who do note the imperative of creating democratic armies seldom identify, let alone discuss, the principal issues involved.

To be sure, there are many studies that describe the efforts of politicians and civic leaders in different countries to transform the armies from being the servants of the old anti- or pre-democratic regime into obedient supporters of the new democratic (or democratizing) political order. A number of more ambitious works – often edited collections by groups of authors – have analyzed the same process on a larger scale, comparing the democratization of military establishments in two or more countries of the same region. Insightful single-country and regional analyses like these are, of course, indispensable building blocks of a further expanded and even more general study that aims to understand democratizing armies and civil-military relations on a global scale. Developing civil-military relations that are marked by the armed forces' steadfast support of democratic rule is a quintessential prerequisite without which the democratization project itself cannot succeed. Only a broadly comparative analysis that encompasses the different political environments and geographic regions in which democratization may occur can generate the proper appreciation and explanation of the critical necessity as well as the tasks and challenges of building democratic armies.

The regular armed forces are one of the most important institutions authoritarian polities maintain. Because the majority – although certainly not all – of these states enjoy little popular legitimacy, they must rely on the agents of coercion of which the most powerful and comprehensive is the military establishment. What can be done with these armies in a democratizing socio-political environment? How can a "democratic" army be built? The answer to these questions is complex and depends to a considerable extent on the sort of political and social foundations or settings upon which democratic armies are built. There are at least five different types of such environments:

1) post-war (e.g., Germany and Japan);
2) post-colonial (e.g., India and Pakistan);
3) post-praetorian (e.g., Chile and Argentina);
4) post-communist (e.g., Russia and Romania); and,
5) post-civil war (e.g., Bosnia and Lebanon).

Some profound disparities between these settings appear even at first glance. For instance, in the first case outside powers took on the responsibility of building new armed forces. External influence was considerable in some cases, whereas in others, such as the countries of post-colonial South Asia, the project of building democratic armies was managed mostly internally. Nonetheless, there are a number of issues that had to be tackled in all of these political environments.

The key tasks of building democratic armies involve fundamental questions of institutional power-balance and civilian oversight. What powers will the executive and legislative branches possess vis-à-vis the armed forces? How are responsibilities between the Minister of Defense and the Chief of the General Staff divided? In what ways can the legislature's control of the defense budget be ensured? How can the state generate a pool of independent civilian defense experts needed for knowledgeable and impartial assessments of the military's financial affairs, weapons programs, operational activities, and so on? How can the fiscal accountability of the defense ministry be established and enforced?

I make three fundamental arguments. First, building democratic armies is a critical issue in democratic transitions and consolidation, although more so in some contexts than others. Second, those settings are very different and thus pose dissimilar challenges to those crafting democratic armies and civil-military relations. And, finally, providing substantive and useful explanations of civil-military relations in such diverse political and socio-economic environments is impossible for a general theory. In fact, the field of civil-military relations ought to restrain ambitions of devising "grand theories" and, instead, encourage openness to the idea of a variety of theoretical constructs with more modest claims but enhanced utility.

This is a vast subject and the scope of this chapter does not permit an exhaustive examination of many relevant and important issues, nor does it allow for analyses of cases belonging to all of the five different types of political environments identified above. Consequently, my objectives are limited to sorting out some of the essential normative, theoretical, and empirical concerns pertaining to the building of democratic armies. I proceed as follows: First, I outline the basic attributes of democratic civil-military relations answering the question "what does a democratic army look like?" Second, I identify some theoretical contributions that are useful to understanding the tasks necessary to build democratic armies in post-praetorian and post-communist contexts and help us appreciate the particular challenges different polities have encountered. Finally, I illustrate my arguments with brief comparative sketches of the actual experiences of building democratic armies in these types of settings.

One terminological caveat needs to be entered here. Strictly speaking, "democratic army" may sound like an oxymoron as armed forces are inherently hierarchical and nondemocratic institutions. Military personnel do not vote for their superiors and their compliance with orders is seldom optional. What I mean when speaking of "democratic armies" is "democratic civil-military relations," that is, the nexus or connection between state and society on the one hand and the military establishment on the other, which rests on democratic principles.

WHAT DOES A DEMOCRATIC ARMY LOOK LIKE?

There is no simple answer to the question in this subheading. There are, to be sure, a number of basic requirements: the protection of the rights of personnel, the accountability of officers and men, fair promotion practices, etc. In a more general sense, however, there *are* several contextually determined variables that can influence what constitutes a democratic army. Let us consider the most important of these before addressing more conventional civil-military relations issues.

Conscripts or Volunteers?

The importance of whether an army's personnel is drafted or comprised by volunteers was appreciated already by Niccolò Machiavelli, an early champion of the popular militia (1964: xiii, 22). This, indeed, is one of the key questions regarding a democratic army. There are sound arguments for both conscription-based and volunteer armies and one is not necessarily more or less democratic than the other. As much as possible, democracies should promote policies ensuring that professional armies reflect the social, ethnic, and geographic composition of society (Young 2006: 28). In states facing severe external threats, where military training for most citizens is considered socially desirable and strategically necessary, and where there is no overwhelming popular opposition to the draft, universal conscription is usually the preferred option. Democratic states must ascertain that the draft is fairly implemented and individuals whose personal or religious convictions forbid bearing arms or performing military service are given the option of unarmed service in the military or work assignment in some socially useful area (such as in health care or education), respectively. Conscript armies tend to be less effective and require more resources on a per-soldier basis for the amount of military capability they provide. They often serve as *de facto* training institutions maintained at the expense of defense modernization because of societal support for mandatory service. Draft-based armies tend to attract more active societal scrutiny given that virtually every citizen will have served or had a close relative who served in the armed forces.

Ethno-Religious Divisions

It would seem beyond debate that a democratic army should be equally open to individuals with diverse ethno-religious identities. Those who want to serve as professional soldiers should be judged by the same criteria. In conscription-based militaries, the rules governing the draft ought to be equitable to all. These basic principles seem simple enough, yet the situation is rarely as uncomplicated as they would indicate. A number of additional questions need to be sorted out in multiethnic and/or multi-religious societies that do not have standard answers. For instance: should the state involve itself in cases where members of one nationality are disproportionately represented in the officer corps not because of governmental manipulation, but owing to greater interest in the profession? Should soldiers be given the opportunity to serve in their own ethnic/ religious region or should they – perhaps for integration purposes – be stationed in ethnic/religious areas different from their own? Alternatively, should individual units be staffed by soldiers of different ethnicities and religions or should they share the same ethno-religious background? If we base our response on the United States' experience, we might well come up with different answers than if we considered contemporary Iraq or Indonesia; our reasoning, too, might be entirely different.

Gender and Sexual Identity

In recent decades a number of publicly debated questions have centered on the gender and sexual orientation of prospective soldiers. Should women be allowed to serve in combat positions? How far should the armed forces go to accommodate female soldiers? Should soldiers be forced to divulge their sexual orientation? Should the military open its doors to openly gay soldiers? The rule of thumb seems to be that in a democratic state the popular will should determine the answer to these questions. Societies, even democratic societies, may hold quite different values and support different approaches and, thus, it is hardly surprising that the citizens of the Netherlands and of the United States think differently about these issues.

The Military as Social Laboratory

An important but rarely-pondered question is whether the armed forces should be used by the state to implement progressive policies that may be controversial in society. The rationale is that although democratic polities enjoy only limited influence over their societies, they do control the armed forces. Consequently, the successful introduction of democratic but contentious social programs in the military might serve to eventually persuade the rest of society of its correctness. For instance, racial integration in the U.S. armed forces was begun by President Truman long before mainstream society – especially in some regions of the country – was ready for such a step. The military became the first large-scale organization in America where blacks were guaranteed equal opportunity to succeed. This policy was a resounding success both because it was "right" and because it enhanced the armed forces' effectiveness (Moskos and Butler 1996; Burk 2001: 270–272).

The issue of using the military as a testing ground for social policy directs our attention to the triangle of linkages between state, society, and the armed forces, in other words, civil-military relations. Like democracy itself, civil-military relations continue to evolve and always have room for improvement. Nonetheless, the standard issues of military politics are fundamentally the same in all democracies (Bruneau 2006: 3). What, then, are they?

Scholars have approached the question of "ideal" civil-military relations differently. For our purposes, perhaps, it may be best understood as a system of dual imperatives: reducing the prerogatives of the armed forces and establishing the civilians' control over them. Naturally, this is not an easy undertaking and the variety of possible environments in which democratic armies may be built complicates matters further still. Let us first look at the military side of the equation and then examine the tasks of civilians.

MILITARY PREROGATIVES

In virtually all authoritarian systems, military officers enjoy numerous political and/or socioeconomic prerogatives. The aim of democratizers is to "roll back" the army's privileged status and establish armed forces that are reliable and capable, but also valued and respected servants of the state and its citizenry. The military must become accountable before the law and its professional responsibilities must be constitutionally regulated. Reducing the mission of the armed forces to the defense of the nation from its *external* enemies and banishing it from domestic politics is critical. If a military establishment shows symptoms of boredom or discontent, signing it up for international peace-keeping duties is a good way to make them feel both useful and appreciated. Insofar as the military is to have any internal function at all, it must be limited to disaster relief and ought not include participation in domestic programs such as rural development or policing functions that might foster its politicization. In particular, the armed forces should have no role in anti-drug-trafficking and manufacturing policies because such activities inevitably increase the likelihood of corruption and, besides, they should be the responsibility of internal security forces.

The military's size should correspond to the challenges it might face ensuring that it can keep up key capabilities. A state that maintains an unnecessarily large standing army and, especially, a bloated officer corps, is not only squandering resources but – depending on the political environment – might also be asking for trouble. It is important that chains of command *within the armed forces* are clearly spelled out and potential ambiguities are eliminated. The Chief of the General Staff – the top-ranking uniformed person in the military – should be subordinated to the *civilian* defense minister, a cabinet member who represents the government in the armed forces and the armed forces in the cabinet. The critical objective of democratizing states is to increase the armed forces' professionalism. This may be done in partnership with the top brass by devising an appropriate system of military training and education, promoting an organizational culture of self-restraint, deference to the constitution, and active recognition of the sacrifices society makes for its own defense.

Timing is important and rushing these reforms – especially in democratizing countries emerging from military rule – may well turn out to be counterproductive (Agüero 1995). In a political context in which the armed forces are threatened by aggressive civilian interference in its internal affairs, some changes might be best postponed. In an ideal civil-military relations scenario, the military stays away from politics and is content with its conditions of service. To that end, the state should extend the armed forces' high professional status through the provision of up-to-date equipment and decent salaries and benefits; raise the social esteem of the military profession; avoid intruding in the army's internal affairs – such as training and routine promotions – and using the military as a tool in domestic political competition.

Finally, in the context of democratizing states, the armed forces' political allegiances must be addressed. It is important to underscore that in a political environment that is transitioning from some type of authoritarianism toward a democratic form of government, a politically neutralized army is not desirable. Democratizers should not want an army that passively stands by if democratic rule is challenged. Rather, the new

democratic leaders should want an army that is unambiguously supportive of the new democratic regime. Toward that end, the military – and
especially its leadership – should be engaged by the democratic political
class and made to understand that its backing is not only highly valued
but it is indispensable for the success of democratic consolidation.

CIVILIAN OVERSIGHT

An essential condition of democratic governance is that civilian control
over the armed forces be shared by the executive and legislative branches
of government. The head of state is the military's commander-in-chief
and the civilian minister of defense is responsible for the day-to-day running of the armed forces. Selecting a defense minister who possesses
a measure of expertise or, at the very least, some demonstrated interest in defense-security matters signals to the armed forces that the state
takes them seriously. Ideally, the defense minister and his ministry are
integrated into the governmental power-structure and hold the executive's confidence (Bruneau and Goetze 2006: 88). Although the ministry
is a part of the executive branch, its relationship with the legislature is
exceedingly important because, in democracies, parliaments debate and
formulate defense-related laws, decide and oversee the budget and monitor its implementation, and hold the government and the armed forces
accountable for their actions. The parliament's authority to prepare, enact
into law, disburse, and scrutinize the military's management of the budget is its most powerful tool for controlling the armed forces. Finally, in
most democracies only the legislature has the power to declare war and
states of emergency (Welch 1976: 7).

   Within the legislature defense-related committees and their staffs are
the key players because they exercise actual civilian oversight and they
are the loci of military expertise. The democratic state must promote the
acquisition of civilian acquaintance with defense matters because only
equipped with this sort of knowledge can the legislature become an
informed and capable overseer of the armed forces. Such expertise in parliament and in non-governmental organizations (NGOs) also prevents the
executive branch from dominating the military sphere (Giraldo 2006: 43).
There can be no robust civilian oversight without strong political institutions. Fledgling democracies, where the military has a tradition of political intervention and retains extensive political and economic influence,
face an especially dangerous and difficult challenge (Diamond 1999: 113).
External actors – such as a military alliance that newly democratizing

states wish to join or democratic states interested in spreading democracy – may be able to positively influence the evolution of democratic civil-military relations. But, the best preventive medicine for the military's political intrusiveness is effective democratic governance and what Juan Linz called "loyalty" to the democratic system on the part of all major political actors (1978: 30).

In sum, civil-military relations in a democracy must satisfy the following standards: 1) the armed forces must be subordinated to institutionalized control balanced between the executive and legislative branches; 2) the military's chains of command and the political institutions' areas of responsibility over the armed forces must be codified for all potential scenarios (peacetime, emergencies, war); 3) the conditions that warrant the use of the military in peacetime must be constitutionally regulated; 4) the executive and legislative branches must share exclusive fiscal responsibility over defense expenditures; 5) the armed forces must be depoliticized and its members must not be permitted to play any political role other than exercising their civic right to vote, and; 6) civilian experts must be trained to provide objective advice to politicians and the public on defense-related issues and to staff pertinent state institutions (including the Ministry of Defense) and NGOs.

EXPLAINING MILITARY POLITICS IN DIVERSE CONTEXTS

The existing body of knowledge of civil-military relations yields little by way of a formal theory or universally applicable principles. There is a notable theoretical literature on the conditions that motivate military personnel to overthrow their governments and on the timing, strategy, planning, and execution of coups. But, the armed forces' political activism can take much more nuanced forms than *coups d'état* or their absence, and ought to be viewed as taking place along a continuum of multiple variables, such as scale, means, and organizational prerogatives. "Military influence," the range of institutional behavior that falls between the extremes of violent *coup d'état* and the army's compliance with its civilian masters, has proved far more difficult to theorize about, even though it is perhaps the most important concern of civil-military relations scholars.

One of the key problems is that accurately measuring the gradations between the two endpoints of the coup/no-interference spectrum is extraordinarily difficult given the complexity of cases, the number of potential explanations for the military's political intervention, and the varying importance of these explanations relative to one another. If we

just consider the five vastly different political contexts in which democratic armies may be built – for instance in post-World War II Japan
or post-communist Romania – the virtual impossibility of constructing
a theory possessing any measure of explanatory power soon becomes
apparent.

In fact, the field of civil-military relations promotes an appreciation of
the importance of theoretical flexibility. What one finds in many cases is
that attempts to "force" one theory to explain or "fit" diverse cases are seldom productive and make one realize that the best explanations of varying contexts are often generated by different theoretical constructs that
may or may not come from scholarly domain of civil-military relations.
Obviously, it cannot be my purpose here to canvass the many theoretical
constructs that might possibly be useful given space limitations. Instead,
I suggest that robust explanations for the various cases in the two post-
authoritarian environments under consideration are yielded by different
theoretical frameworks.

CRAFTING CIVILIAN CONTROL OVER
THE POST-PRAETORIAN MILITARY

Harold Trinkunas (2005) explains in a recent work on Latin American
regimes the dynamics of formulating civilian control in various political
settings. He argues that when democratizers are backed by high levels of
civilian mobilization and the military is weakened by disunity within the
incumbent authoritarian regime, the former enjoy an excellent opportunity to craft lasting and robust civilian control.[1] He contends that democratizers benefit from a broad opportunity structure when the military is
fragmented and civilians reach a consensus on democratization. If a military regime compiles a record marked by political and economic failures and, especially if the generals are unsuccessful on the battlefield, it is
likely to be riddled with cleavages and its position in the transition process
is going to be weak. In contrast, narrow opportunity structures are found
in transitions where the armed forces had pursued solid socioeconomic
policies during their rule. In such contexts, the military's position in the
transition process is likely to be stronger and democratizers are likely to
be divided in their assessment of the military's role.

Democratizers who act strategically can maximize their leverage over
the military by combining high levels of civilian supervision of defense

[1] This section draws on Trinkunas (2005: 4–24).

activities with stiff sanctions against rebellions and dissident officers. Another strategy that may be advantageous in the appropriate context is closely monitoring the military through a variety of surveillance methods and agents, and pitting factions within the armed forces against one another to deter military intervention in politics. The weakest strategy is to appease the military. Trading off civilian control in exchange for regime survival is nearly always a poor tactic for a democratizing state to adopt.

The institutionalization of civilian control is a difficult process and democratizers who possess capable political leadership, ample institutional resources, and personnel with expertise in defense matters will be more successful than those who do not. What strategy *is* available to democratizers largely depends on the context, the relative political influence civilians and the military possess at the time of transition. Trinkunas devised a helpful typology (2005: 17–20) that explains how, with the increasing of civilian leverage vis-à-vis the armed forces, democratizers will be able to successfully pursue ever stronger strategies from appeasement to active civilian supervision of military affairs going through the stages of "regime at risk," "regime persistence," "civilian control by containment," and "civilian control by oversight."

Classificatory Schemes, Borrowed Theories, Miscellaneous Insights

Although measuring military interference in the aforementioned spectrum demarcated by the endpoints of *coup d'état* and no interference is difficult, some scholars succeeded in shedding light on the progressive stages of military influence by providing useful classificatory schemes. The most useful of these is Alfred Stepan's work (1988: 92–7) that lists eleven "military prerogatives" where the military assumes the right or privilege to exercise control over its own internal governance and to play a role in extra-military jurisdictions within the state bureaucracy that are germane to its interests. These spheres, where the military has a formal or informal claim to dominate, include the army's constitutionally sanctioned role in the political system; its relationship to the chief executive, the government, and the legislature; and its role in intelligence, police, state enterprises, and the legal system.

Understanding the concept of military influence is particularly important in polities to which coup theories provide no useful guide simply because the military in these states have not staged a successful *coup d'état* in ages. The absence of coups in states where politicians subject the armed forces to humiliating treatment (meager resources, low prestige) is in itself perplexing. Brian Taylor (2003: 17) contends that organizational culture theory offers the most persuasive explanation to this conundrum because it emphasizes "the unique experiences in the life of an organization as an explanation for subsequent behavior."

The military is first and foremost a state institution and, thus, it is not surprising that the new institutionalist approach helps explain the changes that take place as armed forces undergo democratic reforms. For institutionalists, change is path dependent, that is, when a policy is being formulated or an institution is established, certain choices are made that are difficult to reverse. The importance of path dependence is that it focuses our attention on the formative moments or "critical junctures" (Pierson 1992: 602) for institutions and organizations when the path is set, confirmed, or changed. As North (1990: 100) put it, "[P]ath dependence means that history matters."

When looking for additional insights to help us understand civil-military relations in democratizing states, it is necessary to distinguish post-praetorian from post-communist regimes. In the former, where generals were the de facto state rulers, the *demilitarization of politics* was the objective of pro-democracy reformers. In the latter, where the military was an institutional servant of the communist party, the goal has been the *depoliticization of the military* (Barany 1997: 26–28). Democratization theorists tend to agree that civil-military relations is one area in which the post-communist past is beneficial rather than detrimental for democratizing states (Huntington 1991: 232; Bunce 2003: 175). In the *ancien régime*, the reasoning goes, the armed forces were under firm civilian (i.e., communist party) oversight and kept in check by the internal security forces and other control mechanisms. In short, civilian control was not endangered and this fact, as conventional wisdom would have it, must bode well for the democratic era.

COMPARING CASES OF DEMOCRATIC ARMY-BUILDING

Of the different political environments in which democratic armies may be built, the present framework permits only a brief comparative sketch of the post-praetorian and post-communist political settings. My objective is to show some of the similarities and differences in the challenges democratizing regimes face in building new armed forces and structuring appropriate civil-military relations.

Post-Praetorian Polities

The most important project for democracy builders in countries previously ruled by armed forces elites is to demilitarize politics. The best predictor of the military's role in the new democratizing regime is the kind of socio-economic and political legacy generals leave behind. Societies in Latin America and elsewhere had experienced vastly different kinds of military rule. Given the dissimilar political and socioeconomic performance of these regimes, it is hardly surprising that their transitions away from praetorianism and toward democracy were also quite different and they followed distinctive approaches to the task of building democratic armies.

We may think of the two neighbors, Chile and Argentina, as the pivotal cases here. As Trinkunas suggested, military regimes like Chile (1974–1990) and Brazil (1964–1983) that compiled relatively successful socioeconomic records and retained a significant degree of societal support, were able to *control* the transition to democracy and convert their strong position into political leverage in the transition and post-transition phases. Under these conditions democratizers faced narrow opportunity structures and had to appease military commanders. It also stands to reason that democratic transitions following relatively successful praetorian regimes tend to be gradual and prolonged as military rulers carefully prepare their abdication of power; those in the wake of failed military regimes, on the other hand, are usually of short duration.

Praetorian rulers who performed poorly – Argentina (1976–1983), Greece (1967–1974) – were usually afflicted by a fragmented military establishment, were in a weak bargaining position, and did not possess sufficient leverage to preserve a broad array of their privileges, even in the short run. In these situations democratizers enjoyed extensive opportunities to craft lasting civilian control. Regardless of these differences, perhaps the most prominent trait of political transition from dictatorship to democracy was the peaceful manner in which the armed forces – gradually in some cases, more rapidly in others – abdicated their position in institutions and political life and accepted the establishment of civilian supremacy.

What can successful military regimes obtain for their strong political position? The Chilean case offers an instructive example. General Pinochet's regime was characterized by military unity, an effective and hierarchically organized institutional apparatus, highly centralized powers in his hand, and flexible and relatively successful social and economic policies. He and his government were able to plan and control a slow transition which, in 1990 – when Patricio Aylwin was inaugurated as president – seemed to amount to "more a change of administrations than a change of systems"[2] (Arceneaux 2001: 106). The main components of this process were the extrication of thousands of military personnel from the bureaucracy who, having lost their positions and clout, would become Pinochet's allies vis-à-vis the emerging democratic regime; the *leyes de amarre* (binding laws) passed without negotiation that profoundly restricted the future actions of the new regime; and, because his government had less control over it, a somewhat less successful constitutional reform battle (from Pinochet's perspective) that largely played out in the public domain. More specifically, the new democratic regime had to respect the constitutional functions granted to the armed forces; could not replace service commanders; was to maintain the prestige of the military and protect it from political attacks; and had to refrain from meddling in defense policy, budgetary provisions, and the armed forces' internal affairs along with a host of other restrictions. In other words, as Trinkunas argued, democratic reformers were forced to trade off civilian control of the armed forces for short-term regime survival (2005: 4).

In stark contrast, ineffective military rulers have few options to shield their prerogatives from successor regimes. The *collapse* of the Argentine military regime was triggered by a miscalculated war ending in a humiliating defeat. The transition to civilian rule was initially hampered by the culture of fear bred by the brutality of military rule. Nonetheless, divisions within the armed forces and the opposition's response to the generals' calls for negotiation with mobilization sealed the regime's fate. In its waning days, the military government issued decrees that gave itself amnesty for human rights violations, but these were quickly pronounced illegal by Raúl Alfonsín's cabinet that – unlike Aylwin's in Chile – represented a clean break with the past.[3] The new government brought to justice all of the superior officers who ruled Argentina in 1976–1982, while trying to: a) limit both the duration of the trials and the number of the accused; b) differentiate between those who issued orders violating human rights and those who carried them out, and; c) reassure the armed forces that their legitimate role in the nation was not questioned (Alfonsín 1995: 23–24).

Even though military governments might have been afflicted by weaknesses prior to giving up power – for instance, João Baptista

---

[2] Interview with Carlos Cáceres (Santiago, June 23, 2008).
[3] Interview with Edgardo Boeninger (Santiago, June 27, 2008).

Figueiredo's administration in Brazil was beleaguered by economic problems, military disunity, and growing doubts of their own capacity to govern – this does not necessarily mean that the *regime* itself is weak (Arceneaux 2001: 177). Relatively strong military regimes – such as the Brazilian in the early 1980s – can retain some control over a wide array of political institutions even after they leave the scene. In Brazil, the military was able to maintain three separate service ministries whose leaders remained members of the cabinet along with two of their colleagues, the Chief of the General Staff and the head of the "military household" or *casa militar* (a liaison between the service chiefs and the president and responsible also for the latter's security) (Hunter 1997: 32–33). The armed forces managed to keep a controlling position over the National Security Council and various intelligence and internal police agencies as well. Civilians could not actively supervise the military, and only in 1999 was a civilian defense minister appointed to head the newly formed unitary defense ministry. Until then, defense reform had to take a back seat to economic crises and other more pressing problems on the administration's agenda. Following failed military regimes, on the other hand, the generals – owing to their absent political leverage and the perceived urgency of establishing robust civilian control over them – are typically treated with far more firmness and resolve by their democratic successors.

In all post-praetorian regimes the formation of a civilian-controlled defense ministry is an important objective. In post-Franco Spain, the transition to and consolidation of a democratic regime depended largely on the organization of a powerful defense ministry. The legal context for the military's subordination to civilian authority was established in 1977–1982 and entailed: a) the creation of the Ministry of Defense (replacing the three separate service ministries); b) the definition of the government's role as director and executor of defense policy, and; c) the outlining of the basic norms governing internal armed forces operations. In 1982–1985, the authority of the civilian defense minister was expanded along with civilian participation in the ministry. The outcome was the emergence of a powerful central bureaucracy capable of reinforcing and securing civilian oversight authority of the armed forces (Barany and Graham 1994: 123). These changes effectively established meaningful civilian control of the military and helped obtain public support for Spain's full-fledged Euro-Atlantic participation. In Argentina, too, decision-making authority over the military budget, defense industries, and the setting of defense priorities was transferred from the generals to a civilian-led ministry of defense.

Control over the defense budget is one of the most important components of civilian oversight of the armed forces. In this respect, too, there are wide disparities among post-praetorian states. It does sound counterintuitive, but one of the reasons why the Brazilian armed forces left power was to increase their budget. Although in the first decade of military rule (1964–1974) defense expenditures increased, they declined precipitously thereafter and by the mid-1980s Brazil had the lowest defense budget in GDP terms in South America.[4] This actually led some officers to believe that their budget might increase in a civilian regime where the military's lobbying would be viewed as more legitimate (Arceneaux 2001: 177). In the colonels' Greece, on the other hand, per capita military expenditure was one of the highest in NATO even though the country was one of the poorest in the Atlantic Alliance (Veremis 1997: 164). Not surprisingly, in the new democratic era failed military regimes fared poorly in terms of defense outlays. The Argentine armed forces, for instance, had to make do with drastically reduced budgets both under Alfonsín and Carlos Saúl Menem (between 1982 and 1990, their share of public sector expenditures had plummeted from 32.3% to 18.4%) (Hunter 1997: 162). At the same time, a law passed in Chile before the military left politics guaranteed a fixed floor to the defense budget and supplemented it with a fixed percentage of profits from copper exports.

The development of independent civilian expertise on defense matters remains a thorny problem in most Latin American post-praetorian states where there is no tradition of education on military subjects for civilians. Even in Greece, three decades after the fall of the colonels' regime, no community of independent civilian defense experts has emerged.[5] The situation is somewhat better in Spain and Brazil; although, the rich variety of educational institutions and NGOs that exists in many European and North American democracies, where individuals without military ties may acquire defense-related expertise, has yet to take shape.

Another way successful military regimes, like Chile, are able to influence post-praetorian legislatures is through devising electoral systems that privilege the allies of the *ancien régime*, arrangements for non-elected senators, and setting requirements that impede constitutional reform (Agüero 2002: 123–4). Following failed praetorian regimes, however, the circumstances are far more favorable for the evolution of new democratic

---

[4] Actually, as Stepan (1988: 81) points out, the situation was quite similar in Spain under the last years of Franco's rule.
[5] Interview with Thanos Dokos (Athens, March 13, 2007).

parliaments. The best example is Argentina under President Alfonsín who, given the magnitude of the military regime's breakdown and of his own electoral mandate, was able to vigorously pursue the demilitarization of politics. During his presidency, the legislature passed the National Defense Law (1988) that separated external defense from internal security, banning the military from the latter, and denied the seat for the armed forces on the National Defense Council, thereby civilianizing defense policy (Giraldo 2006: 52). In fact, the Argentine Congress repeatedly rejected Alfonsín's nominees to the high command owing to their past human rights violations and thereby might have indirectly precipitated several unsuccessful coup attempts. Such fledgling coup attempts in Argentina and Spain in the early 1980s provided important lessons to the new political elites who severely punished coup plotters and thereby successfully discouraged further recurrences (O'Donnell 1986).

Unusual circumstances, such as the perceived presence of enduring security threats, can make a parliament reluctant to be assertive on defense issues. In some cases, the legislature's political frailties add to this problem. The biggest problem in the institutional arrangements of civil-military relations in present-day Greece, for example, is that the legislative branch is far weaker than it ought to be. The parliamentary Committee on Foreign Affairs and Defense possesses only limited powers to block governmental decisions. Moreover, national defense is one of the few issues on which there is something of a traditional consensus between the government and the opposition, but this is for reasons unique to Greece. Namely, it is considered disloyal to squabble about military issues given that many Greeks think that their country is under constant threat from Turkey and no political force wants to appear "unpatriotic."

To what extent has the West encouraged the building of democratic armies in post-military regimes? The answer depends not only, naturally, on individual cases, but also on the historical context. During the Cold War, for instance, Western democracies – particularly the United States – were far more reluctant to condemn military regimes and/or aid them in building democratic armies than afterwards. NATO never publicly complained about the frighteningly incompetent human rights-trampling military junta that ruled Greece in 1967–1974, although the European Economic Community and the Council of Europe did.[6]

On the other hand, the extensive contacts of Spanish officers with foreign colleagues from the 1960s onward encouraged changes in their

---

[6] Interview with Thanos Veremis (Athens, March 13, 2007).

political attitudes during Spain's transition to democracy.[7] Although Spain was excluded from NATO until 1982, military contact programs exposed younger officers to Western militaries, especially to U.S. military personnel serving on American bases in Spain. As the senior military cadres with civil war experience retired, many of these younger officers moved up through the ranks and were able, once the opportunity came, to open up Spain to the outside world and to respond with new training initiatives, proposals for reorganization, and a willingness to work with civilian counterparts. They were to form the core of advocates within the military institution for integration into NATO and participation in U.N. peacekeeping operations. Elsewhere, too, the international community has been quite helpful in trying to divert the attention of some Latin American armed forces (especially those of Brazil and Argentina) from politics to something more constructive, such as international peacekeeping.

Since the end of the Cold War, U.S. policy toward post-praetorian states has been reconsidered. In terms of civil-military relations, the West (and especially the United States) has been far more interested in promoting democratization programs. The new strategic objectives of the U.S. Southern Command include not only the general aim of strengthening democratic institutions but also to "enhance the role of the military in democratic society" (Ramos et al. 1992: 34). This objective focuses on assisting South American armed forces to restructure and redefine their roles in support of developing democracies and to protect and promote the human rights of their citizens (Ramos et al. 1992: 38).

AFTER COMMUNISM

In contrast with post-military regimes, in polities emerging from state-socialism where the military did not enjoy an *independent* political role, the key task of democratizers is to depoliticize the armed forces. Although most post-communist states – many of which have become NATO members in the past decade – have succeeded in establishing democratic armies and civil-military relations, these feats have not been accomplished anywhere without problems or controversy. As it turns out, the argument that the communist era's firm civilian control of the military predicts few problems for democratizers has severe limitations. For one, legal regulations, including those governing civil-military relations, meant little

---

[7] Interview with General Francisco Laguna (Madrid, March 11, 1993).

owing to the communist party's domination of the judiciary (Nichols 1993: 11–12). Moreover, although party-states did maintain strong control over the armed forces, this type of oversight was not balanced between branches of government, but was exercised by the party only and thus it is hardly an example for newly democratizing states to emulate.

One of the many differences between the post-communist world and post-praetorian regimes is that the former includes the successor states of three erstwhile federal states (Czechoslovakia, the Soviet Union, and Yugoslavia) that broke down to their constituent parts in ways ranging from "velvet divorce" to the most destructive war fought in Europe since World War II. Building democratic armies in a newly independent state has posed several distinctive challenges that were more or less amicably resolved in former Czechoslovakia where the assets of the armed forces were divided according to a two to one (Czech to Slovak) ratio. Still, one can appreciate the difficulties when considering that independent Slovakia had no military academy for training ground forces, little defense infrastructure (especially for the air force), and no Ministry of Defense or General Staff, given that those were based in Bohemia. For the Yugoslav successor states things could not have gone less smoothly as they – with the exception of Macedonia – were involved in a string of very different wars that were not followed, needless to say, by an orderly and proportionate distribution of military assets. The collapse of the Soviet Union, on the other hand, put a tremendous burden on Russia in several respects, not the least of which was the repatriation of hundreds of thousands of military personnel and their dependents from the internal and external Soviet empire who needed jobs, housing, and socioeconomic infrastructure.

In most of the region, executive-legislative relations were sorted out early on. Given the different amount of power vested in the presidency (ranging from largely ceremonial head of state in Slovakia to strong executive authority in Poland), one cannot generalize about its influence on defense issues. In Slovenia, for instance, the president is the titular commander-in-chief of the armed forces but has no specific power relations to the armed forces. Romania's president, on the other hand, is not only the commander-in-chief, but, according to the July 1994 Law on National Defense, also acts as the guarantor of the country's territorial integrity, chairs the Supreme Council of National Defense, and, in exceptional cases, can mobilize the military and not seek parliamentary approval for five days. At the other end of the spectrum, the successive constitutional decisions political elites took in the late Soviet period and at the birth of the new Russia – such as ambiguously differentiated roles between the legislative and executive branches – in effect, led to the 1993 crisis that hastened the executive's acquisition of super-presidential powers (Colton and Skach 2005: 117–119). Civilian control there has become synonymous with presidential control given that the legislature's independent authority has shrunk to pre-Gorbachev Soviet levels.

The power of the Duma – the Russian legislature's lower house – to oversee military affairs has been gradually reduced since the 1993 Constitution removed its controls over the armed forces. The 1996 Law on Defense entrusted only two important powers to parliament pertaining to the military: to pass the defense budget and to write pertinent laws. Still, even though the Duma is formally responsible for overseeing the budget, it has no effective means to investigate or control how disbursed funds are spent – the Constitution does not permit parliamentary inquiries – and no authority to elicit illuminating details from the Defense Ministry. Especially since Vladimir Putin's accession to the presidency in 2000, the Duma's legislative function has become perfunctory. New laws and regulations are, in fact, the result of executive branch initiatives, not that of independent parliamentary deliberations. In short, under Putin the Duma has turned into a pliant presidential tool described by one expert as "little more than a Kremlin-controlled puppet show" (Shepherd 2005).

In other post-communist states, the legislature has become a more meaningful locus of civilian oversight as parliamentary defense committees have begun to exercise their authority to oversee military affairs. Nonetheless, the scope of their activities is in many cases narrower than would be ideal. Some of the reasons have to do with the institutional arrangements hammered out at the beginning of post-communist transition processes that favored the executive branch. In Hungary, the parliamentary Defense and Security Committee's control over the military budget is still quite limited, but it is a great deal more substantive than in other Central European states (Simon 2003: 36). On the other hand, Romanian MPs serving on defense committees – especially if they sat on the wrong side of the aisle – at times did not even have access to pertinent legislation prior to submission for vote until recently. As democratic consolidation progresses, these issues have been gradually worked out, but it has often proved difficult to change laws and practices.

The relative dearth of independent civilian defense-related expertise is an important reason for limited legislative oversight of defense establishments, although in this respect, too, there is a broad spectrum of cases. The Yugoslav successor states are unique – not just among post-communist states but, more generally, among post-authoritarian states – to the extent that they have benefited from a Yugoslav government policy that established defense studies departments in all republic capitals (except for Montenegro) starting as early as the mid-1970s, and thus have trained civilian defense experts for decades. In Romania and Poland, military academies have started to accept civilians into their programs in a conscious attempt to increase the pool of civilian defense experts. This effort has been accompanied by the gradual process of civilianizing the ministries of defense in the region. Bulgaria, where the ministry's workforce is still largely made up of uniformed personnel, has been a laggard in this respect. In Slovenia, on the other hand, the civilianization of the defense sector might have gone too far as critics charge that some politicians in their zeal to fill the Ministry of Defense with civilian workers may have overlooked their qualifications (Barany 2003: 110). Russia is an "outlier" in this regard as well, given that its political elites have forcefully discouraged the rise of civilian specialists on military-security issues because they have nothing to gain and much to lose from the independent scrutiny of the defense establishment.

Establishing straightforward chains of command over and inside the military at times has also been difficult owing to a number of reasons, such as legislative lacunae or ambiguities, individual misconduct, or lacking understanding of democratic procedures. Croatia, at the declaration of its independence in 1991, had no military of its own and its command structure and arsenal were created haphazardly as its war with Serbia (1991–1995) was unfolding (Perry and Keridis 2004: 165–6). Even in Slovenia, in many ways the most successful former communist state, numerous troublesome incidents occurred in the mid-1990s, chiefly connected to Defense Minister Janez Janša, who utilized a legal void created by the new constitution – which was not accompanied in time by new corresponding legislation – as he effectively made himself the commander-in-chief. Janša deprived President Milan Kučan of relevant information and issued major orders without proper authorization (Bebler 1996: 208). Perhaps the most serious transgressions in this regard occurred in Russia, where a serious rift developed between Defense Ministers Igor Sergeev and Sergei Ivanov on the one hand, and Chief of the General Staff Anatolii Kvashnin on the other. Until Putin eventually dismissed him in mid-2004, Kvashnin repeatedly violated the chain of command – leaving the minister out of key decisions and resisting the implementation of defense reforms – and fueled the tension between the Ministry and the General Staff.

In most East-Central European states civilian defense ministers replaced active-duty military officers at the beginning of the transition to democracy. Elsewhere, however, generals continued to head the ministries, as in Romania until 1994, to "avoid political debates and due to views that a civilian defense minister would be incompetent and arrogant."[8] Such arguments were not entirely without merit considering the lack of prior expertise or even demonstrated interest in military affairs of some post-communist defense ministers. (One example is Hungary's first post-communist defense minister, Lajos Für, a scholar of nineteenth century agricultural history.) The need – indeed, the Western expectation – to switch to civilian defense ministers in accord with accepted international standards was nonetheless clear to all East European states and eventually they replaced active-duty generals everywhere.

In contrast, the Russian top brass publicly opposed the idea of a civilian defense minister throughout the 1990s. Technically, General Igor Rodionov, became Russia's first civilian defense minister in December 1996, when Boris Yeltsin transferred him to the reserves to "reflect the progress of Russian democracy." The emptiness of this gesture was demonstrated by the fact that the Defense Ministry had continued to be staffed entirely by military men and by the active-duty status of Rodionov's successor, Igor Sergeev. Russians finally got a civilian defense minister of sorts in March 2001, when Putin appointed his close associate, Sergei Ivanov, a retired KGB general to the post. Ivanov, in turn, was followed in February 2007, by Anatoliy Serdiukov, a bona fide civilian – his military background was limited to an 18-month conscript service – who previously headed the Federal Tax Service (Barany 2008: 596).

Like the United States in Iraq, the new East European polities encountered the "red or expert" problem, forcing them to make difficult choices about retaining competent officers who were loyal to the *ancien régime*. In several states, as in Hungary, officers were required to sign loyalty oaths to the democratic state or be dismissed. Depoliticization, however, did not always proceed free of problems. In 2001, for instance, it was discovered that fifteen employees of the Slovak Ministry of Defense were agents of the former communist counterintelligence agency. Moreover, the Czechoslovak practice of screening officers did not continue in independent Slovakia. Because background screening was a promotion-requirement, many younger Slovak officers, untainted by their political

---

[8] Interview with Larry L. Watts (Bucharest, May 31, 1993).

past, encountered a new obstacle to their professional advancement. In fact, NATO's Office for Security expressed its apprehension about the approximately 5,000 Slovak officials with access to classified information who were exempted from security background checks (Barany 2003: 69). Another problem has been breaking the bonds between senior East European military officers and their colleagues in Russia. This was a particular concern in Bulgaria, whose army was more closely integrated with Soviet forces and more effectively socialized by them than any other in the region.

Having said this, in the past two decades, all East European militaries have been convincingly depoliticized. In Russia, however, Yeltsin's policy of neglecting the armed forces resulted in conditions that comprised a textbook case for coup incentives – interference by political actors, drastic budget reductions, humiliating treatment by political leaders and the media, and unpopular deployments – but, the generals were not interested in overthrowing the regime. This may be best explained by the organizational culture perspective that focuses on the Russian military's institutional culture, which has traditionally viewed armed intervention against the country's civilian leaders as fundamentally wrong. Nonetheless, a coup-averse military does not mean a depoliticized military. In Russia, three presidential decisions signified "formative moments" that demarcated the military's undemocratic path. First, in the late-1980s, Mikhail Gorbachev invited the armed forces to voice their own political concerns, which led to the unprecedented politicization of the Russian officer corps. Second, Yeltsin not only failed to block the military's political participation, but permitted the development of a polity in which armed forces personnel could play a legitimate political role (running in elections, acquiring consequential political positions, etc.). Third, Putin confirmed this role by appointing senior officers to political posts and allowing the military as an institution to continue to oppose state policy, such as the formulation and implementation of a comprehensive defense reform (Barany 2007: 19–20).

Although East European states satisfy Stepan's criteria for democratic civil-military relations, his classificatory scheme helps to recognize the dramatic increase in the armed forces' political influence in post-Soviet Russia. According to his construct, the Russian armed forces' political role is especially troublesome in two respects: the defense ministry's refusal to provide the legislature with information that would allow actual oversight of military expenditures and the absence of civilian participation in the defense-security sphere (1988: 94–97). The political clout of the

Russian armed forces is a good deal less than militaries hold in praetorian dictatorships, but a lot more than they possess in democracies.

Unlike in some of the other contexts of building democratic armies – such as in post-imperial India or Pakistan or post-praetorian Latin America – in post-communist states, the West (meaning established democracies) had important leverage with which to influence democratization processes. I am referring here not so much to the economic aid conditionally offered by Western democracies or even the more general role played by the European Union (EU). Rather, what I have in mind is the quintessential and overwhelmingly positive role NATO has played in the democratization of post-communist military affairs and, more specifically, civil-military relations (Barany 2006). Given that all of the non-Soviet members of the former Warsaw Pact states identified NATO membership as one of their crucial foreign policy objectives, the Atlantic Alliance possessed powerful bargaining chips, and it has used them well.

NATO's various programs – Partnership for Peace (PfP, launched in 1994) and Membership Action Plan – specified the goals individual states needed to satisfy, provided on-going advice and evaluation, and offered tangible assistance in a variety of ways such as multi-level officer training, surplus equipment, and grant programs. The United States played an important and positive role setting up offices of Defense Cooperation in U.S. embassies where Security Assistance Officers evaluated, supported, and financed programs that fostered the establishment of democratic civil-military relations and professional competence (the big-ticket item was often English-language training).[9] In July 1994, President Bill Clinton announced the Warsaw Initiative, financed by Congress, that disbursed $570 million between 1994 and 2000 to twenty-two partner states to support equipment grants, training, and information technology (U.S. Government 2001: 22).

Several states requested teams of defense experts from NATO member states that assisted their preparations for membership. In Romania, for instance, a small delegation of officers and civilian experts from the British Ministry of Defense provided a resident advisory role to their colleagues in the Romanian defense ministry (UK Ministry of Defense 1997). Another example of success is the George C. Marshall European Center for Security Studies in Garmisch-Partenkirchen, Germany, that since 1993 has enlightened hundreds of high-ranking officers and public

---

[9] Interview with Lt. Col. Deborah Hanagan, a former SAO in Slovenia (Palo Alto, May 15, 2008).

servants from post-communist states about the proper place of the armed forces in a democracy. At the same time, U.S. defense consultants offered help to a number of states in the region to deliberate issues ranging from defense legislation to procurement imperatives (Perry and Keridis 2004: 129). The West's help to the post-communist East in placing their military establishments on democratic foundations were even more direct though unofficial in the several cases when senior American officers returned to their East European birthplaces to assume leading positions in the emerging democratic armed forces.

CONCLUSION

Establishing public order and building democratic armies are critical components of promoting democracy. The United States made two extraordinarily costly mistakes after the 2003 invasion of Iraq from which it has yet to recover; both were directly relevant to the larger issue of security. First, it did not anticipate the widespread looting and disorder and failed to deploy forces in adequate numbers and configuration to deter it (Fukuyama 2006: 234). The second blunder was the decision to dismiss the Iraqi Army. The perfectly foreseeable consequences of this error were overlooked by the American political – although not the military (Diamond 2005: 271) – leadership. The age old questions of whether to: a) destroy the old army first and build a new one from the ground up, or b) work, at least temporarily, with the available personnel and continue shaping it thereafter is crucially important. Most regimes, from Bolshevik Soviet-Russia to post-Raj India took the latter route. Two weighty reasons favoring this choice are that in a fluid political situation security must be maintained at all costs and that discharging the extant army creates a large group of discontents with military training and ready access to weapons.

The dismissal of the Iraqi Army without providing any alternative security force to take its place has been called "one of the greatest errors in the history of U.S. warfare" (Phillips 2005: 153). The termination of salary, retirement, and benefit payments to its members added insult to injury and set off a catastrophic chain reaction. In brief, it

- created a crushing security and public safety vacuum;
- produced a vast pool of trained, armed, humiliated, antagonized, and desperate individuals many of whom saw joining the insurgency as a logical choice;

- generated an economic crisis for approximately 8 percent of the work-force and their dependents;
- lost important intelligence information that could have been gained from the dismissed soldiers and officers;
- prevented coalition forces from controlling and "keeping an eye on" the Iraqi officers and soldiers;
- opened the floodgates for foreign fighters to enter Iraq;[10] and
- destroyed the only national institution in a deeply divided society, an institution with organization, infrastructure, and transportation facilities that would have enabled it to actively participate in post-war reconstruction.

Many of these problems were the logical results of poor decisions reached without reflection or consultation. As Francis Fukuyama notes, it is quite remarkable that none of the major problems the United States had encountered or created in Iraq were either new or unfamiliar, suggesting that there has been little institutional learning since America first tried its hand at nation-building in the aftermath of the Civil War (Fukuyama 2006: 8).

The heavy price the U.S.-led coalition and Iraqis continue to pay on a daily basis for the mistakes made early on in the conflict is an on-going reminder of the importance of establishing public order and forming a democratic army. The many political, socioeconomic, and security contexts in which these tasks have needed to be sorted out in the past also call attention to the tremendous differences between cases and the need to learn from the failures and successes of earlier experiences. What worked in post-imperial India did not work in Nigeria, what seemed like a relatively straightforward process in post-World War II Japan may have very little relevance to post-war scenarios elsewhere. The point – that should be so obvious, but, amazingly, continues to escape many policy-makers – is that learning about individual contexts and judiciously applying the lessons of the past may make or break the given democratization project.

The study of civil-military relations in newly established democracies also shows the wisdom, indeed, necessity of close familiarity with individual contexts. Although some modest and tentative generalizations might be offered, there is no single prescription of civilian control that can be devised to apply to or "fit" the large variety of political settings. Claude Welch cautioned decades ago that just as political systems are unique in

[10] By January 2004, every sixth person apprehended in the so-called Sunni Triangle was a foreign volunteer (Mendelson Forman 2006: 204).

their combinations of circumstances, so are the precise ingredients affecting the formulation of civil-military relations: the strength and unity of the military, the political strength of civilian institutions, the resources available, and so on (Welch 1976: 313).

Of course, it makes an enormous difference whether the new army is created by an outside power or as a result of domestic transition. Foreign involvement should be carefully tailored to the specific local conditions. In some settings – e.g., post-World War II Germany – it is necessary for foreign actors to be decisive, assertive, and to stay until democracy is consolidated. In others – e.g., post-communist Bulgaria – it is important to tread lightly, avoid the appearance of dominating the process, and provide only the assistance that is requested. One tentative generalization that *can* be made is that there is a considerable opportunity for advanced industrial democracies to help stabilize emerging democracies by furthering the development of regime capacity, particularly in the area of civilian expertise on defense-security issues (Trinkunas 2005: 17). The probability of successful formulation of democratic armies and civil-military relations clearly increases with the number of civilians who understand the importance and complexity of these processes.

9 Democratization, Conflict, and Trade[1]

In recent years, promoting democracy has become a cornerstone of United States foreign policy. In his 1994 State of the Union address, President Bill Clinton identified the absence of war among democracies as a principle reason to foster democratization throughout the world. President George W. Bush has pursued this goal even more forcefully, arguing that democracy in the Middle East and elsewhere will enhance the security of the United States. In many ways, these calls are hardly new. Early in the twentieth century, Woodrow Wilson advanced the view that democracy and peace were mutually reinforcing. Near the end of the Cold War, Ronald Reagan echoed this claim. Equally, Western policy makers and various international institutions have argued that democratization should be encouraged because it yields economic reform and prosperity. Among the hopes expressed by these individuals is that democratization will prompt the liberalization of foreign commerce, thereby expanding and deepening the open international trading system.

There is ample reason to expect that, in the long run, political liberalization culminating in the establishment of stable, mature democracies will widen the zone of peace and prosperity. In the short run, however, democratic transitions frequently promote war and undermine economic reform. Of course, not all democratic transitions are tumultuous. Those that occur in the face of strong, stable domestic institutions are often peaceful and facilitate improved economic performance.

---

[1] Portions of this paper draw on Mansfield and Snyder (2002 and 2005).

For helpful suggestions, we are grateful to Nancy Bermeo and the other participants at the conference on "Exporting Democracies: What Democracies Can and Cannot Do," held at the University of Texas. For research assistance, we are grateful to Kaija Schilde and Matthew Tubin.

However, political conflict and protectionist policies are especially likely outcomes in states that are starting to democratize and that lack the institutional infrastructure needed to manage this process.

When these institutions are deformed or weak, politicians are better able to resort to nationalist appeals, tarring their opponents as enemies of the nation, to prevail in electoral competition. War can result if elites then become caught up in the belligerent politics that nationalist rhetoric can unleash. In the same vein, the outset of a democratic transition occurring in the face of weak domestic institutions limits the ability of public officials to resist the demands of interest groups, including those pressing for protection from foreign competition. Moreover, officials in such states are especially likely to use protectionist trade policies to build popular support. As such, the initial stage of democratization often promotes belligerence at home and abroad, as well as impeding commercial liberalization.

DEMOCRATIZATION AND WAR

That democracies rarely fight each other is one of the best-known findings in the social sciences. Two explanations have been offered for what has been dubbed "the democratic peace" (Doyle 1986; Russett 1993). First, wars impose costs on a country's citizens. In a democracy, leaders abstain from wars because the populace – which bears the human and economic costs of international conflict – will vote public officials who decide to engage in war out of office. Further, the checks and balances inherent in democracies are expected to constrain heads of state who are considering the commitment of troops to battle. Second, other observers argue that democracies are characterized by norms regulating internal conflict and that such norms also guide their relations with other democracies in the global system (Owen 1997). Democracies come to view each other as inherently pacific, thereby helping to defuse tensions and foster political cooperation among them.

Debates regarding the sources of the democratic peace have yet to be resolved. Nonetheless, there seems to be widespread acknowledgment that mature democracies rarely come to blows with one another. This, however, does not imply that democratic transitions promote peace. On the contrary, the early stages of such transitions are often quite violent, especially if the institutional infrastructure needed to help manage regime change is lacking.

The democratic peace rests on the presence of strong domestic institutions that regulate mass political participation, including the rule of law, civil rights, a free and effective press, and representative government. These institutions ensure that the individuals who make foreign policy are accountable to the mass public. Even those observers who stress the importance of liberal norms in promoting the democratic peace realize that these norms only function in conjunction with effective democratic institutions (Owen 1997: 155).

In some cases, demands for broader political participation that arise as an autocracy breaks down can be managed through institutions that already exist or that can be rapidly established. Democratic transitions in nineteenth century Great Britain and contemporary South Africa, for example, were facilitated by the prior establishment of various institutions needed to make a representative government work. In other cases – such as the post-Communist Czech Republic – a highly literate, politically sophisticated, large, urban middle class may have the skills needed to create such institutions quickly. If so, democracy may be consolidated relatively smoothly and peacefully.

More commonly, however, demands for broadening political participation arise in countries where authoritarian rule has broken down, but the institutional prerequisites for effective democracy are absent. The rule of law is poorly established, state officials are corrupt, elections can be rigged, militaries or warlords threaten to overturn electoral outcomes, and journalistic media are unprofessional and depend on the state or economic elites. As Samuel Huntington (1968), has pointed out, when rising levels of mass political participation outstrip the ability of weak institutions to manage political activity, the result is not democracy, but a free-for-all in which each social grouping may threaten to take unilateral action to protect its interests: workers may strike, ethnic groups may riot, and militaries may make coups. Governing in this setting requires an ideological basis for popular political support. Under these circumstances, ideology helps to fill the gap between high levels of participation and weak political institutions. Only a well-institutionalized democracy can guarantee rule "by the people," but a populist ideology can promise the plausible-sounding substitute of rule "for the people."

This ideology may appear in several forms, but most frequently it takes the form of some variety of nationalism (Snyder 2000). Nationalism is a state-building ideology that holds out the promise of either gaining a state for a people that lack one or strengthening the capacity of an existing state to better serve the distinctive aims of a people. As such, it can close the gap between popular demands and weak institutions. Nationalism, however, does not necessarily promise to do so by enacting a system of civil rights and strict accountability to the median voter. On the contrary, many forms of nationalism base their appeals on the political exclusion of ethnic or ideological "enemies of the nation," and, in this way, set up the possibility of abridging rights of political participation. According to this ideology, governing "for the people" may require placing limits on government "by the people."

The precise content of nationalism depends on the nature of both the post-authoritarian political setting and the "enemies" to be excluded. For example, French revolutionary nationalism branded aristocratic opponents of the revolution as enemies in league with foreign foes; counter-revolutionary German nationalism appealed to the middle class against anti-national revolutionary workers; and ethnic Serbian nationalism based its exclusions and enmities on ethnic grounds. Religious fundamentalism – which Mark Juergensmeyer (1993) argues is a form of religious nationalism – can serve similarly as a populist, but exclusionary state-building strategy through its anti-secularist ideology. Elsewhere, as in Argentina, military populism played an analogous role (Levy and Vakili 1992).

Facing the institutional challenges of a post-authoritarian environment, elites of all sorts may perceive an incentive to turn to populist or nationalist ideologies of these kinds. Such ideologies may appeal to rising elites representing formerly excluded social groups, such as ethnic minorities, as well as to elites threatened by the collapse of the prior regime, who are trying to find a basis of mass political support. Nationalism offers the latter elites a way to evade strict democratic accountability, while giving the appearance of being responsive to popular interests. Nationalism may also serve as a useful vehicle for old elites who have a parochial interest in military, imperial, or protectionist enterprises that lay at the heart of the former authoritarian state and its ruling coalition.

This kind of nationalist politics in a weakly institutionalized post-authoritarian setting can lead to belligerence abroad through several related mechanisms. One is nationalist outbidding: both old and new elites may bid for popular favor by advancing bold proposals to deal forcefully with threats to the nation, claiming that their domestic political opponents will not vigorously defend the national interest. Another mechanism is blowback from nationalist ideology: nationalists may find themselves trapped in a rhetoric that emphasizes combating threats to the national interest because both the politicians and their supporters have internalized this worldview. A final mechanism is logrolling. Frequently, nationalist coalitions include military, imperial, or protectionist groups that are held together by logrolling. Such tactics increase the prospects of embroiling the state in foreign disputes (Mansfield and Snyder 1995, 2005).

THE DANGERS OF INCOMPLETE DEMOCRATIZATION

In previous work, we have distinguished between complete and incomplete democratic transitions (Mansfield and Snyder 2002, 2005). A complete transition culminates in the establishment of coherent democratic institutions soon (within five years or so) after its launch. As democratic institutions take root, leaders become accountable to the mass public and the watchdog press limits the ability of politicians and interest groups to succeed with the strategies of rule that we outlined in the previous section. An incomplete transition, in contrast, is marked by a breakdown of autocratic institutions that stalls prior to the establishment of democratic institutions. Instead, the transition yields a mixed regime with both autocratic and democratic features. In this setting, weak participatory institutions create both the motive and opportunity for political strategies that heighten the likelihood of international conflict.

Among the many instances of countries that experienced an incomplete democratic transition at some point over the past half century and subsequently became involved in interstate hostilities are Greece, Turkey, Ecuador, Peru, Argentina, revolutionary Iran, revolutionary Nicaragua, and Pakistan. In most of these cases, the breakdown of authoritarian rule gave rise to democratic procedures that were intermittent, manipulated, and animated by nationalist or other populist ideologies. Equally, most of these cases were marked by weak political institutions at the outset of the transition from autocracy.

Indeed, we have found considerable evidence that turbulence during the initial phase of a democratic transition is particularly likely if little domestic political power is concentrated in the hands of public officials and a country's political institutions are weak or deformed (Mansfield and Snyder 2005). Statistical tests covering all countries throughout the nineteenth and twentieth centuries reveal that in states marked by little institutional strength or centralization, an incomplete democratic transition yields between a four-fold and a sixteen-fold increase in the likelihood of an external war compared to states that do not experience a

regime change, depending on which measure of regime change we analyze. Furthermore, an incomplete democratic transition is between 50%
and 200% more likely to precipitate war than any other type of regime
change (complete democratization, complete autocratization, or incomplete autocratization).[2]

These results are robust to a wide variety of changes to the sample of
countries being analyzed, the estimation techniques and modeling strategies that are used, the control variables that we include, and whether
world wars are excluded. Equally, our results refute the view that transitional democracies are simply inviting targets of attack because of their
temporary weakness: in fact, they tend to be the initiators of war. We also
are able to exclude the possibility that the observed effect of democratization on war actually reflects the influence of war on democratization:
our findings indicate that war has very little bearing on either the occurrence of democratic transitions or whether those transitions that do occur
yield coherent democratic institutions (Mansfield and Snyder 2005, and
forthcoming).[3]

The tendency for democratizing states to become involved in wars is
partly rooted in the entrance of new social groups and classes onto the
political stage. Also crucial in this regard, however, is the tendency for
democratization to weaken the central governmental bodies that regulate the policy process and its outputs. But, different episodes of democratization have led to vast differences in the extent to which central governmental bodies have been weakened. In contemporary Latin America,
for example, democratic transitions have been relatively orderly and
smooth processes leading to relatively little political instability. In many
other cases, however, these transitions have been accompanied by considerable institutional instability and the substantial weakening of central

---

[2] In a study covering the period since World War II, we also found evidence that incomplete
democratization stimulates the onset of militarized interstate disputes, a broad class of
events ranging from wars to threats to use force that generate no fatalities. See Mansfield
and Snyder (2002).

[3] The impact of war on democratization is an important, but complex issue. In a few cases,
war has stimulated democratization, for example, through the military defeat of authoritarian states by democracies (e.g., Germany and Japan at end of World War II). In other
cases, governments seeking to mobilize popular support for a war effort have granted the
middle class or the working class greater opportunities to participate in politics. See, for
example, Anderson (1967) and Feldman (1966). However, war can also promote nonliberal nationalist attitudes, strengthen militarist institutions, and serve as a justification
for curtailing political liberties on national security grounds. What matters for the limited
purposes of this paper is that war does not have a systematic effect on democratization
that influences the validity of our findings. For a more systematic analysis of this issue,
see Mansfield and Snyder (forthcoming).

governmental authority. Democratization is more likely to promote war if it is accompanied by considerable institutional decay and a much-weakened central government.

DEMOCRATIZATION AND WAR IN HISTORICAL PERSPECTIVE

Virtually every great power has gone to war during the initial phase of its entry into the era of mass politics. Mid-Victorian Britain, poised between the partial democracy of the First Reform Bill of 1832 and the full-fledged democracy of the later Gladstone era, was carried into the Crimean War by a groundswell of belligerent public opinion. Napoleon III's France, drifting from plebiscitary toward parliamentary rule, fought a series of wars designed to establish its credentials as a liberal, popular, nationalist brand of empire. The ruling elite of Wilhelmine Germany, facing universal suffrage, but limited governmental accountability, was pushed toward World War I by its escalating competition with middle-class mass groups for the mantle of German nationalism. Japan's "Taisho democracy" of the 1920s brought an era of mass politics that led the Japanese Army to articulate an imperial ideology with broad-based appeal. In each case, the combination of incipient democratization and the material resources of a great power produced nationalism, truculence abroad, and major war.

The contemporary era provides additional evidence that incomplete democratization can be an occasion for the rise of belligerent nationalism and war. In 1991, Yugoslavia broke up into separate warring nations within six months of elections that had confirmed the power of ethnic nationalism (Woodward 1995: 17). In the wake of the Soviet collapse, popular sentiment expressed in the streets and at the ballot box fueled warfare between Armenia and Azerbaijan over the disputed enclave of Nagorno-Karabakh (Kaufman 2001: chap. 3). Troubled elected governments of Peru and Ecuador, democratizing fitfully during the 1980s and 1990s, gained popularity through a series of armed clashes that culminated in a small war in the upper Amazon in 1995 (Mares 2001: chap. 7). Several years after the collapse of Ethiopia's Derg dictatorship, its elected government fought a bloody border war from 1998 to 2000 with Eritrea, forestalling the implementation of Eritrea's newly adopted, democratic constitution (Negash and Tronvoll 2000).

In an especially worrisome case, the nuclear-armed, elected regimes of India and Pakistan fought the Kargil War in 1999 when Pakistani forces infiltrated across the mountainous frontier in northern Kashmir.

The death in 1988 of Pakistani military dictator Zia ul-Haq had ushered in a series of revolving-door elected civilian governments that presided over a rise in militant Islamic efforts to liberate majority-Muslim Kashmir from Indian control. In Kashmir itself, the restoration of elections after Indira Gandhi's period of "emergency" authoritarian rule unleashed a political polarization that led to violent conflict between Muslims and the state. These turbulent processes of democratization culminated in war, notwithstanding constitutional changes in Pakistan in 1997 that were intended to strengthen the powers of elected civilian rulers.[4]

In addition to these wars *between* states undergoing traumatic experiments with democratization, the 1990s also witnessed civil wars and violence *within* democratizing states, many of which had significant international dimensions. Internationally mandated elections in Burundi in 1993 led to ethnic polarization and some 200,000 deaths. In East Timor, in 1999, an internationally sponsored referendum on separation from Indonesia precipitated large-scale violence and a refugee crisis. Elsewhere in Indonesia, the replacement of the Suharto dictatorship by a series of weak, chaotic, elected governments coincided with a rise in separatist warfare in the provinces of Aceh and West Papua and the outbreak of intercommunal fighting in the outer islands of the Indonesian archipelago. In Nigeria, the return to electoral politics after a period of military rule sparked violence between ethnic and religious groups.[5] Newly democratizing Russia fought two wars against its breakaway province of Chechnya, with Vladimir Putin winning election in 2000 as Russia's president mainly on the strength of his popular war policy.

More generally, we have found that over the course of the nineteenth and twentieth centuries, incomplete democratic transitions have been a potent source of civil war (Mansfield and Snyder 2007). States experiencing this type of transition are more than twice as likely to become embroiled in a civil war as a stable regime and between two and a half and four times more likely to experience such a war than an autocratizing country.[6] In many cases, states undergoing an incomplete democratization become involved in civil wars for the same reasons that this process yields interstate war (Snyder 2000).[7]

---

[4] On India, see Talbot (2000); on Pakistan, see Rizvi (2000). Russett and Oneal (2001: 48) discuss whether the fighting in Kashmir should be considered a war between democracies.

[5] Between 1999 and fall 2002, 10,000 Nigerians were killed in ethnic and religious clashes. Noritmitsu Onishi, "Ethnic Clenching," *New York Times*, October 1, 2002, p. A12.

[6] Only in comparison to instances of complete democratization does an incomplete democratic transition have relatively little effect.

[7] For a related discussion of how establishing a democracy can promote communal violence and civil unrest, see Chirot (this volume).

DEMOCRATIZATION AND ECONOMIC PERFORMANCE

Even in countries where the initial stage of a democratic transition has not stimulated war, this process often has had other adverse consequences. For example, the same properties of incomplete democratizers that give rise to both interstate and civil war also predispose such states to engage in atrocities and massive human rights violations. Genocides and other atrocities take place in autocracies, but they also occur in states undergoing incomplete democratization. These abuses can result from the ethnic nationalist politics stirred up in the early stages of the transition process in weakly institutionalized political systems where elites are threatened by the prospect of political change. Yugoslavia and Central Africa have been prominent recent cases.

In addition, incomplete democratization can have adverse economic consequences. In this section, we analyze how incomplete democratization can undermine economic reform efforts, placing particular emphasis on trade policy. During the past decade or so, various international organizations, including the World Bank and the International Monetary Fund (IMF), have pressed countries to liberalize both their political and economic regimes as a condition for the receipt of aid. Along with many government officials, they have viewed democratization as likely to promote economic reform. By increasing the political accountability of government officials to a country's populace, democratization is expected to provide these officials with incentives to implement policies that enhance a country's economic performance.

In contrast to this view, however, the experiences of various countries in Africa, Latin America, and elsewhere during the post-World War II era provide ample evidence that incomplete democratization has often undermined economic reform. During transitions from nondemocratic to democratic rule and before the establishment of stable democratic institutions, public officials may be tempted to engage in rent-seeking. Faced with the prospect of being driven from office, government officials are likely to discount heavily the future benefits of enhancing macroeconomic performance and to view the transition period as an opportunity to allocate rents (Alesina 1991; Haggard and Kaufman 1992: 34; Kaufman and Stallings 1991: 26–27). One means of doing so is by taxing an economy's resource-intensive sector, which is its primary source of exports, thereby shifting rents from this sector to the government and restricting trade for the country as a whole (Findlay 1991: 28–30).

However, once democratic transitions have been completed and democracy is consolidated, public officials generally have less ability to engage in rent-seeking, including the imposition of taxes on trade. The actions of policy makers are much more transparent in democracies than other regime types. Further, economic predation is likely to degrade a country's economic performance. Both factors hamper incumbent officials' capacity to distort the economy for their personal benefit and win re-election.

In addition, the frailty and fragmentation of democratizing regimes often limit the ability of policy makers to undertake economic reforms, which are facilitated by a strong and centralized state (e.g., Haggard and Kaufman 1995; Maravall 1994). These conditions also compel governments in emerging democracies to consolidate power and build popular support or face the prospects of reversals of democratization, including the restoration of autocracy (Mansfield and Snyder 2005; Przeworski 1991). Distributing economic favors to influential groups in society is one means available to build such support. These favors are likely to include commercial protection for relatively uncompetitive sectors of the economy and for elite groups that thrived under autocratic rule and pose a threat to a new democracy (Haggard and Kaufman 1995: 152–59). That democratizing regimes will need to generate the support of many groups within society suggests that protection may be relatively widespread.

Compounding this tendency is the fact that democratization elicits demands for greater political participation and the reduction of central authority, both of which often are difficult to reconcile with economic reform programs that impose substantial costs on society (Nelson 1993). Moreover, incompletely democratizing regimes often fail to develop social welfare policies needed to buffer these costs (Bresser Pereira, Maravall, and Przeworski 1993). Because commercial liberalization may create greater political pressure than such regimes are able to bear, it may be postponed until after democracy is consolidated.

Still another reason why incomplete democratic transitions hamper economic reform is that this process promotes uncertainty on the part of firms and investors about the government's ability to consolidate power, thereby dampening investment and hampering commerce. Investors are likely to be discouraged from locating productive assets that generate tradable goods in such countries until clear signs exist that democracy is sustainable (e.g., Alesina 1991; Haggard and Kaufman 1995: 152). Otherwise, they face the risk that political instability and the rollback of political liberalization will threaten the integrity of their assets.

Finally, commercial liberalization is likely to be dampened in democratizing states because, as we discussed earlier, public officials in these countries often use nationalist appeals to consolidate power and generate public support. Nationalists tend to oppose market-oriented reforms, such as trade liberalization, that enhance the susceptibility of domestic firms to overseas competition and increase the participation of foreigners in the economy (Nelson 1993: 443).

DEMOCRATIZATION AND TRADE IN HISTORICAL PERSPECTIVE

Related to the use of nationalist strategies is the tendency for elites in incompletely democratizing countries to rely on economic populism. This involves the use of economic instruments by government officials to generate improvements in a country's economic performance, however fleeting, for the purpose of attaining or maintaining power (Dornbusch and Edwards 1991; Rabello de Castro and Ronci 1991: 151). Heightened trade barriers are among the steps often taken in populist economic packages (Kaufman and Stallings 1991). A number of studies have concluded that stable regimes, whether democratic or autocratic, tend to be shielded from economic populism. Political transitions – especially democratic transitions – however, render countries particularly susceptible to economic populism (Kaufman and Stallings 1991; Rabello de Castro and Ronci 1991). As Robert Kaufman and Barbara Stallings (1991: 26) point out, "in the new democracies, institutional uncertainties tend to shorten the time horizons of both the incumbent government and their opponents. For such governments, there is a premium for meeting distributive expectations early in the administration and a substantial discount for the political risks attached to later problems with the balance of payments and inflation." There is reason to expect that these factors will be magnified in countries where democratic transitions are underway, but have not yet been completed, that is, in countries experiencing incomplete democratization.

Although there has not been a systematic empirical test of this argument to date, a number of cases serve to illustrate how incomplete democratization can inhibit the openness of international trade. Consider, for example, Brazil. Based on the Polity data, Brazil underwent an incomplete democratic transition in the mid-1970s (Jaggers and Gurr 1995; Marshall and Jaggers 2005). This coding seems to accord with the view of various experts. Many scholars date the inception of Brazilian democracy in 1985, when José Sarney assumed the presidency. But as Juan Linz and Alfred Stepan (1996: 167, 168) argue, "[t]he Brazilian transition from authoritarianism began with the inauguration of General Ernesto

Geisel as president on March 15, 1974.... The democratic transition in Brazil was not completed until the directly elected president, Fernando Collor de Mello, assumed office on March 15, 1990." Huntington (1991: 126) concurs, noting that throughout the period from the Médici government's conclusion in 1973 until Collor's election in 1989, there occurred a "creeping democratization.... In fact, the genius of the Brazilian transformation is that it is virtually impossible to say at what point Brazil stopped being a dictatorship and became a democracy."

During the period from 1964 to 1974, Brazil placed a heavy emphasis on export promotion and the reduction of import restrictions. Especially important was a series of reforms in 1967 that slashed many tariffs by more than half and spurred the growth of trade (Coes 1991; Muñoz 1994). But as Donald Coes (1991: 15; see also Clements 1988) argues, "[i]n the following decade, Brazil reverted to a much more restrictive policy on imports, while exports lost the momentum they had gained in previous years." The introduction of these restrictions was partly a reaction to the mounting current account deficit caused by the first oil shock (Coes 1991; Muñoz 1994: 66; Rabello de Castro and Ronci 1991). However, domestic political factors also contributed to this retreat from commercial liberalization, which occurred during a period characterized by extensive economic populism (Bresser Pereira 1993: 55; Rabello de Castro and Ronci 1991: 163).

Import-substitution policies implemented by Geisel led to a almost two-fold increase in tariffs on intermediate and consumption goods, and yielded successive reductions in imports during each year of his administration (Clements 1988: 18–19). Central to these policies was the government's shift from supporting industrialists located in the southeast portion of Brazil, who were hesitant to accept the risks associated with a new round of import substitution, to supporting new industrial centers in the center-north and northeast parts of the country, where the government located much of the investment associated with its Second Development Plan (Sola 1994: 162). This course of action met with some resistance on the part of workers and industrialists in the southeast. But Geisel was committed to gradual political liberalization, and these commercial policies served a useful purpose in the face of domestic political opening. In Lourdes Sola's (1994: 162) words, they "broaden[ed] the scope of regional alliances. The broadening secured both a comfortable majority in Congress and the support of the relevant state governors." The need to expand the geographical basis of the government's support took on newfound importance in light of the incomplete democratic transition that had taken place.

Based on the Polity data, Argentina also experienced an incomplete democratic transition during the mid-1970s. This change coincided with the call for elections by the military regime in 1972 and the victory of Hector Cámpora, the first of four Peronist presidents to hold office until the military reasserted control in 1976. Whereas this election marked a shift away from autocracy, the Peronists' "tolerance and even encouragement of the para-military violence of the Montoneros" and their lack of respect for minority rights clearly does not accord with most definitions of democracy (Linz and Stepan 1996: 199). Thus, characterizing Argentina as having undergone an incomplete democratic transition seems reasonable. And, there is little doubt that this transition was accompanied by increases in commercial protectionism and a reduction in trade openness.

The Three-Year-Plan advanced in 1973 called for extensive state intervention in the economy and reduced dependence on international trade, including an increase in tariffs and government control over exports (Sturzenegger 1991: 83–85). The Peronist base of support emanated largely from urban workers. As William Smith (1989: 225) explains, "The leaders of organized labor were thus essential interlocutors; no Peronist government was possible without their participation and consent." This, in turn, led to a reliance on economic populism, particularly on policies to protect workers and other segments of the coalition supporting the government. Especially pertinent for present purposes is this Plan's call for the imposition of "tariffs with a social purpose" and other economic policies designed to transfer wealth to urban workers and entrepreneurs (Sturzenegger 1991: 85, 115). These policies were initially popular with the Peronists' chief constituencies, but they left Argentina on the brink of economic collapse by the end of 1976. Moreover, these policies represented a break from recent attempts to liberalize trade. Oscar Muñoz (1994: 67) points out that "trade liberalization was first attempted in the late 1960s, during the military regime of the time, but was reversed as strong opposition mounted and the second Juan Perón government (1973–1974) was installed. During the military regime that followed, a new attempt at trade reform was started in 1976." Indeed, in vivid contrast to Argentine trade policy during the period from 1973 to 1976, Smith (1989: 233) argues that "[t]he basic orientation of post-1976 economic policies was actually of quite old vintage, dating back to the 'free trade' doctrine of classical liberal orthodoxy."

Economic populism, however, was only one reason why the incomplete democratic transition inhibited trade liberalization in Argentina. As noted earlier, democratic transitions can increase uncertainty, thereby reducing investment and dampening openness. In fact, during the period from 1973 to 1983, economic uncertainty increased because of the rise in discretionary actions by the government, the reduced ability of the judiciary to resolve disputes among firms, and heightened domestic political instability (de la Balze 1995: 54). These developments increased the risks faced by private investors, thereby distorting investment flows and generating capital flight. This, in turn, augured poorly for promoting commercial openness.

Finally, consider Senegal, which the Polity data codes as experiencing an incomplete democratic transition in the mid to late 1970s. This accords with Thomas Callaghy's (1993: 496) view that "[i]n the late 1970s, President Léopold Senghor started a halting process of democratization." Senghor was succeeded by Abdou Diouf in 1981; he aimed to both continue the process of democratization and institute an economic reform program. The effort at economic reform continued in fits and starts for more than a decade, but never succeeded. As Callaghy (1993: 498) argues, the reforms failed because they were:

> badly conceived and poorly implemented, especially a trade liberalization that was much too rapid. Compensating policies that were to mitigate the loss of protection were poorly formulated and only partially implemented, for reasons of politics and state capacity. A number of the old, mostly foreign, trading houses and light industrial firms simply went out of business; others survived only by obtaining protection and subsidies via old clientelist networks.

By the late 1980s, opposition to the reforms had begun to mount in large measure because of "the explosion of associational life that resulted from the democratization process" (Callaghy 1993: 500). Unemployment became a growing concern on the part of the government and social tensions started boiling over. These developments led the government to begin raising trade barriers in 1989, and by 1991 the reform effort had been largely abandoned. Although democratization was not the primary reason for its failure, experts view it as an important contributing factor (Callaghy 1993).[8]

---

[8] Of course, it is important to ensure that the effects of incomplete democratization on trade policy do not stem from some factor that influences both regime change and foreign economic policy. Although a systematic treatment of this issue is beyond the scope of our

Although incomplete democratic transitions pose substantial impediments to trade liberalization, complete democratization can generate similar problems. In general, it is only when democracy is consolidated that its beneficial effects on foreign commerce become evident (Mansfield, Milner, and Rosendorff 2000, 2002; Milner with Kubota 2005). For example, the inception of democracy in Argentina and Brazil did little to promote trade liberalization (Kaufman and Stallings 1989, 1991; Muñoz 1994: 75–79). Commercial reforms in both countries were deferred until a second democratically-elected government took office (Muñoz 1994: 70). Anne Krueger (1993) argues that democratization in Brazil during the 1980s weakened the state, thereby limiting the extent to which policy makers could implement economic reforms that would harm key interest groups. Indeed, even when faced with an economic crisis, "the resistances to change were great. Industrial leaders opposed reform plans that would have opened the economy and threatened Brazil's highly protected import-substitution firms" (Krueger 1993: 115; see also Bresser Pereira, Maravall, and Przeworski 1993: 47–50). In a similar vein, Stephan Haggard and Robert Kaufman (1995) maintain that, during the 1980s, government officials in newly democratic Argentina, Brazil, Bolivia, and Peru faced potent domestic political obstacles to economic liberalization. These and other nascent Latin American democracies tended to have extensive trade barriers at the time when democracy was first established (Przeworski 1991: 142). In those cases, like Peru, in which commercial liberalization was attempted, opposition from groups that had benefited from trade barriers and import-substitution led to its reversal (Haggard and Kaufman 1995: 189).

Not until the mid-1980s did fears of an autocratic backlash diminish and did expectations that contested national elections would occur on a relatively regular basis take hold in these countries. Of course, electoral institutions were not equally strong in these new democracies. But, because the specter of regular and competitive elections tends to reduce

paper, one possibility that we can address in a preliminary fashion, is that international financial institutions (IFIs) are reluctant to aid states in the throes of an incomplete democratic transition because such states are unstable and unlikely to make the policy changes that these institutions would prefer. Equally, reduced aid by IFIs may promote protectionist policies. At least in the three cases that we have analyzed, however, there is little support for this hypothesis. We collected data on the indebtedness of Argentina, Brazil, and Senegal to the IMF and World Bank as a percentage of their national incomes from the World Bank's *Global Development Finance Online* (2007). In none of these three cases did this percentage decline during the period in which the country experienced an incomplete democratic transition. For Senegal, this percentage actually rose quite a bit. As such, a decline in lending by IFIs is not driving the results of our case studies.

the incentives for rent-seeking by government officials, including protectionist policies, it is not surprising that they engaged in sustained trade liberalization only after 1985 (Haggard and Kaufman 1995: chap. 6).

In addition to Latin America, democratization did little to promote commercial liberalization in Southern Europe. Transitions to democracy occurred in the face of economic crises in Greece, Portugal, and Spain. New democratic governments in these states faced severe pressures from groups that had borne the costs of crisis and that had been shut out of the political process prior to the advent of democracy, as well as from antidemocratic groups that threatened the new regimes (Bresser Pereira, Maravall, and Przeworski 1993: chap. 2).[9] The influence of these groups and the fragile democratic institutions in Greece, Portugal, and Spain contributed to the inability of governments to engage in substantial economic reforms, including commercial liberalization. Like the Latin American countries discussed above, only after democracy was consolidated in these countries did they engage in trade and other economic reforms (Bresser Pereira, Maravall, and Przeworski 1993: 92–104).

CONCLUSION

The past three decades have been marked by a wave of democratization throughout the international system. This development has been heralded by scholars and policy makers alike, who hope that it will promote peace and prosperity. In the long run, it may. In the short run, however, the initial stages of democratic transitions can precipitate both domestic and external conflict and undermine a country's economic performance. Creating techniques to manage these problems is among the most important challenges facing Western policy makers.

The dangers of democratization are especially acute when transitions are not sequenced properly. Not only does an out-of-sequence transition run the risk of failing to culminate in a consolidated democracy, but it also risks triggering intense nationalism and war. This is most likely to occur when a country's political institutions are especially weak at the outset of the transition from autocracy to a partially democratic regime and when elites are threatened by democratization.

Our argument has prescriptive implications for those instances where policymakers have some latitude about the timing and sequencing of a

---

[9] See also Haggard and Kaufman (1995) on how economic crises influenced the ability of democratizing states in Latin America and East Asia to liberalize.

transition. In cases where the institutional requisites for successful consolidation are not yet in place, it is best to forge them before embarking on mass political contestation. Likewise, in cases where powerful potential spoilers could be severely threatened by a democratic transition, it is best to find ways to safeguard their interests, although preferably not their power, under the anticipated democratic regime. Although transitions do not necessarily have to proceed slowly and conservatively, they do have to build on sound foundations and effectively neutralize spoilers through some combination of constraints and inducements (Bermeo 1999; Stedman 1997).

These prescriptions for sequencing, tactics, and pacing of a transition are important from the vantage point of both the short and the long run. In the short term, transitions that flout them risk stalling and degenerating into the politics of war-prone nationalism. Over the longer term, a failed, violent transition may leave a legacy of nationalist ideology, militarized institutions, undemocratic rules, and foreign enmities that will make democratic consolidation less likely and war more likely during subsequent attempts at transition.

Although incomplete democratization tends to stimulate political conflict and protectionism, the successful consolidation of democracy is often accompanied by peace and open trade (Mansfield and Snyder 2005; Milner with Kuboto 2005). This suggests that the relationship between democracy and both conflict and trade liberalization may be characterized by a J-curve (Bremmer 2006). The initial phase of a democratic transition provokes both political and economic turbulence, but the consolidation of democracy and the strengthening of democratic institutions dampen conflict and promote economic reform. If so, it is all the more important to design policies that facilitate the successful completion of democratic transitions and avoid the adverse consequences of incomplete democratization.

MITCHELL A. SELIGSON, STEVEN E. FINKEL, AND
ANÍBAL PÉREZ-LIÑÁN

10 Exporting Democracy

Does It Work?

The chapters in this book are focused on two broad themes. First, should democracy be promoted? Second, how should democracy be promoted? This paper asks and attempts to answer a third question: Does democracy promotion work? In many ways, this is really the prior question, because if democracies cannot be promoted, if their emergence, consolidation and breakdown are entirely random, or follow a pattern that cannot be altered by human intervention, then the prior questions are, after all, moot.

In the field of democracy studies, there is perhaps no more controversial and unsettled question than that of how democracies emerge, consolidate and breakdown. The literature is vast, growing in important ways with each passing month. Consider, for example, the role of economic development, just one of the many factors that have been thought to be important for the emergence and/or stability of democracy. The classical literature dates back to Lipset, who found empirical support for the notion that higher levels of economic development were strongly linked to the transition from dictatorship to democracy (Lipset 1959). Over the years some scholars confirmed this finding, whereas others refuted it. By the mid 1990s, however, larger databases with more sophisticated statistical techniques seemed to demonstrate that Lipset was indeed correct (Lewis-Beck and Burkhart 1994; Muller 1997). Then, the academic bombshell hit in 2000 when Przeworski and his co-authors presented the most comprehensive data set (and arguably the most sophisticated

This study was supported by a grant from the Association Liaison Office (ALO) to Vanderbilt University, the University of Virginia and the University of Pittsburgh. We thank Margaret Sarles, David Black, and Andrew Green of USAID for their support and assistance, and Dinorah Azpuru, Michael Bratton, Michael Coppedge, Pamela Paxton, for their expert advice and criticism. The analysis and opinions expressed here do not necessarily coincide with those of USAID.

statistical design) to support their findings that economic development had no impact on the probability that a dictatorship would "die" and give birth to a democracy, although once established, more prosperous democracies were less likely to collapse (Przeworski et al. 2000). Just as those findings were becoming "conventional wisdom," taught worldwide in graduate seminars, newer research undermines them almost completely. A spate of articles has found that the results were affected by selection bias and the lack of critical control variables (Boix and Stokes 2003), the need for a longer term perspective (Gerring et al. 2005), and the importance of moving away from a strict democracy/dictatorship dichotomization (Epstein et al. 2006). Each of these new papers also presents persuasive theoretical challenges to the Przeworski et al. arguments on the impact/non-impact of development on democracy. So, once again, for the moment at least, it now appears that the conventional "conventional wisdom" was indeed correct, and economic development helps produce democracy.

Into this theoretical and empirical morass came studies that look at the impact of foreign assistance on democracy. This is certainly a much smaller literature, as it deals with a far more limited issue, one that involved only the handful of advanced industrial democracies that have been investing in democracy promotion activities. Democracy promotion itself is certainly not a new activity as its origins go back at least to the post-World War II program to democratize Japan and Germany (Lowenthal 1991; Lowenthal 1991; Merritt 1995). After that major effort, however, Cold War politics predominated, and little effort was made to weaken dictatorships of the right (Schoultz 1981; Schoultz 1987), whereas dictatorships of the left became targets of largely propagandistic efforts, such as the broadcasts of Radio Free Europe.[1] There was, nonetheless, a continued effort to promote subnational democracy in such programs as the establishment of agrarian cooperatives and labor unions (Carothers 1991).

This paper reports on a component of a much larger research project that seeks to determine if there is solid evidence to support the hypothesis that democracy promotion works.[2] This might sound like a simple

---

[1] As Schoultz (1981) has documented, only during brief periods in the Cold War, such as the first two years of the Carter administration, did concerns with human rights trump national security interests defined in terms of an anticommunist alliance.

[2] In addition to the two authors, Professor Neal Tate and Dinorah Azpuru have been involved with various aspects of the project. The National Academy of Sciences in 2006–2007 brought together a panel of experts (on which one of the authors of this paper, Mitchel Seligson, serves) to develop a systematic methodology for testing the impact

question, but it is not. At least since September 7, 1854, when Dr. John Snow persuaded the Board of Guardians of St. James's Parish in London to remove the handle from the community water pump well on Broad Street and, thus, ended one of the worst outbreaks of cholera in that city's history (Tufte 1997: 27–37), scientists have been seeking to demonstrate that their research can lead to good public policy. In the case of public health, the evidence of success is overwhelming, as one disease after another has been tamed. In other fields, the story is not as clear. Consider the tangled case of the Head Start program, one in which "early intervention" in breaking the cycle of poverty in the U.S. inner cities has not yet, after decades of research, been proved to be effective.

The research problems in the case of Head Start range from serious issues of "selection bias" (students who enter the program are different from those who do not), to the complexities of detecting the impact of preschool education many years later in life (e.g., at the time of completion of college studies). In the field of democratization research, the barriers to measuring success or failure are even higher than they are in the Head Start area. In Head Start, it was easy to specify benchmarks of program impact; did participants get better grades or more advanced degrees or end up with higher annual salaries than those who did not participate? In the democracy arena, however, what are we to use as a criterion for impact? Are we satisfied to use a narrow standard (e.g., free and fair elections are regularly held), or are we interested in a broader definition that might encompass the extent to which citizens enjoy a wide range of civil liberties and human rights protection, as well as a system in which political parties are genuinely competitive? Many researchers would be dissatisfied with the limited standard, but that is the one that is easiest to measure objectively. The more we move into broader and broader definitions of democracy, including respect for minority rights, protection of vulnerable groups, etc., the more complex the measurement of the dependent variable (in this case, democracy) becomes.

Without a universally agreed upon standard for defining the dependent variable, the more difficult it is to measure the impact of democratization programs. However, there are further complexities that cloud any study of the impact of democracy assistance efforts, and those deal

of democracy assistance programs. At M.I.T., the Abdul Latif Jameel Poverty Action Lab serves as a focal point for development and poverty research based on randomized trials.

with a myriad of confounding variables. Democracy assistance certainly does not go on in a vacuum. Nations have histories, including colonial origins (Weiner 1987; Weiner and Özbudun 1987; Boix 2003; Gerring et al. 2005) that may make them more inclined or less inclined to follow a democratic trajectory. Nations also can be richer or poorer, less or more equal in their distribution of income, have lower or higher levels of ethnic fragmentation, are more or less dependent on other nations, and so on. The challenge, then, is to isolate the impact of democracy assistance from each of these other variables.

A final difficulty needs to be noted before we turn to the literature review about democracy assistance itself. Many analyses of development projects rest on a "rate of return" evaluation of costs and benefits. That is, when one builds a road, one attempts to determine its economic benefits vs. its economic cost. More recently, other elements have been factored into the equation, such as environmental impact. In the democracy area, however, we cannot produce a dollar value of democratic growth. In this study, we use as our dependent variable commonly used and, we think, very reasonable measures of democracy (Freedom House and Polity IV). We hasten to add, however, that democratic growth can have an intrinsic value that is hard to quantify. One frequently cited study (Rummel 1994), for example, has counted the tens of millions of citizens murdered by their own authoritarian governments in the twentieth century versus the very small number of citizens murdered by democracies. In addition, the so-called "second-order" benefits of democracy vs. dictatorship are very much clouded in academic controversy. On the one hand, whereas the literature on the "democratic peace" is enormous, and it is probably the case that democracies are unlikely to make war on each other, it is far less clear if democracies are less likely to go to war with other countries that are not democracies themselves (Russett 1993; Brown, Lynn-Jones, and Miller 1996; Henderson 2002; Moore 2004; Rasler and Thompson 2005; Geis, Brock, and Müller 2006). Our effort in this paper merely strives to respond to the more limited question on the impact of democracy assistance on the level of democracy.

The paper is divided into three sections. The first briefly reviews the literature on democracy promotion. The second looks at the main independent variable, namely, the level and nature of the investment in democracy building by the U.S. government. The third presents key findings of the research program to date on the impact of foreign assistance on democracy.

PRIOR RESEARCH: WHAT HAVE WE LEARNED?

To date, research to measure the effects of democracy assistance has been limited in scope. The majority of research has been qualitative, with much of it coming to very critical conclusions regarding USAID's and other Western countries' efforts to promote democracy. Those who have evaluated the research have been critical of its quality (Crawford 2001), whereas others have argued that despite that criticism, democracy is becoming an internationalized norm that one way or another will involve international actors, so democracy assistance is a fact of life with which nations will need to learn to live (McFaul 2004). In looking at the research as a whole, we came to three general conclusions. First, much of the literature is more concerned with the motivations behind the assistance than its impact. This literature is overwhelmingly critical, viewing with great suspicion the motivation for such assistance, viewing it as being entirely self-serving (i.e., pursuing single-mindedly the U.S. "national interest" as it would be defined by international relations experts of the "realist" school) (Morgenthau 1982; Morgenthau and Thompson 1993). The literature tends to assume that what is good for the U.S. cannot be, or probably cannot be, good for the recipient countries. This is, however, an empirical question. Whether the U.S. has the "right" motivations to pursue democracy-promotion policies is a different issue from whether such policies succeed or fail in particular contexts. "Skeptical realists" can equally invoke hidden motivations to explain policy success (in situations in which the U.S. arguably has a vested interest in fostering democracy) or failure (in situations in which U.S. national security or economic goals presumably clash with the stated pro-democracy policy). Although "true" historical motivations are very hard to assess (because foreign policy is often formed in multiple layers of decision-making), the impact of such policies can be documented through proper empirical analysis.

The second difficulty we found with the literature is that the great bulk of it is qualitative, which in itself is not a problem, as qualitative methods can tease out the mechanisms by which the foreign assistance works or does not work. However, when searching for worldwide, cross-time patterns, which are the focus and the current research effort, it is very difficult to "add up" the qualitative literature and find those patterns. It seems to us that the qualitative evidence is crucially important once it is known if foreign assistance does or does not produce greater levels of democratization, and in what areas it works or does not work, and in what regions of the world it works better or worse.

Third, among the few works that use rigorous quantitative methods, we found significant weaknesses. Perhaps, the most serious problem is the data on which prior research has been built. Much of the quantitative work limits itself to either a short period of time, or a regional subset of the world. Those few studies that are worldwide and include a wide range of years use data on foreign assistance that is highly aggregated. Such works used an estimated overall figure for U.S. assistance on the (in our view mistaken) assumption that general official development assistance should produce democratization.[3] A further limitation of the quantitative studies, as a whole, is that they tend to under-specify their models by failing to include a sufficient number and variety of control variables, and they use statistical techniques that do not allow for the clear specification of the "added value" of foreign assistance.

Our approach has been to develop a data set that reflects USAID's expenditures on democracy promotion worldwide, for an extended period of years. We separate all USAID obligations in the democracy sector from those in areas such as education, health, and economic development, and include expenditures in each of these areas, as well as a wide range of control variables, in the statistical models.[4] This is the first comprehensive examination, then, of the specific effects of U.S. *democracy* assistance on levels of democracy in recipient countries.[5] Moreover, we further separate the amount of assistance in each of the specific sub-sectors in the USAID democracy portfolio – Elections and Political Processes, Rule of Law, Civil Society, and Governance – and assess the effects of each on countries' general levels of democracy, as well as their effects on additional variables that represent counties' levels of democratic development *on those specific sub-sectoral dimensions*. Thus, we show the impact of elections assistance on countries' level of free and competitive electoral processes, the impact of civil society assistance on the freedom and independence of countries' civil society sector, the impact of governance assistance on governance-related democratic outcomes, and so forth. None of these kinds of critical analyses for the overall assessment of USAID democracy efforts have been conducted previously.

---

[3] As an interesting exception, Scott and Steele (2005) analyze the impact of NED funds, but this is a very small proportion of U.S. democracy promotion programs worldwide (on average, less than 5 percent in the 1990s).

[4] Note that "obligations" is used throughout this study to refer to "actual appropriations," or the amount for which USAID is allowed by Congress to incur obligations for specified purposes.

[5] Paxton and Morishima (2005) conducted analyses on a preliminary version of the data base we utilize here, and we relate our findings to theirs at several points in the report.

Turning now to the qualitative literature itself, one of the earliest works in the field is an edited collection with the well chosen title of *Exporting Democracy* (Lowenthal 1991; Lowenthal 1991). In this edited collection, reflecting the broader trend in much of the qualitative literature, the authors express deep skepticism of the motivations of the United States in attempting to promote democracy in Latin America. Certainly this skepticism is understandable, given the record of the U.S. in the nineteenth and much of the twentieth centuries in supporting a wide variety of dictatorial/military regimes in Latin America (Schoultz 1987; Schoultz 1998). Therefore, in this early study, with most of the papers written only a short time after U.S. policy had resolved to make democratization a high priority in its foreign policy, the authors were concerned far less with the question "did it work?" than the question, "why is the U.S. doing it?"

Diamond's (1992) seminal piece in *Foreign Policy* is another early effort that expresses skepticism of the motivations of the U.S. His main contribution, however, is to distinguish between "exporting democracy," the theme of the Lowenthal collection and "promoting democracy." Diamond urges policy makers to avoid the export model, and instead to support groups and even individuals in authoritarian regimes that are attempting to move in a democratic direction. This implies, argues Diamond, that much of the assistance should be channeled through non-governmental organizations (NGOs) such as civic associations, trade unions, the media, etc. Diamond's critique of USAID is that it is not light enough on its feet to be able to program the aid to where it is needed most. He recognizes, as do many of those inside and outside of USAID, that Congressional mandates, earmarks, and other limitations, especially foreign policy considerations mandated by the State Department, make it difficult and sometimes impossible for USAID to dedicate its democracy resources where they seem to be needed the most. Another early and frequently cited paper is also prescriptive rather than evaluative. Graham Allison and his co-author Robert Beschel, Jr. (Allison and Beschel 1992) establish ten principles or guidelines for promoting democracy, describing how the external environment, the infrastructure and the strategies can be programmed for maximum effectiveness. Again, however, this work largely avoids any effort to evaluate the impact of foreign assistance on democracy, focusing instead on making the argument on the need for the U.S. to become heavily involved in the effort.

The most extensive, detailed evaluative work emerges in the several works of Thomas Carothers (Carothers 1991; Carothers 1996; Newberg and Carothers 1996; Carothers 1999; Ottaway and Carothers 2000; Carothers 2004; Carothers and Ottaway 2005). Carothers has been studying the role of the U.S. government in general, and USAID in particular, for over 15 years. During that period, he has developed a body of work that suggests a common theme, namely that U.S. democracy promotion is worth doing because when done well, it can work, but much of the time, it is not done well and fails. In a paper with Paula Newberg (Newberg and Carothers 1996), for example, he argues that in the former communist countries of central and eastern Europe, the level of assistance was moderate, and the effects were of the same magnitude, being most notable in the area of elections where free and fair elections have emerged. In a more extensive, book-length treatment, Carothers (1999) agrees with the earlier themes of Lowenthal and Diamond, both cited before that the U.S. is engaged in a process of "exporting" rather than promoting democracy. The weakness of this model, argues Carothers, is that "one size does not fit all." As a result, the effectiveness of the democracy efforts is hamstrung. In a more recent volume (Carothers 2004), he echoes the theme raised in the Lowenthal, as well as the detailed studies by Schoultz, namely that the U.S. has conflicted goals, which are to promote democracy on the one hand, but to focus first and foremost on U.S. national security interests. According to Carothers, the U.S. continues to tolerate and even support dictatorial regimes, the most infamous of which have been oil-exporting nations in the Middle East and the important case of China, whereas promoting democracy most heavily in countries of little direct strategic or economic interest.

The Carothers work, taken collectively, provides what is arguably the most detailed case study material available outside of the evaluations written under contract by USAID itself (i.e., end of project evaluations carried out by USAID contractors). The record is a mixed one, as it is in virtually all development projects, be they economic, social or, in this case, democracy focused. Although this work therefore offers some important lessons for those who implement programs, it is difficult to determine from it if "aid works" or if "aid does not work."

Additional qualitative studies seem to be uniformly negative. A book by Sogge finds that aid has failed to promote democracy because donor countries place their own interests first (Sogge 2002), a theme mentioned earlier, and one that is the focus of a paper and a book by Peter Burnell (Burnell 1997; Burnell 2000). An even more negative assessment is found in a study of foreign assistance to South Africa (Hearn and Third World Quarterly 2000). According to this study, foreign assistance has focused on the establishment of political stability at the cost of the creation of an effective opposition. As a result, competitive democratic development has been constrained in South Africa. This thesis is echoed in the work of Carapico, focused on the Middle East (Carapico 2000), where she finds that democracy assistance to NGOs has produced more conflict between government and these organizations and less democratization.

Turning now to the limited number of quantitative studies that have attempted to evaluate the impact of foreign assistance on democracy, we find a mixed assessment of the effects of foreign assistance on democracy-related outcomes. The earliest study we could find deals in only an indirect way with the question, as it does not focus on foreign assistance, per se, but on military intervention. This research harkens back to the discussion of the role of the U.S. in promoting democracy in post-World War II Germany, Italy, and Japan, in which the military defeat of these nations was followed by a *military* effort at promoting civil society and democracy more generally. Thus, the research deals with the *military* delivery of foreign assistance on democracy. The work of James Meernik, published in 1996 (Meernik 1996) tackles this question. Using a probit model with an N of 27, Meernik finds strong evidence that over the long run, invasions (and their presumable democratization efforts) help promote democracy, and that the effect is especially strong when the stated goal of the intervention is democracy and when the U.S. is opposed to the regime in power at the time of the invasion. Democracy is measured using the Gurr Polity II data series.

Only few published studies, to our knowledge, deal directly with the issue of U.S. civilian assistance and democratization. The first (Goldsmith 2001) is limited to Sub-Saharan Africa, and focuses not on democracy assistance but overall levels of assistance, regardless of its country source. The author wrestles with the question that foreign assistance might actually promote dictatorships by shoring up weak regimes. The dependent variable in the analysis is democracy measured using the Freedom House scores as well as the Gurr democracy index. The results show a positive effect of assistance on democracy, even when a number of control variables are introduced into the OLS regression equations (initial Freedom House score, logged GDP per capita (PPP), urbanization, percentage of Catholic, percentage of Muslim, log of population, and log of land area). Goldsmith concludes that those who see foreign assistance as promoting dictatorships are wrong, at least as far as Sub-Saharan Africa is concerned.

A more recent study (Knack 2004), focusing on a larger set of countries for a longer period of time, comes to an opposite conclusion. Using a variety of methods suitable for longitudinal data analysis and total OECD aid from 1975–2000 as his primary explanatory variable, Knack finds no effect of foreign assistance on democratic outcomes over the entire period, and no impact even if the study is confined to the post-Cold War period.

Paxton and Morishima (2005) argue that the Knack results are flawed because the independent variable is *all* foreign assistance from all OECD countries, regardless of whether the assistance involves obligations related to democracy. Using an earlier version of the data set that we deploy in the analysis here, and on a somewhat smaller pool of countries, they find a small but positive impact of democracy assistance on overall levels of democracy, a finding that holds after using several different statistical procedures to replicate and extend the Knack (2004) analyses. In turn, Scott and Steele (2005) analyzed the effect of funds allocated by the National Endowment for Democracy (NED) in the 1990s. Their findings did not identify a positive impact of NED investment on democratization, but rather an attempt by NED to invest in "hard cases" to resist authoritarianism.

Several other studies relate to the general topic of democracy and foreign aid, but do not provide direct tests of the impact of assistance on democratic outcomes. Jakob Svensson (1999: 293–294) focuses on the growth impact of foreign assistance. The paper finds that democracy matters in producing growth, such that, "the long run growth impact of aid is conditional upon the degree of political and civil liberties." This means that democracy conditions growth rather than the other way around. The author concludes that "democracy promotion may not only have a value in it, it may also increase the long-run growth impact of foreign assistance." When aid is not conditioned by democracy, then the aid merely serves to increase corruption. The paper shows, then, that aid needs to be given to promote democracy, because not only does it achieve its objective, it will help achieve other key foreign assistance objectives. The paper does not demonstrate, however, that aid produces democracy, only that democracy is needed for growth. Similar findings are reported by Kosack (2003). In this study, the dependent variable is "quality of life" as measured by the Human Development Index. The data set covers the period 1974 through 1985. Once again, the findings do not speak to the question of the impact of aid on democracy, but rather show that aid improves quality of life more in democratic systems.

Summarizing what we know from the prior research, we can draw the following conclusions. First, there has been little research on the impact of democracy promotion on democracy. This result is disappointing given the importance that democracy promotion has taken in U.S. foreign policy in recent years, and the enormous volume of research on democracy and democratization in general. Second, much of the work has been qualitative rather than quantitative. Third, the qualitative work is largely negative in its evaluation of the impact of democracy assistance, whereas the quantitative research has shown at least some suggestions of positive findings, especially if foreign assistance is disaggregated into democracy and non-democracy elements.

Our analysis extends all of these previous efforts in two important ways, as we stress in the sections that follow. First, we have far better measures of the independent variables (i.e., United States foreign assistance for democracy) and a far more comprehensive set of dependent variables (i.e. democratic outcomes) than have been used to date. Second, we make use of more appropriate statistical procedures that allow us to test with greater rigor the hypothesis that democracy assistance leads to positive democratic outcomes, controlling for the confounding effects of many other variables and controlling for each country's own specific democratic trajectory over time. We turn to describing our data set, first in terms of what it contains (and does not contain), and then in terms of its basic descriptive characteristics.

U.S. FOREIGN DEMOCRACY ASSISTANCE: HOW MUCH?

To carry out this analysis we employed a newly constructed data set that covers 165 countries over the entire post-Cold War period (1990–2005). Excluded are an additional thirty advanced industrial democracies, countries that are not and would not be the recipient of foreign assistance over the time span covered by our data set. The core of the data set is a comprehensive and inclusive listing of USAID spending in the field of democracy promotion, as well as information on all other non-democracy expenditures, comprising 44,958 separate budgetary records divided into the following areas: 1) Democracy and Governance (DG) spending at the country level; 2) DG sub-sectors (Elections, Rule of Law, Civil Society, and Governance) at the country level; 3) Non-DG Sectors (Agriculture and Economic Growth, Education, Environment, Health, Humanitarian Assistance, etc.) at the country level; 4) Programs that operate at the regional level (in any of the fields just described); and 5) Programs that operate at the subregional level (in any of the fields). In addition, we used USAID's congressional reports (the so-called "Greenbook") to document U.S. official development assistance not channeled through USAID, excluding the funding through the National Endowment for Democracy (NED).[6] All variables were measured in millions of constant 2000 U.S. dollars. The primary dependent variables of the analysis are the Freedom House democracy ratings as well as the Polity IV ratings. The data set also includes dozens of additional variables employed as controls, which help us measure the relative level of economic growth, military assistance, political violence, etc. In addition, we use relatively simple country characteristics, such as their prior level of democracy, prior USAID presence, population size, territorial size, level of development, ethnic fractionalization, income inequality and state failure. Full details describing the data base as well as the data set itself can be found at: http://www.pitt.edu/~politics/democracy/democracy.html.

It has often been noted that total U.S. foreign assistance is small by the standards of many other advanced industrial nations, but, our concern lies in a different direction. We want to know how important democracy assistance is relative to all other foreign assistance granted by the U.S. government. Between 1990 and 2005, democracy aid averaged 7.7 percent of total aid. However, the trend is for increasing proportions to be spent on democracy; by 2004, it has reached a high point of 12.3 percent, much of that driven by the wars in Afghanistan and Iraq. This has meant that democracy assistance has increased from $128 million in 1990 to $902 million in 2005, in constant (2000) dollars, and in current dollars to more than one billion in 2005. This suggests that although foreign assistance in the democracy area is growing in importance, it is far behind other areas, such as health, in which it represents only 41 percent of the levels of funding in that area.

Worldwide, the distribution of democracy assistance varies somewhat. For the entire period under study, the largest aggregate proportion of democracy assistance, at 20%, went to Latin America and the Caribbean, while Asia received the smallest proportion, 12 percent. But, because the number of countries per region in which USAID spends its funds differs sharply, a more meaningful number is the average funding per recipient, 1990–2005 (in constant 2000 dollars). These figures are shown in Figure 10.1. As can be seen, per-country assistance to African countries was

---

[6] That funding in the period 1990–2004 amounted to about 5.1% of the USAID expenditures.

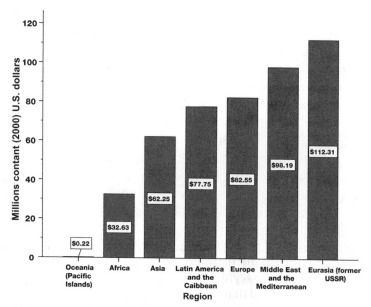

Figure 10.1: Average funding per recipient country, 1990–2005 – by region.

only a small proportion of what it was to the bloc of nations that make up the former Soviet Union. These figures also hide some important variations in the pattern, such as a dramatic increase in spending in 2004 for the Middle East (Iraq, which represented 86 percent of the entire Middle East democracy budget in that year), and the steady decline in funding for Latin America. These shifts reflect many factors in the priority of U.S. foreign policy, but also the reality of the more robust consolidation of democracy in much of Latin America compared to patterns in Africa and the Middle East.

USAID has distributed its foreign assistance among several overall categories, as noted above. For the time period being studied, the largest proportion of funds was expended on civil society (38 percent of the total), followed by governance at 29 percent (increasingly focused on anti-corruption and decentralization activities), and trailed by rule of law at 19 percent and only 14 percent on elections. However, these numbers do not necessarily reflect favoring one component of democracy over another, but rather reflect differences in costs and opportunities. For example, whereas free and fair elections are widely considered a *sine qua non* of democratic rule, assistance is often fairly inexpensive, limited to the establishment of voter registration systems, printing and counting the ballots. Other forms of assistance, such as civil society are more long term and cost intensive, involving as they often do long-term efforts to promote civil society organizations that are labor intensive and hence high cost. Moreover, shifts among these programs are evidenced, with governance after 2003 overtaking civil society.

DEMOCRACY ASSISTANCE: WHAT IMPACT?

Estimation

To determine the impact of foreign assistance on democracy requires much care in the treatment of the data. Our main concern is to isolate the impact of foreign assistance from over-time patterns that are going on both within a country and worldwide. To address this concern, we collected systematic information for the 165 countries in our database over the period 1990–2003 (yielding 2,310 observations; information for 2004 and 2005 was not available for all items). Our dependent variable is the level of democracy measured through Freedom House scores. (Freedom House indices of civil liberties and political rights were inverted and added up to create a measure of democracy ranging between 1 and 13, with 13 being the most democratic score). We estimated the level of democracy observed in any given country-year as a function of five types of factors:

1) USAID investment in democracy programs:
   - Annual obligations for democracy programs in the country (measured as an average for the current year and the previous year, in millions of 2,000 dollars);
   - Annual funding for democracy programs that operate at the regional or subregional level.
2) Other forms of foreign assistance:
   - USAID investment in development programs not oriented toward democracy (health, education, agriculture, etc.);
   - Annual funding for nondemocracy programs operating at the regional or subregional level;
   - U.S. assistance not channeled via USAID;
   - Non-U.S. foreign aid for democracy programs (a gross estimate based on OECD data);
   - Non-U.S. foreign aid for other development programs.
3) Other control variables expected to affect democracy (and to change on a yearly basis):
   - Annual growth in per capita GDP;

- The percentage of U.S. military and counter-narcotics grants allocated to a particular country during the year (as a measure of U.S. military assistance priorities);
- An index of political violence created by Arthur Banks that summarizes information on political assassinations, general strikes, guerrilla warfare, government crises, purges, riots, revolutions, and antigovernment demonstrations;
- A dummy indicating the occurrence of ethnic or revolutionary wars, genocide episodes, or violent regime changes in any given year (data from the Political Instability Task Force);
- A measure of democratic diffusion, capturing the average level of democracy in all other countries in the world during the previous year, weighted by the distance from the country in question.

4) Control variables considered "fixed attributes" for a country (i.e., not changing over time):
- The size of the country's territory;
- The number of years the country was rated "free" by Freedom House in 1972–1989;
- Total U.S. development assistance during 1960–1989;
- Population (in thousands);
- The average per capita GDP for 2000–2005;
- Ethnic Fractionalization (between 0, or ethnic homogeneity, and 1, or fractionalization);
- The share of income received by the top 20 percent of the population;
- The number of years between 1960 and 1989 that the country suffered political anarchy or foreign intervention (according to the Polity IV database)

5) A unique country trend (or rate of democratization), captured by a linear time counter.[7]

The fifth factor is crucial, because it identifies the underlying pattern of democratization over the 14-year period, regardless of the specific conditions (including the level of investment and the behavior of the other control variables) in any particular year. We captured the unique trend in each country by allowing the coefficient for the time counter variable to change across cases. As an example, consider Figure 10.2, which plots

---

[7] This variable is coded so that year 1990 = 1, 1991 = 2, 1992 = 3, etc. If the coefficient for this variable is allowed to change across countries, then the distinctive slope for each case indicates the average yearly change in democratization in the particular country during 1990–2003, after we control for all other factors.

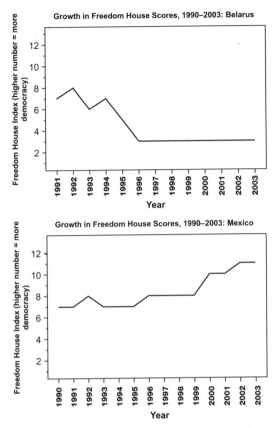

Figure 10.2: Growth in freedom house scores, 1990–2003: Belarus, Mexico.

the trend in Freedom House scores of Belarus and Mexico in the 1990–2003 period. The two countries had roughly the same level of democracy in 1990 (a score of 7), but the rate of change in democratization for the countries is starkly different. In Belarus, the "slope" for the effect of time is strongly negative, reflecting the sharp decline in Freedom House ratings between 1990 and 1996 before leveling off at the score of 3. By contrast, Mexico's growth over time is sharply positive, reflecting the gradual increase from 7 to 10 in Freedom House scores over the 14-year period. Our statistical model accounts for these kinds of country-specific trends, and estimates the "added value" of USAID Democracy and Governance assistance on Freedom House ratings, controlling for the country's underlying growth trajectory and controlling for other variables that also may influence democratic outcomes over time.

To carry out such an estimation of impact using standard ordinary least squares (OLS) estimation would be inappropriate because of the complex nature of the combined ("mixed") model's error term.[8] To resolve this problem, we used an approach based on hierarchical linear models using maximum likelihood estimates. Whereas the details are complex, and can be seen on the web site noted earlier, our model is able to capture country-level growth (or decline) in democracy along with inter-country democratic growth (or decline) over time, and sort out the contribution of U.S. foreign assistance from other factors that could be producing change in democracy.[9]

The distinctive advantage of hierarchical models is that we can estimate the coefficient for the time trend in each nation (illustrated in Figure 10.2) as a function of variables that are fixed characteristics of the country (the size of the territory, the overall level of development, the historical experience with democracy, etc.). Thus, the fourth group of variables presented above was used to estimate not only the expected level of democracy for each country, but also the expected *rate of change* of the level of democracy for each country. The results of the estimation are presented in the Appendix.

Results

We found, using the Freedom House 13-point scale, the average country increased by about .04 points per year, so that over the period of study, the average country increased its level of democracy by about .6 units. This result indicates a slow but consistent world-wide increase in democracy over time. Our findings also suggest that during the 1990s, smaller and ethnically diverse countries seemed to democratize at a faster pace.

The second and most important step in our analysis was to look at the impact of democracy assistance and other variables over and above this overall trend line of democracy. What we found provides very strong evidence that such assistance, on average, works. Moreover, only democracy assistance increases democracy. No other form of assistance (e.g., economic growth, health, the environment, etc.) makes any significant impact. We re-ran our models using Polity IV as the dependent variable, and found effects of almost the same magnitude, once the Polity measure is scaled the same way as is Freedom House. This finding demonstrates

---

[8] The approach we use is known as "hierarchical longitudinal growth modeling," also called "individual growth curves."

[9] In additional models, we also went to considerable length to be sure that U.S. assistance was not the effect of change in democracy rather than the cause. That is, we carefully tested for "endogeneity" in our models, which could have emerged as a result of the U.S. government deciding to spend its democracy funds in places where democracy was doing the best, and cut it back where it was doing the worst. The results held in every case.

rather clearly why prior analyses got it wrong, because nearly all of them lumped together democracy assistance with all other forms of assistance. Doing so obscured entirely the impact of the democracy programs. It may well be that these other forms of assistance may have indirect effects; as Lipset suggested, economic growth may help produce democracy, but we did not find any direct effect of those forms of assistance, and if there is an effect, it is likely mediated through the democracy assistance.

We also found that countries whose economies grew faster and were situated in regions of the world that were more democratic (as measured by the diffusion variable) experienced higher levels of democratization than countries that grew slowly and were located in regions with a lower level of democracy. Also, we determined that political violence strife hurts democratic development in the short-term. But, these findings are not surprising, and conform to our general notion of the factors that stimulate democracy. What was not previously established, however, was the positive impact of democracy assistance. We should also note that in our studies of endogeneity, we did not find that the level of aid was a result of USAID "going with the winners." Indeed, we found just the opposite; as countries such as Poland and others in Eastern Europe consolidated their democracies, U.S. assistance was terminated because these countries were considered to have "graduated." As a result, USAID tended to shed the successful cases while concentrating on the more difficult ones.

Statistical significance is not the substantive significance, so we wanted to know how much of an impact on democracy does foreign assistance have above and beyond other factors in our model. What we found is that 10 million dollars of democracy assistance increases the 13-point Freedom House index by about one-quarter of a point. Another way to assess the substantive impact of democracy programs is by comparison to the main counterfactual – the expected rate of democratization for the average country in the sample. The investment of 1 million dollars is expected to increase the typical rate of democratization by 65 percent in any given year (.026/.040).

We hasten to temper these conclusions with a dose of reality. The powerful impact of democracy aid on the growth of democracy needs to take into consideration that, although $10 million of DG assistance increased the Freedom House scores far more than the normal trend line predicts, the average country received only $2.07 million in the period 1990–2005. Thus, as we stressed in the previous section, democracy assistance is a small proportion of overall assistance, and U.S. assistance itself is small relative to the size of its economy when compared to other advanced industrial nations.

CONCLUSIONS

The results from our study are comforting for the intellectual work of this conference. We began our paper by stating that the two main questions at the conference (Should democracy be promoted? How should democracy be promoted?) would have little meaning if democracy promotion does not work. What we have found is that it does. We have found this pattern for the world as a whole, even when controlling for all other major suspected influences on the growth of democracy and on all other forms of foreign assistance. We have also found that the effect is powerful when compared to the "normal" trend line of democratic growth.

This suggests that we should indeed turn our attention to the "should" and "how" questions. Although our paper does not concern itself with either, we have a very strong bias toward answering the first question with a "yes." That is, we believe that there are a very large number of ethical reasons for preferring democracy over dictatorship, not the least of which, as noted, is the far lower probability that democracies murder their own citizens. The "how" question can also be answered, in part, with our data set, as it contains information on subsectoral democracy assistance, allowing us to look at which form of assistance (civil society, elections, rule of law, etc.) works best, and under what conditions. That analysis and discussion, however, is for a different paper.

APPENDIX 1: Growth curve model estimates

Dependent variable:	Freedom House (1–13)	
	Coefficient	Std. error
Level 1		
Democracy and Other Assistance		
USAID DG	.026**	.006
USAID Non-DG	.001	.001
Non-USAID US	.0001	.0005
Regional-Subregional DG	.010	.130
Regional-Subregional Non-DG	−.010	.014
Other Donor Assistance DG	.0004	.0004
Other Donor Assistance Non-DG	3.12E-5	5.60E-5
Economic and Political Factors		
GDP Growth Per Capita	.008**	.003
Democracy Diffusion	.237**	.088
U.S. Military Assistance Priority	−.029	.021
Extent of Political Violence	−.001**	.0004
State Failure	−.772**	.085
Level 2		
Effect on (Level-1) Intercept		
Average Intercept	6.866**	.247
Prior Democracy	.312**	.050
Pre-1990 USAID	4.77E-5	4.71E-5
Population	−3.2E-6	2.49E-6
Size in Squared Km	−3.0E-6	.0002
Income Per Capita	.097*	.052
Ethnic Fractionalization	−1.882*	1.040
Income Inequality	.052	.033
State Failure, Pre-1990	−.200	.132
Effect on (Level-1) Slope		
Average Slope for Growth Curve	.040**	.017
Prior Democracy	−.004	.003
Pre-1990 USAID	−1.9E-6	2.74E-6
Population	1.47E-7	1.50E-7
Size in Squared Km	−1.6E-5*	9.71E-6
Income Per Capita	.003	.003
Ethnic Fractionalization	.112*	.063
Income Inequality	.0004	.002
State Failure, Pre-1990	−.006	.008
Model Statistics and Variance Parameters		
Approx. Level 1 R-squared	.40	
Random Variance (Intercept)	5.955**	.939
Random Variance (Slope)	.013**	.003
Autocorrelation (rho)	.794**	
Model Deviance\AIC	6256.052	6290.052

NANCY BERMEO

Conclusion

Is Democracy Exportable?

Whether we assess the evidence from the essays in this book or from examples in the world around us, we are forced to conclude that democracy is not exportable. Export involves crafting a product in one location, finding a buyer willing to pay for it in another location, and conveying it intact. Democracy simply does not fit the metaphor. First, democracy is not a singular product, but a complex set of institutions and behaviors that can only be put in place by local individuals acting on their own accord. Second, democracy has no single local buyer. Many may seek it, but their visions of its institutional composition will vary, and many pivotal local actors may not seek democracy at all. Indeed, these actors may be willing to pay a high price to prevent democracy and, thus, make the costs of creating democracy too high even for those who desire it dearly. Finally, institutions rarely journey from one setting to another unchanged. Forms might remain the same, but content and function will vary dramatically.

The ever present problems with the export model have been exacerbated by the war in Iraq. Although, as Marc Plattner points out, attempts to establish democracy through invasion have been "exceedingly rare" (Plattner, this volume), the Iraq war is still seen by many as emblematic of the West's, or more specifically, the United States' export efforts. Export initiatives of very different types have been tainted by the Iraqi experience, as well as by the deeply problematic multilateral initiative in Afghanistan.

Even though democracy is not exportable, its prospects in any individual country can be helped (or hindered) by other countries near and far.

Note: The author thanks Joshua Woodward of Oxford University for valuable research assistance.

242

It thus makes sense to distinguish between three terms that are often used interchangeably, but which, in this essay at least, will be used to indicate different projects: 1) the *export of democracy,* meaning wholesale system transfer; 2) *democracy promotion,* meaning the ideational project of framing democracy as the best form of government; and 3) *democracy assistance,* meaning support for the various interrelated institutions and behaviors, which emerging democracies are thought to require.

Although the export of democracy has proved impossible, the spread of democracy as an idea has been impressive and democracy assistance has had some success. Using the chapters in this volume as its foundation, this essay analyzes the success and the failure of the export, promotion, and assistance projects and offers some modest proposals for how democracy might best be advanced in the future.

DEMOCRACY AS AN EXPORT

The problems with the idea of exporting democracy go far beyond those of an ill-fitting metaphor and are rooted in the complexity of democracy itself. Robert Dahl's widely accepted definition of democracy highlights no fewer than seven institutional components. According to Dahl, modern democracy is a type of regime in which: "1) Control over government decisions ... is constitutionally vested in elected officials. 2) Elected officials are chosen in frequent and fairly conducted elections. ... 3) Practically all adults have the right to vote ... 4) Practically all adults have the right to run for elective office ... 5) Citizens have the right to express themselves on political matters broadly defined, including criticism of officials ... 6) Citizens have a right to seek out alternative sources of information [which] are protected by law and 7) ... Citizens ... have a right to form relatively independent associations and organizations including political parties and interest groups ... " (Dahl 1982: 11). Constitutions, fair elections, voting rights, access to office, freedom of expression, freedom of information, and freedom of association must be rooted and reflected in local behaviors and norms to be meaningful. Because these institutions require voluntary cooperation, they cannot be imposed, even in conditions of extreme asymmetries of power. Postwar Japan exemplifies the point. Even in an occupied land laid waste by conventional and nuclear bombs and led by a Supreme Commander with a level of authority that would be unthinkable today, local institutions sometimes exercised a stubborn and even determinant resistance. The devastated nation's constitution was written in six days by a team of Americans sequestered in a Tokyo ballroom, but even the Supreme Commander who ordered the initiative recognized that the document had to be presented to the nation by Emperor Hirohito and that it "was acceptable only because it retained the throne in its transcendent splendor" (Dower 1999: 389). Context always matters.

Because "foreign involvement should be carefully tailored to the specific local conditions" (Barany, this volume) and because institutions crafted in one place can be "useless" or dysfunctional elsewhere (Chirot, this volume), the wholesale export of even one of democracy's many institutional components is likely to be highly problematic. The powerful effects of context are further illustrated by the many disastrous elections held in the wake of foreign pressure to democratize quickly. "Quick elections" imposed "by outsiders who do not know the local situation" (Chirot, this volume) are often the spark that sets long simmering struggles ablaze. The essays in this volume remind us that internationally mandated elections in Burundi led to the death of 200,000 in 1993, that the internationally sponsored referendum in East Timor provoked widespread killing and dislocation in 1999 (Chirot, this volume), and that imposed "elections can exacerbate ethnic conflict" in a wide variety of states (Moser, this volume). Likewise, internationally mandated elections in Angola, in 1992, ignited new fighting that claimed over one thousand lives daily, drove 2 million people from their homes, and brought 3 million people to the point of starvation (Pycroft 1994: 241). Even when quick elections do not trigger new violence, they may give legitimacy to violent leaders instead. Hastily imposed elections in Bosnia in 1996 were manipulated "from start to finish" by antidemocratic elites and served in the end only to "legitimize the results of ethnic cleansing" (Manning 2004: 64).

Even though the international community has learned from past mistakes and is now more likely to resist pressures to hold "instant" national elections (Reilly 2004: 117), we still see democracy being exported piecemeal and proving to be dysfunctional. For example, although the July 2006 elections in the Democratic Republic of Congo were 3 years in the making, produced a clear winner, and proceeded with only sporadic violence, 18 months later a devastating war was ravaging the country once again. Over half a billion dollars in aid and a UN peacekeeping force of 17,600 proved insufficient to compensate for the absence of the other institutions and behaviors that a peaceful democracy requires (Kaplan 2007: 299–300).

Given the violence and regime breakdown that often follow elections, it is not surprising that Mansfield and Snyder insist that a wide range of "institutional requisites" be forged "before embarking on mass political contestation" (Mansfield and Snyder, this volume). Yet, imposed grad-ualism may be as problematic as imposed elections. On what moral or practical basis can international forces restrain a people from holding elec-tions if they seek to do so? Robert Dahl highlighted the dilemma before the third wave of democratization even began, noting that the ideal, grad-ual path to polyarchy was no longer politically possible (Dahl 1971). Michael McFaul reminded us of this more recently asserting that there is "no just or practical way to ask citizens to accept disenfranchisement" (McFaul 2007: 166). The popular interest in holding elections and the many sacrifices ordinary people make to topple dictatorships and choose their own leaders highlight the popularity of democracy as an idea.

DEMOCRACY AS AN IDEA

The idea of democracy, as a general formula for governance, has undeni-ably broad appeal. Guillermo O'Donnell is right to assert that democracy "has won the war of ideas nearly worldwide" (O'Donnell 2007: 7). This victory derives, in part, from deliberate attempts to promote democracy as a good and even grand idea. In this narrow sense, democracy promo-tion appears to have been extremely successful. Marc Plattner's assertion that "democracy is the only political system with a plausible claim to uni-versal legitimacy" (Plattner, this volume), is sustained by evidence from public opinion polls and by the language, if not always the behavior, of international actors and domestic elites.

POPULAR VIEWS OF DEMOCRACY

There is no alternative mode of political organization that approaches democracy in its appeal across regions. Recent cross-national research on thirteen post-communist states found that democracy was "favored by 82% of those surveyed with only 7% favoring dictatorship and 11% favoring something between the two" (Rose 2007: 113). Despite high lev-els of distrust toward politicians and political parties, levels of support for nondemocratic forms of governance are extremely low. Ninety percent of post-communist citizens reject the idea of military government and 80% reject a return to communism. In the Czech Republic, Hungary, Slovakia, Slovenia and Romania, more than 75% reject strongman rule. In the ten new European Union (EU) member states, over two-thirds of the citi-zenry reject all three alternatives to democracy (Rose 2007: 114-5).

Despite the poor performance of many new democracies in Africa, the largest and most recent public opinion survey of the continent found that a solid 61% of citizens interviewed prefer democracy to any other form of government. Respondents who were most familiar with how the concept was defined in the West supported democracy at a rate of 75% (Bratton 2007: 100). The high level of support for democracy in Africa is not a function of widespread misunderstanding of what democracy involves. Africans were, for the most part, well aware of the shortcomings of their own political systems and the gulf between the real and the ideal. Michael Bratton's research shows a remarkable match between popular and expert perceptions of democracy in specific African states (Bratton 2007: 104). Just as important, Africans reject other forms of rule by wide margins. Nearly three-quarters reject military rule, and on average, 71% reject one-party rule. An impressive 78% reject one-man rule. Over half of the people surveyed rejected all three alternatives (Bratton 2007: 102).

The three alternatives to democracy were rejected by over half of the respondents in the latest Asian Barometer polls as well. The percentage of citizens rejecting military rule was over 81%. Those rejecting one party rule numbered 76% and those rejecting strongman rule numbered 65%.[1] More than half of those interviewed agreed that democracy was "always preferable to any other kind of government," and 85% of respondents agreed that a democratic government in their country was desirable (Chang et al. 2007: 70–73). Recent survey research in the People's Republic of China reveals surprisingly similar findings – especially among younger cohorts (Wang 2007).

In Latin America, the most recent cross-national survey data reveal that 72% of the citizenry believe that democracy is the "best system of government" (Latinobarometro 2007: 80). Those who see little difference between authoritarianism and democracy number only 20% (down slightly from a high point of 23% in 2003) and only 17% believe that authoritarian government is ever justifiable (Latinobarometro 2007: 79–81).

In the Arab world, support for democracy is also surprisingly high. Whether we consider the results of the World Values Survey of 1999–2002 or National Science Foundation surveys in 2003 and 2004, the percentage of Arabs believing that democracy is "superior to other political systems" is consistently well above 80% and often in the 90% range. Contrary to what some might expect, support for democracy in Arab countries "does not vary as a function of gender, education and age" (Tessler and

---

[1] These figures are the average of the percentages for Taiwan, South Korea, the Philippines, Thailand, and Mongolia. Japan's results were 65% against strongman leadership, 67% against single party rule, and 95% against military rule (Chang et al. 2007: 73).

Gao 2005: 8). "Citizens who do not support democracy are relatively few in number and are . . . divided roughly equally between secular and religious authoritarians" (Tessler and Gao 2005: 92). In the Muslim world as a whole, a 2007 poll of over 6,000 respondents found that support for democracy was "in the 80% range" in countries as diverse as Indonesia, Jordan, Lebanon, and Morocco, and support for Al Qaeda has dropped in recent years (Pew Global Attitudes Project). Despite decades of anti-democratic Islamist mobilization, a full two-thirds of the world's more than one billion Muslims now live under democratically elected governments (Ibrahim 2007: 6). Survey data from a wide variety of sources suggest that popular support for democracy is strong in every region of the world. (McFaul 2004–05: 152).

DEMOCRACY – INTERNATIONAL ORGANIZATIONS AND GOVERNMENT AGENCIES

The popularity of democracy with ordinary citizens is matched by its status with international organizations and government agencies of varied sorts. As Michael McFaul notes, democracy promotion has become "entrenched" in institutional life across the globe and will thus be a part of the political landscape for some time (McFaul 2004–05: 152). Even though the National Endowment for Democracy was controversial at its founding, organizations that dedicate resources to promoting the values and institutions of democracy have now proliferated throughout the world (Plattner, this volume). The United States and the EU now spend $1.5 billion on democracy assistance annually (McFaul 2007: 47). European countries now devote substantially more funds to democracy promotion than the United States does, and the EU is but one of the many European actors devoting substantial resources to the democracy project. The Organization for Security and Co-operation in Europe is active in democracy assistance in seventeen countries, and spent over 162 million Euro in 2006 alone (Boonstra 2007: 14). Latin American countries in the OAS are officially committed to "promote and consolidate representative democracy" and to defend democracies that appear to be challenged by antidemocratic, extra-legal actors (McFaul 2004: 156–7). The African Union's Constitutive Act commits member states to "respect for democratic principles, human rights, the rule of law and good governance" as well as the "condemnation and rejection of unconstitutional changes of governments" (African Union 2001). The Association of South East Asian Nations (ASEAN) signed a Democracy Charter in December 2005, promising to "strengthen democratic institutions" where they exist and to promote "democracy, human rights . . . transparency and good governance" throughout the region (ASEAN 2005). The United Nations now devotes a great many resources to democracy promotion through new agencies and through new emphases in older programs. Its documents now frame democracy as "essential" to human development (UNDP 2002: 3). The emphasis that the World Bank and the International Monetary Fund now give to good governance is part of this world-wide trend.

Stimulated by the vision that "the advancement of human rights and democracy" constitutes "the bedrock of [the] war on terrorism" (Dobriansky 2001), the United States now has democracy promotion programs in government agencies of all sorts. The 2002 National Security Strategy vowed that "nations moving towards democracy" would be "rewarded for the steps they take," with increased foreign aid (Windsor 2003: 52). President George W. Bush promised that the Millenium Challenge Account will provide up to $5 billion annually to countries that "rule justly" (Windsor 2003: 51). The thinking behind these initiatives helps explain why U.S. spending on democracy assistance increased from $128 million in 1990 to $902 million in 2005 (Seligson et al., this volume). Zoltan Barany's essay teaches us that the formal commitment to democracy has even extended to the U.S. military. Given that the U.S. military was often used to support right-wing dictatorships in the past, it is remarkable that officials from the U.S. Southern Command now see their mission as one of "strengthening democratic institutions" (Barany, this volume).

The success of democracy as an idea is illustrated further in John Carey's work on constitutions. Whereas 76% of the constitutions written between 1789 and 2005 mentioned democracy, a full 94% of the constitutions written between 1990 and 2005 used the term (Carey, this volume). Of course, as Carey states clearly, constitutions are often ignored, but even the act of pretending to be democratic is significant, and the fact that signals have changed over time is not without meaning. Guillermo O'Donnell put it eloquently, "Being democratic or claiming to be is like a currency: credibly holding it adds political capital" (O'Donnell 2007: 6).

Ironically, the triumph of democracy as an idea might best be illustrated by the nature of the political elites who pay lip service to democracy's merits and by the many leaders who feel compelled to hold elections even as they refuse to expose themselves to fully open competition. Premier Wen Jiaobao of China provided powerful evidence of democracy's ideational victory at a press conference following the closing session of the National People's Congress in March, 2007. As if wishing to appropriate what now seems a nearly hegemonic vision of how polities should be organized, Wen stated, "Democracy, law, freedom, human rights, equality and fraternity are not characteristics unique to capitalism. They are the shared fruits of civilization that have come into being in the history of the whole world..." He then went on argue that the advance of a market-oriented economic system should "guarantee people's rights to democratic elections, democratic decision-making, democratic management and democratic supervision" (Wen as quoted in Yang 2007: 61). These words seem to justify Nodia's claim that democracy has become "synonymous with civilization itself" (Plattner, this volume). In any case, they suggest that even "China's ruling elite has no alternative to the global discourse on liberty and democracy" (Yang 2007: 62).

A surprising range of political leaders now seem to believe they have no alternative to elections as a means of legitimating power and, occasionally, policy changes. The flawed elections that plague so many third and fourth wave democracies show the inadequacy of the "export" project, but they also provide perverse proof that the promotion of democracy as an idea has been triumphant.

As Robert Moser reminds us, "elections bestow legitimacy both domestically and internationally" (Moser, this volume); and, currently, *only* elections can perform this role. This is because alternative, global formulas for legitimacy are lacking. "Illiberal democracies" use "elections to legitimize autocracy" precisely because autocrats feel they need this form of legitimization (Chirot, this volume). "Today, as never before," authoritarian rulers render "tribute to virtue by implicitly acknowledging the principle of popular sovereignty" (O'Donnell 2007: 7). This was not always the case.

CAUSE FOR CAUTION

The popularity of democracy among ordinary people throughout the world, the embrace of democracy by international organizations, and the near ubiquity of democratic discourse and signaling among political leaders of varied sorts all testify to the victory of democracy as an idea. Yet, there are reasons to be cautious about the worldwide embrace of democracy and, thus, about democracy promotion's success. First, democracy's popularity is at least partially the result of its multiple meanings. Its advocates have different referents, different expectations, and thus different reactions when and if a regime that calls itself a democracy comes into being. In formerly communist regimes in Eastern Europe, for example, "democracy means...the freedom to do and say what you want; the choice of government by competitive elections; and a welfare state" (Rose 2007: 113). The idea that democracy involves a welfare state is not universally held, but its salience in popular understanding of the term in formerly communist regimes affects citizens' evaluation of regime performance.

A second reason to be cautious about the promotion project is that currently high levels of support for democracy among ordinary citizens may be eroding. The most recent Asian Barometer Survey found that "every indicator of average support for democracy showed a decline" between 2001 and 2006 (Chang et al. 2007: 71). Even though "nearly everyone embraces democracy as an abstract idea,...significantly fewer endorse it as their preferred form of government under all circumstances" and fewer still said that they would "prefer democracy to economic development" if forced to choose between the two (Chang et al. 2007: 72).

In some Latin American countries, populism seems to be posing a challenge to liberal democracy among certain social sectors. A 2006 *AmericasBarometer* survey tapped citizens' support for populism by surveying their willingness to back five measures that would strengthen the power of presidents at the expense of other democratic institutions and the separation of powers more generally. Although over a third of respondents refused to accept any populist measures at all, almost two-thirds were willing to accept at least one such measure and nearly half were willing to accept two measures. Populist sentiment proved to be significantly higher among the "poorer and less educated" and among younger respondents. Even after controlling for wealth and education, younger respondents were significantly more likely to back "populist measures at the expense of liberal democracy" (Seligson 2007: 90). If these attitudes are lasting, they may have serious consequences when this younger cohort constitutes a larger portion of the voting public.

The specter of populism seems to be haunting Central and Eastern Europe as well, where knowledgeable observers write of a "populist backlash" bringing "potentially dangerous outbursts against...liberal-democratic constitutionalism" (Rupnik 2007: 20–24). An extensive 2007 study of twenty-nine post-communist countries and territories in Central Europe and Eurasia concludes that "populism and anti-liberal trends are on the rise" (Freedom House 2007). The saving grace in Eastern Europe and Latin America is that populism means many things. For some, "populism is anti-liberal but not anti-democratic" (Krastev 2007: 60); for others, it is fully compatible with democracy (Schmitter 2006), but for many regional specialists, there is a sense that "democratic improvements have been slowed" by rising populist tendencies among the citizenry (Bútora 2007: 55).

The rising profile of "authoritarian capitalism" in Russia and China provides a third cause for concern about the lasting hegemony of the democratic idea. The capacity of both systems to project an image that combines extraordinary economic dynamism with uncompromised nationalism is appealing to citizens who seek to improve their standard of living, but feel threatened by a liberalized global market politically dominated by Western democracies. Putin's insistence that outsiders have no right to judge his "sovereign democracy" (Sestanovich 2007: 124) allows him to put a patriotic and attractive frame around authoritarianism. These trends have led Thomas Carothers to conclude that we can "no longer assume a consensus about the pre-eminence of democracy among the main geo-strategic actors in the world" and that we must thus "return to the challenge of engaging in global debates over the very value of democracy itself" (Carothers 2007: 115).

The final reason to be cautious about the success of the ideational project is that democracy's current appeal has probably resulted less from deliberate attempts at promotion by governments than from how democracy itself has been seen (and imagined) to work in actual states. It is not coincidental that Thomas Pangle begins his essay with the observation that democracy is "proliferating *itself*" with breathtaking energy (Pangle, this volume) or that Athenian democracy was spread, not simply through force, but "by its own exemplary excellence." Since Athenian times, even subject peoples have been able, to "learn what human flourishing is" through observing (or imagining) the workings of someone else's political system (Pangle, this volume). This is what Ghia Nodia refers to when he argues that democracy spreads through "imitation" (Plattner, this volume) – a process very different from imposition.

With globalized media, the capacities for observation, learning, and imitation are at a new high. Yet, because the free media do not focus on "human flourishing" alone, this heightened capacity carries two serious disadvantages for those who wish to promote the idea of democracy as a superior form of government. Outsiders get to see not just the good, but the bad and, at times, even the ugly. The image and credibility of U.S. democracy have been gravely damaged by a number of highly publicized incidents in recent years, including the heated controversy over the fairness of the 2000 presidential elections, the debate over the Guantanamo detention camps, the debacle following Hurricane Katrina, and the horrific scenes of abuse in Abu Ghraib. These incidents, plus other vivid media images of human suffering in Iraq, may help explain why the 2007 Pew Global Attitudes Project found that over 80% of Turks and 70% of Pakistanis actively "disliked"..."American ideas about democracy" (Traub 2007: 19). Attitudes in a number of Western countries were hardly better. In France, the comparable percentage was 76%. In Argentina and Brazil, the percentage of citizens disliking American ideas about democracy was a full 67%. If, as M. Steven Fish argues, the success of democracy promotion depends on a people's "disposition toward the democratizers," the efforts of U.S. democracy promoters have been seriously compromised by these well documented deviations from the democratic ideal.

Thus, there are several reasons to avoid complacency regarding the successful emergence of democracy as an idea, but they do not add up to an argument for abandoning the ideational project. These notes of caution do not add up to an argument against the more concrete and conscious project of democracy assistance either. They merely make the assistance project more difficult. How might the lessons of past efforts inform future assistance policies?

DEMOCRACY ASSISTANCE

The answer to the question posed above should vary according to the country or countries crafting the assistance policies both because local perceptions of outside actors are highly consequential (Fish, this volume) and because the success of each country's policies in one realm may be affected by its policies in another. Accordingly, the analysis below focuses on the policies of the United States, in particular; although, some of the arguments advanced may be of general applicability.

Despite diversity in focus and method, the essays in this volume offer several consistent themes relevant to the crafting of democracy assistance. Each essay points to serious challenges and pitfalls, but none concludes that democracy assistance is useless or impossible. The chapter by Seligson, Finkel, and Pérez-Liñán suggests that, despite various inadequacies, the financial resources dedicated to U.S. democracy assistance programs have had positive effects. The finding that "1 million dollars in democracy aid is expected to increase the typical rate of democratization by 65% in any given year" is a significant antidote to despair about the utility of the assistance effort (Seligson et al., this volume). In keeping with this theme,

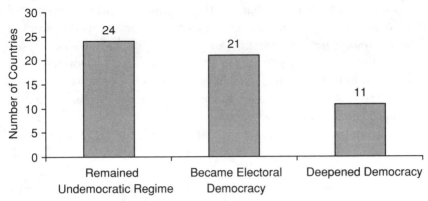

Figure C.1: The magnitude of positive political change in aid recipients (1991–2003).

an overview of political change in countries receiving U.S. Democracy Assistance between 1991 and 2003 shows that of the 98 countries receiving at least 1 year of DG aid, 58% became more democratic, 19% became less democratic and 23% stayed the same. (The measures of change are Polity Scores from the Seligson et al. dataset with a score of 6 representing the threshold for an electoral democracy.)

These figures tell us nothing about causality, of course, but they do show that well over half of the countries receiving democracy assistance actually experienced positive political change in the period under study. Figure C.1 shows that 24 of the 56 countries experiencing positive change remained authoritarian, 21 became new electoral democracies, and 11 improved the quality of an already democratic regime.[2] Coupled with the causal argument presented by Seligson et al., these figures suggest that democracy assistance is sometimes effective. But, how can the assistance project be improved? The essays in this collection suggest several lessons regarding whom to work with, what to do and what to avoid.

WHO?

Working with existing elites is essential to the success of democracy assistance. As Seligman reminds us, local elites "are the carriers of ideological

---

[2] If a country finished <6 = Remained Undemocratic; If a country started <6 and became >6 = Electoral Democracy; If a country started >6 and finished >8 = Deepened Democracy.

programs" in any society (Seligman, this volume). Ignoring them invites trouble even if they are the carriers of ideological programs that seem to have no democratic components. Although the abstract idea of democracy has become widely popular, its "protean" essence (O'Donnell 2007: 6) means that its constituency diverges widely in its concepts of self and thus in the embrace of the individualism that lies at the foundation of the liberal form of democracy described by Pangle. Seligman's focus on non-Western societies reminds us that the agents of democracy assistance often work where individuals do not see themselves as singular, "self-defining moral agents" but primarily as members of ascriptive groups instead. Where and when group-based identities trump individual ones, the future will be shaped, in large part, by group leaders enjoying traditional legitimacy. If these elites are somehow integrated in the new order, it just might last.

The focus on local elites is justified even when traditional authority and legitimacy are not at play. Mansfield and Snyder remind us that trouble may ensue when elites of any sort are "threatened by democratization" and thus that democracy will be advanced if its proponents "find ways to safeguard" the interests of "powerful spoilers" (this volume).

Chirot, writing of divided societies in general, also has a strong message about the need to focus on elites. He argues that elites of various communities have to be assured that they will not "lose their property, their local power or opportunity to gain from being part of the state" (this volume). He also recommends a special focus on younger and better educated elites arguing that they must "be given substantial reasons to participate," presumably to prevent them from directing their mobilizational resources to the antidemocratic projects discussed by Sheri Berman. The need to work with local elites extends even to the military and police. Because basic security must be maintained for democracy to proceed, Barany advocates "working at least temporarily with existing [military] personnel" (this volume).

The emphasis on inclusion that emerges in other essays reinforces the need to think broadly when crafting assistance programs. As Moser reminds us, outlawing certain types of political parties risks making democracy assistance itself seem antidemocratic. When parties are outlawed, international actors are especially likely to be blamed (Moser, this volume). Thus, the U.S. should take care to distance itself from party banning and to advocate inclusive party laws.

U.S. assistance programs should also encourage inclusive processes for the crafting of constitutions; although, on these occasions, elected elites

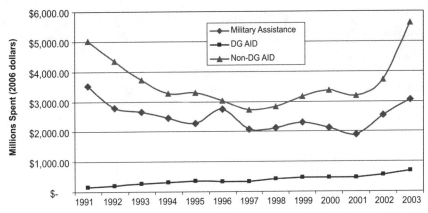

Figure C.2: USAID: Military assistance, democratic promotion, & non-DG AID (1991–2003).

seem to carry the most weight. Carey's finding that "the number of democratically elected actors" included in the promulgation process contributes to "higher levels of subsequent democracy," "greater constraints on government," and increased "constitutional stability," provides additional evidence that inclusion yields rewards (this volume). Inclusion can of course, lead to delay and deadlock, but the risks of exclusion may be even greater. As Chirot puts it, "excluding local ... elites as part of democratization is a prescription for disaster" (this volume).

WHAT TO DO?

This brief essay is not the place to present detailed policy proposals and these should be tailored to individual countries in any case. But, the chapters in this volume do highlight certain prescriptive themes.

One of the most powerful themes is that the success of democracy assistance depends on state capacity. Because democracy involves a formula for governmental institutions rather than state institutions, this dependence is not always obvious, but its implications are great. Zoltan Barany's essay underscores the importance of the state's coercive capacity. Democracy's fundamental institutions, including free elections, freedom of assembly, and freedom of speech each depend on the capacity of the police and armed forces to provide order and contribute to the rule of law. U.S. military assistance dwarfs U.S. democracy assistance, as Figure C.2 illustrates, but because the two initiatives are not coordinated, the former may often undercut the latter.

Table C.1: U.S. military aid to autocracies, 1991–2003
(millions of 2006 dollars)

Algeria	2.3	Oman	132.8
Angola	3.0	Pakistan	623.8
Azerbaijan	14.0	Rwanda	100.7
Belarus	1.1	Somalia	37.6
Cambodia	7.9	Swaziland	1.5
Cameroon	4.5	Tajikistan	4.9
Cote d'Ivoire	7.4	Togo	0.7
Egypt	20,965.9	Tunisia	157.5
Guinea	7.2	Turkmenistan	7.3
Haiti	24.4	Uzbekistan	66.0
Iraq	177.5	Vietnam	3.7
Kazakhstan	26.0	Zimbabwe	6.7
Nepal	24.5		

Note: Autocracies are regimes designated as Not Free by Freedom House in 2006.

The impact of assistance for civic groups, political parties or independent media is inevitably diminished by military aid that supports the rule of authoritarians rather than the rule of law. If military aid is used to professionalize the armed forces and to build the coercive capacity of a democratic state, its effects are positive. Yet, as Table C.1 illustrates, the U.S. sends millions of dollars in military aid to authoritarian regimes as well. Saad Eddin Ibrahim, one of Egypt's leading dissidents, recently suggested that an effective "way of helping Arab democrats would be...to stop sending so much help to autocrats" (Ibrahim 2007: 13). Those who are struggling to improve U.S. democracy assistance should keep this advice in mind, for it is applicable throughout the world.

Weak state capacity in civilian institutions may also compromise democracy and democratic assistance programs. Mansfield and Snyder show that new democracies with weak state institutions risk both war and economic failure. Where institutions are too weak "to manage political activity," bellicose "nationalism" will "fill the gap," and elites will be forced to engage in protectionism and a whole range of policies that impede trade and growth (this volume). Chirot draws our attention to the need for state capacity to provide effective legal protection for property. He writes that the "absence of stable property relations," in a context of scarce resources, makes the mitigation of conflict in a formal democracy "most unlikely" (this volume). Barany also argues for strengthened institutional capacity in his discussion of armed forces reform, reminding us that there "can be no robust civilian oversight without strong political institutions" (this volume).

Sheri Berman highlights the profoundly consequential connections between state institutions, political institutions, and civil society. The lesson from her argument is that assistance to civil society may be counterproductive if state and political institutions are dysfunctional. Strong civil societies do not always work in the interest of democracy. They may even undermine the fragile social and political contract that often undergirds newly democratic regimes. In a context where the state has poor capacity to provide services and justice, civil society organizations may fill the breach and thus erode what little state capacity and authority exists. In a context where parties are weak, civil society may harm democracy by siphoning off the talent and energy needed by parties themselves. Even in a highly problematic political order, civil society may function "in the service of something much worse" (Berman, this volume). Assistance efforts that privilege civil society over political society and state capacity-building may well be misguided. Democratic associational life is an asset for polyarchy, but not all associational life is democratic, and even seemingly neutral associations can be manipulated by authoritarian forces. Seligman's message reinforces this point. He cautions us to "be aware of the particularistic assumptions we bring to the idea of civil society before attempting to promote its virtues throughout the world" (this volume).

Much assistance to civil society has no doubt been well spent. It helps explain why there appears to be some association between the funds spent on democracy assistance and democratization itself. Yet, if the arguments in this volume are correct, efforts to strengthen state capacity and to "build strong parties with staying power and robust linkages to key social constituencies" should take priority (Moser, this volume). Given the United States' tarnished image abroad, its ability to assist political parties may be limited. Actors who are convinced they have a political future on their own merits may not want to risk association with the United States. As a consequence, aid will go disproportionately to "bit players" (Fish, this volume).

Thus, for the United States, democracy assistance that builds state capacity through investment in governance and rule of law programs should be prioritized. Unfortunately, these programs have not been the top assistance priorities in the past. Between 1990 and 2005, only 29% of assistance funds went to governance programs and only 19% of assistance funds went to rule of law programs. Nearly 40% of assistance funds went to civil society programs instead (Seligson et al., this volume). Priorities may be changing, however. A shift in spending from civil society to governance emerged in 2003 (Seligson et al., this volume). This shift may be the result of new restrictions on NGOs imposed by authoritarian leaders following Putin's lead (Gershman and Allen 2006). Yet, if the arguments in this volume are correct, the shift may have positive effects.

WHAT TO AVOID

Positive effects are also more likely if the U.S. avoids at least some of the pitfalls which have hampered the success of democracy assistance in the past. It is essential, for example, that the U.S. refrain from sending signals that democracy is dispensable. Even the most carefully crafted democracy assistance programs are compromised when the U.S. refuses to work with parties who win popular support in free elections. The U.S. reactions to the electoral victories of Hezbollah in Lebanon and Hamas in the Palestinian Authority were seen by many as proof that U.S. support for democracy was false. Coming on the heels of the invasion of Iraq, the U.S. reaction fed cynicism, especially in the Middle East.

U.S. support for the outright ouster of leaders who come to power through the polls is similarly harmful. When the Bush administration openly supported the coup against Hugo Chavez in April 2002, and expressed its willingness to work with a junta that had clearly violated the Venezuelan constitution, it sent a signal that U.S. support for democracy was conditional (Coppedge 2007: 36–38). When Thailand's military ousted Thaksin Shinawatra in 2006, the U.S. sent a signal that its support for democracy was lukewarm. The U.S. complied with existing legislation and suspended $24 million in military aid, but it did not signal opposition to a coup when the move was being planned (Wall Street Journal 2006) and, after the event, the administration's condemnation of the military's action was measured. Indeed, United Nations Ambassador John Bolton spoke of the coup in language reminiscent of the Cold War saying, "We think it important that there be peace in the streets and that their constitution be upheld" (CNN 2006). Signals that democracy can be sacrificed in the interests of "peace in the streets" or in the interests of one set of actors over another undercut the credibility of U.S. democratization efforts. U.S. policymakers should avoid sending them.

U.S. policy-makers should also avoid divorcing programs for democracy assistance from programs for economic development. Scores of studies have shown that economic development boosts both the impulse to democratize and the likelihood of democratic consolidation. The essays in this volume reinforce the theme. Economic growth truly is "vital," as Chirot puts it, and its slowdown in places such as Egypt does, in fact, help account for the rise of extremist groups (Berman, Chirot, and Seligson et al., this volume; Wickham 2002). Yet, currently, U.S. efforts to assist democracy and U.S. efforts to shape economic policy often work at cross purposes. U.S. support for neo-liberal economic reforms has left legacies that undercut the political reforms that democracy assistance promotes. These legacies are apparent within the state and within society.

Within the state, an emphasis on economic liberalization undercuts the very institutions democracy assistance programs seek to strengthen. Economic liberalization programs encourage strong executives who can take tough decisions on technocratic grounds and ignore the pressures of parties, legislatures, and interest groups. Democracy assistance programs seek to strengthen the very institutions neo-liberal reformers often seek to avoid. Strengthening parties, legislatures, and civic groups ranks high among the goals of democracy assistance programs, yet, strengthening these institutions is made difficult by an economic model that privileges technocratic decision-making and executive autonomy. Despite millions of dollars of aid and great effort, political parties, legislatures, and civic groups remain notoriously weak in most new democracies. The fact that our hegemonic economic model privileges executive autonomy helps explain why.

The mismatch between economic development programs and democracy assistance programs also has societal effects that detract from the democratic project. The neo-liberal economic model has boosted economic growth in some countries, but it has also left two legacies that hamper democratic development. The first legacy is a heightened level of perceived economic inequality. Poor citizens who feel left out of the emerging global economy often turn away from politics altogether, focusing instead on the daily struggle to meet basic needs. Impoverished citizens who become politically mobilized often develop an understandable thirst for immediate redistribution. Both of these reactions hamper the advance of the liberal democracy the U.S. wishes to promote. Apathy undermines the possibilities of representation and accountability while hyper-mobilization undermines the possibilities for compromise and contributes to polarization.

A growing (and accurate) awareness that foreign forces of all sorts play a determinant role in national policy making complicates the task of democracy assistance even further. This second legacy of the neo-liberal development model stimulates calls for increased national autonomy – calls that make even well-intentioned U.S. assistance initiatives seem suspect. Combined with the often accurate perception that legislatures and mainstream political parties are impotent, the double drive for the immediate redress of inequalities and increased national autonomy produces a fertile environment for populism. It is not coincidental that Hugo Chavez, Thaksin Shinawatra, Evo Morales, Juan Correa, and other populists derive their popularity from sectors of society that have not seen the benefits of neo-liberal reforms. Nor is it coincidental that all of these leaders make nationalist appeals that color popular perceptions of U.S. democracy assistance programs.

Because the U.S. commitment to the neo-liberal growth model is likely to remain unchanged in the foreseeable future, it falls to the proponents of democracy assistance to shape policies that will compensate for the negative legacies summarized above. Figure C.3 illustrates that these compensatory policies are needed immediately.

Most of the new democracies emerging since 1991 are desperately poor, and very few of these new democracies have enjoyed any substantial increase in GDP per capita in the past 15 years. These new regimes are democracies against the odds. They lack both the institutional and the class structures that have been associated with the democratization of polities in the past. The fact that they have emerged at all is a tribute to the success of democracy as an idea. Yet, if the essays in this volume (and the consensus in the larger literature) are correct, the consolidation of democracy in these states will be extremely difficult if not impossible. If the U.S. is sincere in its determination to assist these democracies, its assistance programs must compensate for the negative legacies of neo-liberalism. They must also be coordinated with economic aid programs that actually boost growth. The meager resources devoted to democracy assistance at the current time are woefully inadequate for these tasks. Budgetary allocation priorities must be changed.

The functionalist arguments used to defend democracy assistance must also be changed for these are also counter-productive. Framing democracy assistance as a weapon in the U.S. war on terror is highly problematic. To begin with, there is little evidence that democracy provides immunity from terrorism. On the contrary, the long histories of the ETA in Spain, the IRA in Britain, the New People's Army in the Philippines, and the Tamil Tigers in Sri Lanka lead us to the opposite conclusion. Even though the key figures in the September 11 bombings came from

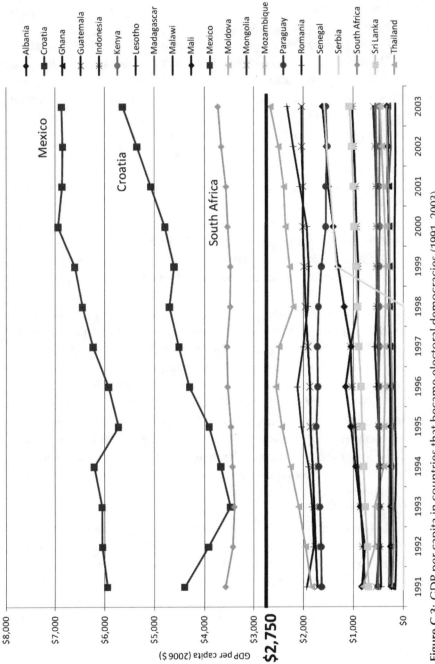

Figure C.3: GDP per capita in countries that became electoral democracies (1991–2003).

261

authoritarian regimes, the actors behind the terrorist bombings in Spain and Britain resided in democracies.

Framing democracy assistance as a weapon to protect the U.S. against terrorism implies a selective reading of history, but because this frame is blatantly self-serving it also implies a misreading of the assistance audience. It suggests that democracy is not being advanced because it is a good in itself, or because it will benefit the countries involved, but because it serves the interest of a super-power. This utilitarian argument may be functional in the U.S. Congress, but abroad, it only hampers U.S. assistance efforts by legitimating skepticism.

The functionalist message that democracy will bring peace (and not simply an end to terrorism) also requires some rethinking. The problem with this message is not that it is self-serving but that it is unrealistic. The evidence that consolidated democracies do not go to war with one another is copious (Doyle 1986), but the regimes receiving democracy assistance are not consolidated democracies. In fact, they may not be democracies at all. The essays in this volume illustrate that the early phases of regime change are very likely to be tumultuous. Mansfield and Snyder argue that inchoate democracies will often be bellicose. Chirot and Berman argue that violence is an integral part of the state-building process that successful democratization requires. Recent quantitative research suggests that in poor countries democracy actually *increases* the likelihood of internal political violence. Poor democracies do not have the state capacity to preempt rebellion, and once rebellion breaks out, they are constrained in their techniques of suppression by the institutions of democracy itself. Even though democracy is "peace-promoting at higher levels of income," democracy actually increases the likelihood of armed rebellion in countries below a threshold of $2,750 per capita GDP (Collier and Rohner 2007: 2–4). All but three of the electoral democracies that have emerged since 1991 are situated in economies that fall below this threshold (see Figure C.3). Not surprisingly, many are suffering from high levels of political violence, and some have already drifted back into authoritarianism. It is essential that U.S. democracy assistance programs be designed with these harsh realities in mind. Strategies that secure peace must become a top priority in democracy assistance programs (Collier and Rohner 2007: 3). These strategies must involve the creation of democratic armies, as Barany points out, but they must also include the strengthening of a wide range of civilian institutions responsible for the rule of law. Establishing lawful democracies has historically required "generations of hard work" (Chirot, this volume), and there is no reason to expect the process to move more swiftly today. In any case, the moving forces behind the establishment of lawful democracies must be local. The United States and other foreign actors must walk the thin line between assistance and interference. They must also debunk functionalist myths about what democracy will bring. Because democracy's effects will always vary across contexts and across time, democracy must be embraced for what it is, and not for what it does.

Bibliography

Absalom, Roger. 1995. *Italy Since 1800: A Nation in the Balance?* New York: Longman.

African Elections Database. 2007 <http://africanelections.tripod.com/>.

African Union. 2007. Meeting of the Draft African Charter on Democracy, Elections and Governance and on the Lomé Declaration, April 6–7 <www.africa-union.org/root/au/conferences/past/2006/april/pa/apr7/meeting.htm>.

Agüero, Felipe. 1995. *Soldiers, Civilians, and Democracy: Post-Franco Spain in Comparative Perspective.* Baltimore, MD: Johns Hopkins University Press.

Agüero, Felipe. 2002. "A Political Army in Chile: Historical Assessment and Prospects for the New Democracy." In Kees Koonings and Dirk Kruijt, eds., *Political Armies: The Military and Nation Building in the Age of Democracy.* New York: Zed Books.

Agulhon, Maurice. 1995. *The French Republic 1879–1992.* Trans. Antonia Nevill. Cambridge, MA: Blackwell.

Ajami, Fouad. 1986. *The Vanished Imam: Musa Sadr and the Shia of Lebanon.* Ithaca, NY: Cornell University Press.

Ajami, Fouad. 1995. "The Sorrows of Egypt." *Foreign Affairs* 74: 72–88.

Alesina, Alberto. 1991. "Comment." In Rudiger Dornbusch and Sebastian Edwards, eds., *The Macroeconomics of Populism in Latin America.* Chicago: University of Chicago Press.

Alfonsín, Raúl. 1995. "The Transition toward Democracy in a Developing Country: The Case of Argentina." In Daniel N. Nelson, ed., *After Authoritarianism: Democracy or Disorder?* Westport, CT: Greenwood Publishing Group, Inc.

Allison, Graham T., Jr., and Robert P. Beschel. 1992. "Can the United States Promote Democracy?" *Political Science Quarterly* 107: 81–89.

Almond, Gabriel, and Sidney Verba. 1963. *The Civic Culture.* Princeton, NJ: Princeton University Press.

Al-Sayyid, Mustapha. 1995. "A Civil Society in Egypt?" In Augustus Richard Norton, ed., *Civil Society in the Middle East.* New York: E. J. Brill.

Anderson, Benedict. 1991. *Imagined Communities.* London: Verso.

Anderson, Olive. 1967. *A Liberal State at War.* London: Macmillan.

Anglin, Douglas G. 1998. "International Election Monitoring: The African Experience." *African Affairs* 97: 471–495.

Arceneaux, Craig L. 2001. *Bounded Missions: Military Regimes and Democratization in the Southern Cone and Brazil.* University Park: Pennsylvania State University Press.

Arendt, Hannah. 1958. *On the Human Condition.* Chicago: University of Chicago Press.

Arendt, Hannah. 1973. *The Origins of Totalitarianism.* New York: Harcourt Brace Jovanovich.

Bagehot, Walter, and Norman St. John-Stevas. 1965. *Bagehot's Historical Essays.* Garden City, NY: Anchor.

Balibar, Etienne, and Immanuel Wallerstein. 1991. *Race, Nation, Class: Ambiguous Identities.* London: Verso.

Balze, Felipe A. M. de la 1995. *Remaking the Argentine Economy.* New York: Council on Foreign Relations.

Banac, Ivo. 1984. *The National Question in Yugoslavia.* Ithaca, NY: Cornell University Press.

Banti, Alberto Mario. 2000. "Public Opinion and Associations in Nineteenth Century Italy." In Nancy Bermeo and Philip Nord, eds., *Civil Society Before Democracy: Lessons from Nineteenth-Century Europe.* New York: Rowan and Littlefield.

Banting, Keith, and Richard Simeon. 1983. "Federalism, Democracy, and the Constitution." In Keith Banting and Richard Simeon, eds., *And No One Cheered: Federalism, Democracy, and the Constitution Act.* Toronto: Methuen.

Barany, Zoltan. 1997. "Democratic Consolidation and the Military." *Comparative Politics* 30: 21–44.

Barany, Zoltan. 2003. *The Future of NATO Expansion: Four Case Studies.* New York: Cambridge University Press.

Barany, Zoltan. 2006. "NATO's Post-Cold War Metamorphosis: From 16 to 26 and Counting." *International Studies Review* 8: 165–178.

Barany, Zoltan. 2007. *Democratic Breakdown and the Decline of the Russian Military.* Princeton, NJ: Princeton University Press.

Barany, Zoltan. 2008. "Civil-Military Relations and Institutional Decay: Explaining Russian Military Politics." *Europe-Asia Studies* 60: 581–605.

Barany, Zoltan, and Lawrence S. Graham. 1994. *Democratic Transitions and Civil-Military Relations: Comparing Eastern and Southern Europe.* Grant report prepared for NATO.

Barber, Benjamin. 1973. *The Death of Communal Liberty: A History of Freedom in a Swiss Mountain Canton.* Princeton, NJ: Princeton University Press.

Barkan, Joel. 1995. "Elections in Agrarian Societies." *Journal of Democracy* 6: 106–116.

Barkey, Karen, and Mark Von Hagen. 1997. *After Empire: Multiethnic Societies and Nation-Building.* Boulder, CO: Westview Press.

Bartholomeusz, Tessa J., and Chandra R. De Silva, eds. 1998. *Buddhist Fundamentalism and Minority Identities in Sri Lanka.* New York: State University of New York Press.

Bayat, Asef. 1998. "Revolution without Movement, Movement without Revolution: Comparing Islamic Activism in Iran and Egypt." *Comparative Studies in Society and History* 40: 136–169.

Bebler, Anton. 1996. "Civil-Military Relations in Slovenia." In Constantine P. Danopoulos and Daniel Zirker, eds., *Civil-Military Relations in the Soviet and Yugoslav Successor States*. Boulder, CO: Westview Press.

Bejczy, Istvan. 1997. "Tolerantia: A Medieval Concept." *Journal of the History of Ideas* 58: 365–384.

Bell, Daniel A. 2006. *Beyond Liberal Democracy: Political Thinking for an East Asian Context*. Princeton, NJ: Princeton University Press.

Bellah, Robert, Richard Madsen, William Sullivan, Ann Swidler, and Steven Tipton. 1985. *Habits of the Heart: Individualism and Commitment in American Life*. Berkeley: University of California Press.

Belmont, Katharine, Scott Mainwaring, and Andrew Reynolds. 2002. "Introduction: Institutional Design, Conflict Management, and Democracy." In Andrew Reynolds, ed., *The Architecture of Democracy: Constitutional Design, Conflict Management, and Democracy*. New York: Oxford University Press.

Berman, Sheri. 1997. "Civil Society and the Collapse of the Weimar Republic." *World Politics* 49: 401–429.

Berman, Sheri. 2003. "Islamism, Revolution, and Civil Society." *Perspectives on Politics* 1: 257–272.

Berman, Sheri. 2008. "Taming Extremist Parties: Lessons from Europe." *Journal of Democracy* 19: 5–18.

Bermeo, Nancy. 1992. "Surprise, Surprise: Lessons from 1989 and 1991." In Nancy Bermeo, ed., *Liberalization and Democratization: Change in the Soviet Union and Eastern Europe*. Baltimore, MD: Johns Hopkins University Press.

Bermeo, Nancy. 1999. "Myths of Moderation: Confrontation and Conflict during Democracy Transition." In Lisa Anderson, ed., *Transitions to Democracy*. New York: Columbia University Press.

Bermeo, Nancy, and Phil Nord, eds. 2000. *Civil Society Before Democracy: Lessons from Nineteenth-Century Europe*. New York: Rowan and Littlefield Publishers.

Bertrand, Jacques. 2004. *Nationalism and Ethnic Conflict in Indonesia*. Cambridge, UK: Cambridge University Press.

Birnir, Johanna. 2004. "Stabilizing Party Systems and Excluding Segments of Society?: The Effects of Formation Costs on New Party Foundation in Latin America." *Studies in Comparative International Development* 39: 3–27.

Black, Earl, and Merle Black. 2002. *The Rise of Southern Republicans*. Cambridge, MA: Harvard University Press.

Blackbourn, David. 1984. "Between Resignation and Volatility: The German Petite Bourgeoisie in the Nineteenth Century." In Geoffrey Crossick and Heinz-Gerhard Haupt, eds., *Shopkeepers and Artisans in 19th Century Europe*. London: Methuen.

Bleicken, Jochen. 1994. *Die Athenische Demokratie*. 2nd ed. Paderborn: Schöningh.

Boix, Carles. 1999. "Setting the Rules of the Game: The Choice of Electoral Systems in Advanced Democracies." *American Political Science Review* 93: 609–624.

Boix, Carles. 2003. *Democracy and Redistribution*. Cambridge: Cambridge University Press.

Boix, Carles. 2005. "Constitutions and Democratic Breakdowns." Working Paper 2005/222. Centro de Estudios Avanzadas en las Ciencias Sociales, Fundación Juan March.

Boix, Carles. 2006. "The roots of democracy." *Policy Review* 135: 3–21.

Boix, Carles, and Susan C. Stokes. 2003. "Endogenous Democratization." *World Politics* 55: 517–549.

Boone, Catherine. 2003. *Political Topographies of the African State*. Cambridge: Cambridge University Press.

Boonstra, Jos. 2007. "OSCE Democracy Promotion: Grinding to a Halt?" *FRIDE Working Paper* 44, October.

Bratton, Kathleen A., and Leonard P. Ray. 2002. "Descriptive Representation, Policy Outcomes, and Municipal Day-Care Coverage in Norway." *American Journal of Political Science* 46: 428–437.

Bratton, Michael. 2007. "Formal versus Informal Institutions in Africa." *Journal of Democracy* 18: 96–110.

Bremmer, Ian. 2006. *The J Curve: A New Way to Understand Why Nations Rise and Fall*. New York: Simon and Schuster.

Bresser Pereira, Luiz Carlos. 1993. "Economic Reforms and Economic Growth: Efficiency and Politics in Latin America." In Luiz Carlos, Bresser Pereira, José María Maravall, and Adam Przeworski, eds., *Economic Reforms in New Democracies: A Social-Democratic Approach*. Cambridge: Cambridge University Press.

Bresser Pereira, Luiz Carlos, José María Maravall, and Adam Przeworski, eds. 1993. *Economic Reforms in New Democracies: A Social-Democratic Approach*. New York: Cambridge University Press.

Brown, Michael E., Sean M. Lynn-Jones, and Steven E. Miller. 1996. *Debating the Democratic Peace*. Cambridge, MA: MIT Press.

Bruneau, Thomas C. 2006. "Introduction." In Thomas C. Bruneau and Scott D. Tollefson, eds., *Who Guards the Guardians and How: Democratic Civil-Military Relations*. Austin: University of Texas Press.

Bruneau, Thomas C., and Richard P. Goetze, Jr. 2006. "Ministries of Defense and Democratic Control." In Thomas C. Bruneau and Scott D. Tollefson, eds., *Who Guards the Guardians and How: Democratic Civil-Military Relations*. Austin: University of Texas Press.

Bruneau, Thomas C., and Scott Tollefson, eds. 2006. *Who Guards the Guardians and How: Democratic Civil-Military Relations*. Austin: University of Texas Press.

Bunce, Valerie. 2003. "Rethinking Recent Democratization: Lessons from the Postcommunist Experience." *World Politics* 55: 167–192.

Bunce, Valerie J., and Sharon L. Wolchik. 2006. "Favorable Conditions and Electoral Revolutions." *Journal of Democracy* 17: 5–18.

Bunce, Valerie J., and Sharon L. Wolchik. 2006. "International Diffusion and Postcommunist Electoral Revolutions." *Communist and Post-Communist Studies* 39: 283–304.

Burk, James. 2001. "The Military's Presence in American Society, 1950–2000." In Peter D. Feaver and Richard H. Kohn, eds., *Soldiers and Civilians: The Civil-Military Gap and American National Security*. Cambridge, MA: MIT Press.

Burke, Edmund. 1839. *Works of Edmund Burke*. Vol. 4. Boston: Little and Brown.

Burke, Edmund. 1958–1978. *The Correspondence of Edmund Burke*. Vol. 7. Thomas W. Copeland, ed. Chicago: University of Chicago Press.

Burnell, Peter. 1997. "The Changing Politics of Foreign Aid: Where to Next?" *State of the Art* 17: 117–25.

Burnell, Peter J., ed. 2000. *Democracy Assistance: International Co-operation for Democratization*. Portland, OR: Frank Cass and Co., Ltd.

Burton, Michael, Richard Gunther, and John Higley. 1992. "Introduction: Elite Transformations and Democratic Regimes." In Richard Gunther and John Higley, eds., *Elites and Democratic Consolidation in Latin America and Southern Europe*. New York: Cambridge University Press.

Buruma, Ian. 2007. "The 'King Never Smiles': A Biography of Thailand's Bhumibol Adulyadej." *New York Review of Books* 54: 43–45.

Butora, Martin. 2007. "Nightmares From the Past, Dreams of the Future." *Journal of Democracy* 18: 47–55.

Caiazza, Amy. 2004. "Does Women's Representation in Elected Office Lead to Women-Friendly Policy? Analysis of State-Level Data." *Women and Politics* 26: 35–70.

Callaghy, Thomas M. 1993. "Political Passions and Economic Interests: Economic Reform and Political Structure in Africa." In Thomas M. Callaghy and John Ravenhill, eds., *Hemmed In: Responses to Africa's Economic Decline*. New York: Columbia University Press.

Campbell, David E., and Christina Wolbrecht. 2006. "See Jane Run: Women Politicians as Role Models for Adolescents." *Journal of Politics* 68: 233–247.

Canon, David T. 1999. *Race, Redistricting, and Representation: The Unintended Consequences of Black Majority Districts*. Chicago: University of Chicago Press.

Carapico, Sheila. 2002. "Foreign Aid for Promoting Democracy in the Arab World." *The Middle East Journal* 56: 379–395.

Carothers, Thomas. 1991. *In the Name of Democracy: U.S. Policy toward Latin America in the Reagan Years*. Berkeley: University of California Press.

Carothers, Thomas. 1996. *Assessing Democracy Assistance: The Case of Romania*. Washington, DC: Carnegie Endowment Book.

Carothers, Thomas. 1997. "The Observers Observed." *Journal of Democracy* 8: 17–31.

Carothers, Thomas. 1999. *Aiding Democracy Abroad: The Learning Curve*. Washington, DC: Carnegie Endowment for International Peace.

Carothers, Thomas. 2004. *Critical Mission: Essays on Democracy Promotion*. Washington, DC: Carnegie Endowment for International Peace.

Carothers, Thomas. 2007. "A Quarter-Century of Promoting Democracy." *Journal of Democracy* 18: 112–115.

Carothers, Thomas, and Marina Ottaway. 2005. *Uncharted Journey: Promoting Democracy in the Middle East.* Washington, DC: Carnegie Endowment for International Peace: Brookings Institution Press, distributor.

Carroll, Royce, Gary W. Cox, and Monica Pachon. 2006. "How Political Parties Create Democracy, Chapter 2." *Legislative Studies Quarterly* 31: 153–174.

Casanova, Jose. 1994. *Public Religions in the Modern World.* Chicago: University of Chicago Press.

Centeno, Miguel A. 2002. *Blood and Debt: War and the Nation-State in Latin America.* University Park, PA: Pennsylvania State University Press.

Chang, Yu-Tzung, Yun-han Chu, and Chong-Min Park. 2007. "Authoritarian Nostalgia in Asia." *Journal of Democracy* 18: 66–80.

Chirot, Daniel. 2006. "The Debacle in Côte d'Ivoire." *Journal of Democracy* 17: 63–77.

Chirot, Daniel, and Clark McCauley. 2006. *Why Not Kill Them All?* Princeton, NJ: Princeton University Press.

Clark, William, and Matt Golder. 2006. "Rehabilitating Duverger's Theory – Testing the Mechanical and Strategic Modifying Effects of Electoral Laws." *Comparative Political Studies* 39: 679–708.

Clay, Henry. 1961. *The Papers of Henry Clay.* 14 vols. James F. Hopkins and Margaret W. M. Hargreaves, eds. Lexington, KY: University of Kentucky Press.

Clements, Benedict J. 1988. *Foreign Trade Strategies, Employment, and Income Distribution in Brazil.* New York: Praeger.

CNN, September 19, 2006.

Cobb, Richard. 1998. *The French and Their Revolution.* London: John Murray.

Coes, Donald. 1991. "Brazil." In Michael Michaely, ed., *Liberalizing Foreign Trade.* Vol. 4. Cambridge, MA: Basil Blackwell.

Collier, Paul, and Dominic Rohner. 2007. Democracy, Development, and Conflict. Working Paper. Oxford University.

Collier, Paul, and Dominic Rohner. 2008. "Democracy, Development, and Conflict." *Journal of the European Economic Association* 6: 531–540.

Colomer, Josep M. 2001. *Political Institutions: Democracy and Social Choice.* New York: Oxford University Press.

Colton, Timothy J., and Cindy Skach. 2005. "The Russian Predicament." *Journal of Democracy* 16: 117–119.

Commonwealth Human Rights Initiative. 1999. *Best Practices of Participatory Constitution Making* <http://www.humanrightsinitiative.org/programs/ai/const/india/practices.htm>.

Coppedge, Michael. 2007. "In Defense of Polyarchy." *NACLA Report on the Americas* 40: 36–45.

Corrales, Javier. 2006. "Power Asymmetries and the Origins of Self-Enforcing Constitutions: Venezuela since 1945, Latin America in the 1990s, and the United States in 1787." Paper presented at the annual meeting of the American Political Science Association, Philadelphia, PA, August 31.

Cox, Gary W. 1997. *Making Votes Count: Strategic Coordination in the World's Electoral Systems.* Cambridge: Cambridge University Press.

Crabtree, John, and Lawrence Whitehead. 2001. *Toward Democratic Viability: The Bolivian Experience.* New York: Palgrave.

Crawford, Gordon. 2001. *Foreign Aid and Political Reform: A Comparative Analysis of Democracy Assistance and Political Conditionality.* New York: Palgrave.

Crook, Richard C. 1997. "Winning Coalitions and Ethno-Regional Politics: The Failure of Opposition in the 1990 and 1995 Elections in Cote d'Ivoire." *African Affairs* 96: 215–242.

Crouch, Harold A. 1996. *Government and Society in Malaysia.* Ithaca, NY: Cornell University Press.

Cunsolo, Ronald. 1990. *Italian Nationalism.* Malabar, FL: Krieger.

Dahl, Robert. 1971. *Polyarchy: Participation and Opposition.* New Haven: Yale University Press.

Dahl, Robert. 1982. *Dilemmas of Pluralist Democracy.* New Haven: Yale University Press.

Dahl, Robert. 1998. *On Democracy.* New Haven: Yale University Press.

Davis, Hannah. 1992. "Taking up Space in Tlemcen: The Islamist Occupation of Urban Algeria." *Middle East Report* 179: 11–15.

De Grand, Alexander. 1978. *The Nationalist Association and the Rise of Fascism in Italy.* Lincoln, NE: University of Nebraska Press.

Dekmejian, R. Hrair. 1995. *Islam in Revolution: Fundamentalism in the Arab World.* Syracuse: Syracuse University Press.

Denoeux, Guilain. 1993. *Urban Unrest in the Middle East: A Comparative Study of Informal Networks in Egypt, Iran, and Lebanon.* Albany: State University of New York Press.

Diamond, Larry. 1992. "Promoting Democracy." *Foreign Policy* 87: 25–46.

Diamond, Larry. 1994. "Rethinking Civil Society: Toward Democratic Consolidation." *Journal of Democracy* 5: 4–17.

Diamond, Larry. 1999. *Developing Democracy: Toward Consolidation.* Baltimore, MD: Johns Hopkins University Press.

Diamond, Larry. 2002. "Thinking About Hybrid Regimes." *Journal of Democracy* 13: 21–35.

Diamond, Larry. 2005. *Squandered Victory: The American Occupation and the Bungled Effort To Bring Democracy to Iraq.* New York: Henry Holt and Co.

Dobriansky, Paula. 2001. Heritage Foundation. Washington, DC, December 21.

Dolan, Kathleen. 2006. "Symbolic Mobilization? The Impact of Candidate Sex in American Elections." *American Politics Research* 34: 687–704.

Dornbusch, Rudiger, and Sebastian Edwards. 1991. "The Macroeconomics of Populism." In Rudiger Dornbusch and Sebastian Edwards, eds., *The Macroeconomics of Populism in Latin America.* Chicago: University of Chicago Press.

Dower, John W. 1999. *Embracing Defeat: Japan in the Wake of World War II* (New York: W. W. Norton).

Doyle, Michael. 1986. "Liberalism and World Politics." *American Political Science Review* 80: 1151–1169.

Eaton, Kent. 2007. "Backlash in Bolivia: Regional Autonomy as a Reaction against Indigenous Mobilization." *Politics and Society* 35: 1–32.

Eckstein, Harry. 1992. *Regarding Politics*. Berkeley, CA: University of California Press.

Edwards, Bob, Michael Foley, and Mario Diani. 2001. *Beyond Tocqueville: Civil Society and the Social Capital Debate in Comparative Perspective*. Hanover, NH: University Press of New England.

Eisenstadt, S. N. 1995. *Power, Trust and Meaning*. Chicago: University of Chicago Press.

Eley, Geoff. 1994. *Reshaping the German Right: Radical Nationalism and Political Change After Bismarck*. Ann Arbor: University of Michigan Press.

El-Khazen, Farid. 2000. *The Breakdown of the State in Lebanon, 1967–1976*. Cambridge, MA: Harvard University Press.

Elkins, Zach, and Thomas Ginsburg. 2007. *Comparative Constitutions Project*. Champaign, IL: University of Illinois.

Elkins, Zachary, Tom Ginsburg, and James Melton. 2006. "The Lifespan of Written Constitutions." Working paper.

Elklit, Jorgen, and Palle Svensson. 1997. "What Makes Elections Free and Fair?" *Journal of Democracy* 8: 32–46.

Ellul, Jaques. 2004. *Islam et judeo-christianism*. Paris: Presses Universitaires de France.

Elster, Jon. 1995. "Forces and Mechanisms in the Constitution-Making Process." *Duke Law Journal* 45: 364–396.

Elster, Jon. 1997. "Ways of Constitution-Making." In Axel Hadenius, ed., *Democracy's Victory and Crisis*. New York: Cambridge University Press.

Encarción, Omar. 2003. *The Myth of Civil Society*. New York: Palgrave.

Entelis, John. 1996. "Civil Society and the Authoritarian Temptation in Algerian Politics." In Augustus Richard Norton, ed., *Civil Society in the Middle East*. New York: E. J. Brill.

Epstein, David L., Robert Bates, Jack Goldstone, Ida Kristensen, and Sharyn O'Halloran. 2006. "Democratic Transitions." *American Journal of Political Science* 50: 551–569.

Ertman, Thomas. 2000. "Liberalization, Democratization and the Origins of a 'Pillarized' Civil Society in Nineteenth Century Belgium and the Netherlands." In Nancy Bermeo and Phil Nord, eds., *Civil Society Before Democracy: Lessons from Nineteenth Century Europe*. New York: Rowan and Littlefield.

Esposito, John L. 1999. *The Islamic Threat: Myth or Reality?* New York: Oxford University Press.

Feldman, Gerald D. 1966. *Army, Industry, and Labor in Germany, 1914–1918*. Princeton, NJ: Princeton University Press.

Fenton, Steve. 2003. *Ethnicity*. Cambridge, UK: Polity Press.

Ferrara, Federico, Erik S. Herron, and Misa Nishikawa. 2005. *Mixed Electoral Systems: Contamination and Its Consequences*. New York: Palgrave Macmillan.

Findlay, Ronald. 1991. "The New Political Economy: Its Explanatory Power for LDCs." In Gerald M. Meier, ed., *Politics and Policy Making in Developing Countries: Perspectives on the New Political Economy*. San Francisco: ICS Press.

Firro, Kais M. 1992. *A History of the Druzes*. Leiden, Netherlands: Brill.

Fish, M. Steven. 2002. "Islam and Authoritarianism." *World Politics* 55: 4–37.

Foley, Michael, and Bob Edwards. 1996. "The Paradox of Civil Society." *Journal of Democracy* 7: 38–52.

Fox, R. L. and Lawless, J. L. 2005. "To Run or Not to Run for Office: Explaining Nascent Political Ambition." *American Journal of Political Science* 49: 642–659.

Franklin, Benjamin. 1959–2003. *The Papers of Benjamin Franklin*. 37 vols. L. Labaree et al., eds. New Haven: Yale University Press.

Freedom House. 2007. "Nations in Transit." Press Release, June 1, <www.freedomhouse.org>.

Friedman, Milton. 2002. *Capitalism and Freedom*. Chicago, IL: University of Chicago Press.

Fritzsche, Peter. 1990. *Rehearsals for Fascism: Populism and Political Mobilization in Weimar Germany*. New York: Oxford University Press.

Fromm, Erich. 1941. *Escape From Freedom*. New York: Rinehart.

Fukuyama, Francis. 1995. *Trust: Social Virtues and the Creation of Prosperity*. New York: Free Press.

Fukuyama, Francis. 2004. *State-Building: Governance and Order in the 21st Century*. Ithaca, NY: Cornell University Press.

Fukuyama, Francis. 2006. "Guidelines for Future Nation-Builders." In Frances Fukuyama, ed., *Nation-Building: Beyond Afghanistan and Iraq*. Baltimore, MD: Johns Hopkins University Press.

Fukuyama, Francis. 2006. "Nation-Building and the Failure of Institutional Memory." In Frances Fukuyama, ed., *Nation-Building: Beyond Afghanistan and Iraq*. Baltimore, MD: Johns Hopkins University Press.

Fukuyama, Francis, ed. 2006. *Nation-Building: Beyond Afghanistan and Iraq*. Baltimore, MD: Johns Hopkins University Press.

Gallagher, Tony. 2001. "The Northern Ireland Conflict: Prospects and Possibilities." In Daniel Chirot and Martin Seligman, eds., *Ethnopolitical Warfare*. Washington, DC: American Psychological Association Press.

Geary, Patrick J. 2002. *The Myth of Nations*. Princeton, NJ: Princeton University Press.

Geis, Anna, Lothar Brock, and Harald Müller. 2006. *Democratic Wars: Looking at the Dark Side of Democratic Peace*. New York: Palgrave Macmillan, 2006.

Gellner, Ernest. 1988. *Plough, Sword and Book: The Structure of Human History*. Chicago: University of Chicago Press.

Gellner, Ernest. 1994. *Conditions of Liberty: Civil Society and its Rivals*. London: Allan Lane.

Gerring, John, Philip Bond, William T. Barndt, and Carola Moreno. 2005. "Democracy and Economic Growth: A Historical Perspective." *World Politics* 57: 323–364.

Gershman, Carl, and Michael Allen. 2006. "The Assault on Democracy Assistance." *Journal of Democracy* 17: 36–51.

Giraldo, Jeanne Kinney. 2006. "Legislatures and National Defense: Global Comparisons." In Thomas C. Bruneau and Scott D. Tollefson, eds., *Who Guards the Guardians and How: Democratic Civil-Military Relations.* Austin: University of Texas Press.

Goldsmith, Arthur A. 2001. "Donors, Dictators and Democrats in Africa." *Journal of Modern African Studies* 39: 411–436.

Greenfeld, Liah. 1992. *Nationalism.* Cambridge, MA: Harvard University Press.

Gries, Peter Hays. 2005. *China's New Nationalism: Pride, Politics, and Diplomacy.* Berkeley, CA: University of California Press.

Gunther, Richard. 1992. "Spain: The Very Model of a Modern Elite Settlement." In Richard Gunther and John Higley, eds., *Elites and Democratic Consolidation in Latin America and Southern Europe.* New York: Cambridge University Press.

Habermas, Jürgen. 2006. *The Divided West.* Trans. Ciaran Cronin. Cambridge: Polity Press.

Haggard, Stephan, and Robert R. Kaufman. 1992. "Institutions and Economic Adjustment." In Stephan Haggard and Robert R. Kaufman, eds., *The Politics of Economic Adjustment.* Princeton, NJ: Princeton University Press.

Haggard, Stephan, and Robert R. Kaufman. 1995. *The Political Economy of Democratic Transitions.* Princeton, NJ: Princeton University Press.

Haider-Markel, D. 2007. "Representation and Backlash: The Positive and Negative Influence of Descriptive Representation." *Legislative Studies Quarterly* 32: 107–133.

Hall, John A., ed. 1995. *Civil Society: Theory, History, Comparison.* Cambridge, England: Polity Press.

Halperin, Morton H., Joseph T. Siegle, and Michael M. Weinstein. 2005. *The Democracy Advantage: How Democracies Promote Prosperity and Peace.* New York: Routledge.

Hamilton, Alexander. 1961–1987. *The Papers of Alexander Hamilton.* 27 vols. Harold C. Syrett et al., eds. New York: Columbia University Press.

Hamilton, Alexander, John Jay, and James Madison. 2001 (1787–1788). *The Federalist.* Indianapolis: The Liberty Fund.

Hardin, Russell. 1989. "Why a Constitution?" In Bernard Grofman and Donald Wittman, eds., *The Federalist Papers and the New Institutionalism.* New York: Agathon.

Harris, John. 2002. "Whatever Happened to Cultural Nationalism in Tamil Nadu." *Commonwealth and Comparative Politics* 40: 97–117.

Harrison, Lawrence, and Samuel Huntington. 2000. *Culture Matters.* New York: Basic Books.

Hartz, Louis. 1955. *The Liberal Tradition in America.* New York: Harcourt, Brace and World.

Hawthorne, Amy. 2004. "Middle Eastern Democracy: Is Civil Society the Answer?" *Carnegie Paper* 44, March.

Hayden, Robert M. 1992. "Constitutional Nationalism in the Formerly Yugoslav Republics." *Slavic Review* 51: 654–673.

Hearn, Julie. 2000. "Aiding Democracy? Donors and Civil Society in South Africa." *Third World Quarterly* 21: 815–830.

Hechter, Michael. 2000. *Containing Nationalism*. Oxford, UK: Oxford University Press.

Hefner, Robert. 2000. *Civil Islam: Muslims and Democratization in Indonesia*. Princeton, NJ: Princeton University Press.

Hefner, Robert. 2005. "Muslim Democrats and Islamic Violence in Post-Soeharto Indonesia." In Robert W. Hefner, ed., *Remaking Muslim Politics*. Princeton, NJ: Princeton University Press.

Helmke, Gretchen, and Steven Levitsky. 2004. "Informal Institutions and Comparative Politics: A Research Agenda." *Perspectives on Politics* 2: 725–740.

Henderson, Errol Anthony. 2002. *Democracy and War: The End of an Illusion?* Boulder: Lynne Rienner Publishers.

Hirschman, Albert O. 1977. *The Passions and the Interests*. Princeton, NJ: Princeton University Press.

Holmes, Stephen. 1988. "Precommitment and the Paradox of Democracy." In Jon Elster and Rune Slagstad, eds., *Constitutionalism and Democracy*. New York: Cambridge University Press.

Horowitz, Donald L. 1985. *Ethnic Groups in Conflict*. Berkeley, CA: University of California Press.

Horowitz, Donald L. 2001. *The Deadly Ethnic Riot*. Berkeley, CA: University of California Press.

Horowitz, Donald L. 2002. "Constitutional Design: Proposals Versus Processes." In Andrew Reynolds, ed., *The Architecture of Democracy: Constitutional Design, Conflict Management, and Democracy*. New York: Oxford University Press.

Hourani, Albert. 2002. *A History of the Arab Peoples*. Cambridge, MA: Harvard University Press.

Howard, Marc. 2003. *The Weakness of Civil Society in Post-Communist Europe*. New York: Cambridge University Press.

Howard, Marc, and Philip Roessler. 2006. "Liberalizing Electoral Outcomes in Competitive Authoritarian Regimes." *American Journal of Political Science* 50: 365–381.

Htun, Mala. 2004. "Is Gender Like Ethnicity? The Political Representation of Identity Groups." *Perspectives on Politics* 2: 439–458.

Hunter, Wendy. 1997. *Eroding Military Influence in Brazil: Politicians against Soldiers*. Chapel Hill: University of North Carolina Press.

Huntington, Samuel P. 1968. *Political Order in Changing Societies*. New Haven, CT: Yale University Press.

Huntington, Samuel P. 1991. *The Third Wave: Democratization in the Late Twentieth Century*. Norman, OK: University of Oklahoma Press.

Ibrahim, Saad Eddin. 1980. "Anatomy of Egypt's Militant Islamic Groups: Methodological Note and Preliminary Findings." *International Journal of Middle East Studies* 12: 423–453.

Ibrahim, Saad Eddin. 1995. "Civil Society and Prospects for Democratization in the Arab World." In Augustus Richard Norton, ed., *Civil Society in the Middle East*. Vol. 1. New York: E. J. Brill.

Ibrahim, Saad Eddin. 1996. "Reform and Frustration in Egypt." *Journal of Democracy* 7: 125–135.

Ibrahim, Saad Eddin. 2007. "Toward Muslim Democracies." *Journal of Democracy* 18: 5–13.

Ignatieff, Michael. 2001. *Human Rights as Politics and Idolatry*. Princeton: Princeton University Press.

Il Giorno. 24.11.2000. "Il sindaco alla larga dalle chiese infedeli."

International Peace Academy. 2005. *Conference Report: Governance and Power After Conflict*. New York: International Peace Academy.

Inter-Parliamentary Union. Parline Website <www.ipu.org>.

Jaggers, Keith, and Ted Robert Gurr. 1995. "Tracking Democracy's Third Wave with the Polity III Data." *Journal of Peace Research* 32: 469–482.

Jefferson, Thomas. 1903. "Letter to Samuel Kercheval, 1816." In Andrew A. Lipscomb and Albert E. Bergh, eds., *The Writings of Thomas Jefferson, Memorial Edition*. Washington, DC: Thomas Jefferson Memorial Association.

Jefferson, Thomas. 1984. *The Writings of Thomas Jefferson*. M. Peterson, ed. New York: Penguin Putnam, Library of America.

Johnson, Jo. 2007. "A Creed of Loathe Thy Neighbor." *Financial Times*, 31 March/ 1 April.

Jomo, K. S. 1997. "A Specific Idiom of Chinese Capitalism in Southeast Asia: Sino-Malaysian Capital Accumulation in the Face of State Hostility." In Daniel Chirot and Anthony Reid, eds., *Essential Outsiders*. Seattle, WA: University of Washington Press.

Jones, Larry Eugene. 1972. "'The Dying Middle': Weimar Germany and the Fragmentation of Bourgeois Politics." *Central European History* 5: 23–54.

Jones, Mark P. 2004. "Quota Legislation and the Election of Women: Learning from the Costa Rican Experience." *Journal of Politics* 66: 1203–1223.

Jones-Luong, Pauline, and Erika Weinthal. 1999. "The NGO Paradox: Democratic Goals and Non-Democratic Outcomes in Kazakhstan." *Europe-Asia Studies* 51: 1267–1284.

Judah, Tim. 1997. *The Serbs*. New Haven, CT: Yale University Press.

Juergensmeyer, Mark. 1993. *The New Cold War? Religious Nationalism Confronts the Secular State*. Berkeley, CA: University of California Press.

Kagan, Donald. 1969. *The Outbreak of the Peloponnesian War*. Ithaca: Cornell University Press.

Kant, Immanuel. 1902. *Kants Werke*. 9 vols. Berlin: Preussischen Akademie der Wissenschaften.

Kasparov, Garry. 2007. "Battling KGB, Inc." *Journal of Democracy* 18: 114–119.

Kaufman, Robert R., and Barbara Stallings. 1989. "Debt and Democracy in the 1980s: The Latin American Experience." In Robert R. Kaufman and Barbara Stallings, eds., *Debt and Democracy in Latin America*. Boulder, CO: Westview Press.

Kaufman, Robert R., and Barbara Stallings. 1991. "The Political Economy of Latin American Populism." In Rudiger Dornbusch and Sebastian Edwards, eds., *The*

Macroeconomics of Populism in Latin America. Chicago: University of Chicago Press.

Kaufman, Stuart. 2001. *Modern Hatreds: The Symbolic Politics of Ethnic War*. Ithaca, NY: Cornell University Press.

Keesing's. 1990–2007. "Various Articles." *Keesing's record of world events*. 36–53.

Kentworthy, L., and M. Malami. 1999. "Gender Inequality in Political Representation: A Worldwide Comparative Analysis." *Social Forces* 78: 235–268.

Kepel, Gilles. 1985. *Muslim Extremism in Egypt: The Prophet and Pharaoh*. Berkeley: University of California Press.

Kepel, Gilles. 2002. *Jihad: The Trail of Political Islam*. Cambridge: Harvard University Press.

Keyder, Cağlar. 1997. "The Ottoman Empire." In Karen Barkey and Mark von Hagen, *After Empire: Multiethnic Societies and Nation-Building*. Boulder, CO: Westview Press.

King, Gary, J. Alt, N. R. Burns, and M. Laver. 1990. "A Unified Model of Cabinet Dissolution in Parliamentary Democracies." *American Journal of Political Science* 34: 846–871.

Knack, Stephen. 2004. "Does Foreign Aid Promote Democracy?" *International Studies Quarterly* 48: 251–266.

Koonings, Kees, and Dirk Kruijt, eds. 2002. *The Military and Nation-Building in the Age of Democracy*. London: Zed Books.

Kornhauser, William. 1959. *The Politics of Mass Society*. Glenco, IL: The Free Press.

Kosack, Stephen. 2003. "Effective Aid: How Democracy Allows Development Aid to Improve the Quality of Life." *World Development* 31: 1–22.

Koshar, Rudy. 1986. *Social Life, Local Politics and Nazism*. Chapel Hill, NC: University of North Carolina Press.

Kostadinova, T. 2007. "Ethnic and Women's Representation under Mixed Electoral Systems." *Electoral Studies* 26: 418–431.

Krastev, Ivan. 2007. "The Strange Death of the Liberal Consensus." *Journal of Democracy* 18: 56–63.

Krueger, Anne O. 1994. *The Political Economy of Reform in Developing Countries*. Cambridge, MA: MIT Press.

Kuzio, Taras. 2006. "Civil Society, Youth and Societal Mobilization in Democratic Revolutions." *Communist and Post-Communist Studies* 39: 365–386.

Kwon, Hyeong-Ki. 2004. "Associations, Civic Norms, and Democracy: Revisiting the Italian Case." *Theory and Society* 33: 135–166.

La Republica. 15.10.2000. "Lodi, la lega alla guara santa."

Latinobarametro. *Informe de Prensa* 2007: 79–81. <www.latinobarometro.org>.

Lawless, J. 2004. "Politics of Presence? Congresswomen and Symbolic Representation." *Political Research Quarterly* 57: 81–99.

Lee, Hock Guan. 2000. "Ethnic Relations in Peninsular Malaysia." *Social and Cultural Issues* (Singapore Institute of Southeast Asian Studies), No. 1, August.

Lenin, V.I. 1939 (1916, 1917). *Imperialism, the Highest Stage of Capitalism*. New York: International Publishers.

Levitsky, Steven, and Lucan Way. 2002. "The Rise of Competitive Authoritarianism." *Journal of Democracy* 13: 51–65.

Levy, Jack S., and Lily Vakili. 1992. "Diversionary Action by Authoritarian Regimes." In Manus Midlarsky, ed., *The Internationalization of Communal Strife*. London: Routledge.

Lewis-Beck, Michael, and Ross E. Burkhart. 1994. "Comparative Democracy: The Economic Development Thesis." *American Political Science Review* 88: 903–910.

Lijphart, Arend. 1977. *Democracy in Plural Societies*. New Haven, CT: Yale University Press.

Lijphart, Arend. 1991. "Constitutional Choices for New Democracies." *Journal of Democracy* 2: 72–84.

Lijphart, Arend. 1994. *Electoral Systems and Party Systems*. Oxford: Oxford University Press.

Lijphart, Arend. 2002. "The Wave of Power-Sharing Democracy." In Andrew Reynolds, ed., *The Architecture of Democracy: Constitutional Design, Conflict Management, and Democracy*. New York: Oxford University Press.

Lijphart, Arend. 2004. "Constitutional Choices for Divided Societies." *Journal of Democracy* 15: 96–109.

Lin, Jih-wen. 2002. "Transition through Transaction: Taiwan's Constitutional Reforms in the Lee Teng-Hui Era." *American Asian Review* 20: 123–155.

Lincoln, Abraham. 1953–55. *The Collected Works of Abraham Lincoln*. 9 vols. New Brunswick, NJ: Rutgers University Press.

Linz, Juan J. 1978. *The Breakdown of Democratic Regimes: Crisis, Breakdown, and Reequilibrium*. Baltimore, MD: Johns Hopkins University Press.

Linz, Juan J., and Alfred Stepan. 1996. *Problems of Democratic Transition and Consolidation: Southern Europe, South America, and Post-Communist Europe*. Baltimore, MD: Johns Hopkins University Press.

Lipset, Seymour Martin. 1959. "Some Social Requisites of Democracy: Economic Development and Political Legitimacy." *American Political Science Review* 53: 65–105.

Lowenthal, Abraham F. 1991. *Exporting Democracy: The United States and Latin America*. Baltimore: Johns Hopkins University Press.

Lowenthal, Abraham F. 1991. *Exporting Democracy: the United States and Latin America: Themes and Issues*. Baltimore: Johns Hopkins University Press.

Lowenthal, Abraham F. 1991. *Exporting Democracy: The United States and Latin America: Case Studies*. Baltimore: Johns Hopkins University Press.

Lublin, David. 1997. *The Paradox of Representation: Racial Gerrymandering and Minority Interests in Congress*. Princeton: Princeton University Press.

Luce, Edward. 2007. *In Spite of the Gods: The Strange Rise of Modern India*. New York: Doubleday.

Lyttelton, Adrian. 2000. "Liberalism and Civil Society in Italy." In Nancy Bermeo and Philip Nord, eds., *Civil Society Before Democracy*. New York: Rowan and Littlefield.

MacFarquhar, Neil. 2001. "To U.S. a Terrorist Group; to Lebanese, a Social Agency." *New York Times*, 28 December <http://www.nytimes.com/2001/12/28/international/middleeast/28LEBA.html>.

Machiavelli, Niccolò. 1964 (1519–1520). *The Art of War*. Trans. Neal Wood. Cambridge, MA: Da Capo Press.

Machiavelli, Niccolò. 1995 (1513/1532). *The Prince*. Trans. David Wootton. David Wootton, ed. Indianapolis: Hackett.

Maddy-Weitzman, Bruce. 1996. "The Islamic Challenge in North Africa." *Terrorism and Political Violence* 8: 171–188.

Madison, James, Alexander Hamilton, and John Jay, eds. 1788 (1961). *The Federalist Papers*. New York: Mentor.

Madrid, Raul. 2005. "Ethnic Cleavages and Electoral Volatility in Latin America." *Comparative Politics* 38: 1–20.

Mainwaring, Scott. 1999. *Rethinking Party Systems in the Third Wave of Democratization: The Case of Brazil*. Stanford: Stanford University Press.

Mainwaring, Scott, and Matthew S. Shugart. 1997. "Juan Linz, Presidentialism, and Democracy: A Critical Appraisal." *Comparative Politics* 29: 449–471.

Mainwaring, Scott, and Edurne Zoco. 2007. "Political Sequences and the Stabilization of Interparty Competition: Electoral Volatility in Old and New Democracies." *Party Politics* 13: 155–178.

Malley, Robert. 1996. *The Call from Algeria*. Berkeley, CA: University of California Press.

Manent, Pierre. 2006. *La raison des nations: réflexions sur la démocratie en Europe*. Paris: Gallimard.

Mannheim, Karl. 1980. *Man and Society in an Age of Reconstruction*. New York: Routledge & Kegan Paul.

Manning, Carrie. 2004. "Elections and Political Change in Post-War Bosnia and Herzegovina." *Democratization* 11: 60–86.

Mansbridge, Jane. 1999. "Should Blacks Represent Blacks and Women Represent Women? A Contingent 'Yes.'" *Journal of Politics* 61: 628–657.

Mansfield, Edward D., Helen V. Milner, and B. Peter Rosendorff. 2000. "Free to Trade: Autocracies, Democracies, and International Trade." *American Political Science Review* 94: 305–321.

Mansfield, Edward D., Helen V. Milner, and B. Peter Rosendorff. 2002. "Why Democracies Cooperate More: Electoral Control and International Trade Agreements." *International Organization* 56: 477–513.

Mansfield, Edward D., and Jack Snyder. 1995. "Democratization and the Danger of War." *International Security* 20: 5–38.

Mansfield, Edward D., and Jack Snyder. 2002. "Incomplete Democratization and the Outbreak of Military Disputes." *International Studies Quarterly* 46: 529–549.

Mansfield, Edward D., and Jack Snyder. 2005. *Electing to Fight: Why Emerging Democracies Go to War*. Cambridge, MA: MIT Press.

Mansfield, Edward D., and Jack Snyder. 2007. "Democratization and Civil War." Ts. University of Pennsylvania and Columbia University.

Mansfield, Edward D., and Jack Snyder. Forthcoming. "Does War Influence Democratization?" In Elizabeth Kier and Ronald R. Krebs, eds., *In War's Wake: International Conflict and the Fate of Liberal Democracy.*

Maravall, José María. 1994. "The Myth of the Authoritarian Advantage." *Journal of Democracy* 5: 17–31.

Mardin, Serif. 1997. "The Ottoman Empire." In Karen Barkey and Mark von Hagen, *After Empire: Multiethnic Societies and Nation-Building.* Boulder, CO: Westview Press.

Mares, David R. 2001. *Violent Peace: Militarized Interstate Bargaining in Latin America.* New York: Columbia University Press.

Marshall, Monty G., and Keith Jaggers. 2005. "Political Regime Characteristics and Transitions, 1800–2004." Center for International Development and Conflict Management, University of Maryland.

Marshall, Monty G., and Keith Jaggers. 2007. *Polity IV Project: Political Regime Characteristics and Transitions, 1800–2004.* George Mason University, Arlington, VA: Center for Global Policy <http://www.cidcm.umd.edu/polity/>.

Martinez, Luis. 2000. Trans. and Pref. Jonathan Derrick. *The Algerian Civil War.* New York: Columbia University Press.

Marx, Anthony W. 1998. *Making Race and Nation.* Cambridge, UK: Cambridge University Press.

Marx, Anthony W. 2003. *Faith in Nation: Exclusionary Origins of Nationalism.* New York: Oxford University Press.

Matland, Richard E. 1993. "Institutional Variables Affecting Female Representation in National Legislatures: The Case of Norway." *Journal of Politics* 55: 737–755.

Matland, Richard E. 1998. "Women's Legislative Representation in National Legislatures: A Comparison of Democracies in Developed and Developing Countries." *Legislative Studies Quarterly* 28: 109–125.

Matland, Richard E., and Donald Studlar. 1996. "The Contagion of Women Candidates in Single Member and Multi-Member Districts." *Journal of Politics* 58: 707–733.

McDowall, David. 1997. *A Modern History of the Kurds.* London: I. B. Tauris.

McFaul, Michael. 2001. "Explaining Party Formation and Nonformation in Russia – Actors, Institutions, and Chance." *Comparative Political Studies* 34: 1159–1187.

McFaul, Michael. 2004–05. "Democracy Promotion as a World Value." *Washington Quarterly* 28: 147–163.

McFaul, Michael. 2005. "Transitions from Postcommunism." *Journal of Democracy* 16: 5–19.

McFaul, Michael. 2007. "Are New Democracies War-Prone?" *Journal of Democracy* 18: 160–167.

McFaul, Michael. 2007. "Ukraine Imports Democracy: External Influences on the Orange Revolution." *International Security* 32: 45–83.

McGarry, John, and Brendan O'Leary. 1995. *Explaining Northern Ireland.* Oxford, UK: Blackwell.

Meernik, James. 1996. "United States Military Intervention and the Promotion of Democracy." *Journal of Peace Research* 33: 391–402.

Meiggs, Russell. 1972. *The Athenian Empire*. Oxford: Oxford University Press.

Mendelson, Sarah, and John Glenn. 2002. *The Power and Limits of NGOs*. New York: Columbia University Press.

Mendelson Forman, Joanna. 2006. "Striking Out in Baghdad: How Postconflict Reconstruction Went Awry." In Frances Fukuyama, ed., *Nation-Building: Beyond Afghanistan and Iraq*. Baltimore, MD: Johns Hopkins University Press.

Merritt, Richard L. 1995. *Democracy Imposed: U.S. Occupation Policy and the German Public, 1945–1949*. New Haven: Yale University Press.

Mill, John Stuart. 1965–81. *The Collected Works of John Stuart Mill*. 33 vols. J. Robson et al., eds. Toronto: University of Toronto Press.

Milner, Helen V., with Keiko Kubota. 2005. "Why the Move to Free Trade? Democracy and Trade Liberalization in the Developing Countries." *International Organization* 59: 107–143.

Moon, Katharine H. S. 2003. "Korean Nationalism, Anti-Americanism, and Democratic Consolidation." In Samuel S. Kim, ed., *Korea's Democratization*. New York: Cambridge University Press.

Moore, John Norton. 2004. *Solving the War Puzzle: Beyond the Democratic Peace*. Durham, NC: Carolina Academic Press.

Moraski, Bryon, and Gerhard Loewenberg. 1999. "The Effect of Legal Thresholds on the Revival of Former Communist Parties in East-Central Europe." *Journal of Politics* 61: 151–170.

Morgenthau, Hans Joachim. 1982. *In Defense of the National Interest: A Critical Examination of American Foreign Policy*. Washington, DC: University Press of America.

Morgenthau, Hans Joachim, and Kenneth W. Thompson. 1993. *Politics Among Nations: The Struggle for Power and Peace*. Brief ed. New York: McGraw-Hill.

Moser, Robert G. 2001. "The Effects of Electoral Systems on Women's Representation in Post-Communist States." *Electoral Studies* 20: 253–269.

Moser, Robert G. 2001. *Unexpected Outcomes: Electoral Systems, Political Parties, and Representation in Russia*. Pittsburgh: University of Pittsburgh Press.

Moser, Robert G. 2008. "Electoral Systems and the Representation of Ethnic Minorities: Evidence from Russia." *Comparative Politics* 40: 273–292.

Moser, Robert G., and Stephanie Holmsten. 2008. "Do Ethnic Parties Discriminate against Women?" Paper presented at the annual meeting of the American Political Science Association, Boston, MA, August 30.

Moser, Robert G., and Stephanie Holmsten. 2008. "The Paradox of Descriptive Representation: Can PR Simultaneously Elect Women and Ethnic Minorities?" Paper presented at the annual meeting of the Midwest Political Science Association, Chicago, IL, April 3–6.

Moser, Robert G., and Ethan Scheiner. 2007. "Electoral Systems and the Representation of Ethnic Minorities: Evidence from Four Mixed Electoral Systems." Paper presented at the University of Texas, February 5.

Moser, Robert G., and Frank Thames. 2001. "The Origins of Russia's Mixed-Member Electoral System." In Matthew Shugart and Martin Wattenberg, eds., *Mixed-Member Electoral Systems: The Best of Both Worlds?* Oxford: Oxford University Press.

Moskos, Charles C., and John Sibley Butler. 1996. *All that We Can Be: Black Leadership and Racial Integration the Army Way.* New York: Basic Books.

Muller, Edward N. 1997. "Economic Determinants of Democracy." In Manus I. Midlarsky, ed., *Inequality, Democracy, and Economic Development.* Cambridge: Cambridge University Press.

Muñoz, Oscar. 1994. "Toward Trade Opening." In Joan Nelson, ed., *Intricate Links: Democratization and Market Reforms in Latin America and Eastern Europe.* New Brunswick, NJ: Transaction Publishers.

Naimark, Norman M. 2001. *Fires of Hatred: Ethnic Cleansing in Twentieth Century Europe.* Cambridge, MA: Harvard University Press.

Nakash, Yitzhak. 2003. *The Shi'is of Iraq.* Princeton, NJ: Princeton University Press.

Namy, Sophie. 2006. "Investigating Tamil Ethnonationalism: Indian Democracy and Sri Lankan Violence." Unpublished paper, Seattle: University of Washington, Henry M. Jackson School of International Studies.

Nasr, Vali. 2006. *The Shia Revival.* New York: W.W. Norton.

Negash, Tekeste, and Kjetil Tronvoll. 2000. *Brothers at War: Making Sense of the Eritrean-Ethiopian War.* Oxford: James Currey.

Nelson, Daniel N., ed. 1995. *After Authoritarianism: Democracy or Disorder?* Greenwood, CT: Praeger.

Nelson, Joan. 1993. "The Politics of Economic Transformation: Is the Third World Experience Relevant in Eastern Europe." *World Politics* 45: 433–463.

Neumann, Sigmund. 1942. *Permanent Revolution.* New York: Harper.

Newberg, Paula R., and Thomas Carothers. 1996. "Aiding – and Defining – Democracy." *World Policy Journal* 13: 97.

Newton, Kenneth. 2001. "Trust, Social Capital, Civil Society and Democracy." *International Political Science Review* 22: 201–214.

Nichols, Thomas M. 1993. *The Sacred Cause: Civil-Military Conflict over Soviet National Security, 1917–1992.* Ithaca, NY: Cornell University Press.

Nipperdey, Thomas. 1976. "Verein als soziale Struktur in Deutschland im späten 18. und frühen 19. Jahrhundert: Eine Fallstudie zur Modernisierung." In Thomas Nipperdey, ed., *Gesellschaft, Kultur, Theorie: Gesammelte Aufsätze zur neueren Geschichte.* Göttingen: Vandenhoeck & Ruprecht.

Nirenberg, David. 1996. *Communities of Violence: Persecution of Minorities in the Middle Ages.* Princeton: Princeton University Press.

Nohlen, Dieter, ed. 2005. *Elections in the Americas: A Data Handbook.* Oxford: Oxford University Press.

Nohlen, Dieter, Florian Grotz, and Christof Hartmann, eds. 2001. *Elections in Asia and the Pacific: A Data Handbook.* Oxford: Oxford University Press.

Nohlen, Dieter, Michael Krennerich, and Bernhard Thibaut, eds. 1999. *Elections in Africa; A Data Handbook.* Oxford: Oxford University Press.

Norris, Pippa. 2004. *Electoral Engineering: Voting Rules and Political Behavior.* Cambridge: Cambridge University Press.

Norris, Pippa, and Ronald Inglehart. 2002. "Islamic Culture and Democracy: Testing the 'Clash of Civilizations' Thesis." *Comparative Sociology* 1: 235–263.

North, Douglass C. 1990. *Institutions, Institutional Change, and Economic Performance.* New York: Cambridge University Press.

North, Douglass C., William Summerhill, and Barry Weingast. 2000. "Order, Disorder, and Economic Change: Latin America vs. North America." In Bruce Bueno de Mesquita and Hilton L. Root, eds., *Governing for Prosperity.* New Haven, CT: Yale University Press.

Norton, Augustus Richard, Roger Owen, Diane Singerman, and James Gelvin. n.d. *The Civil Society Debate in Middle Eastern Studies.* Los Angeles: UCLA Near East Center Colloquium Series.

O'Donnell, Guillermo. 1986. "Modernization and Military Coups: Theory, Comparisons, and the Argentine Case." In Abraham F. Lowenthal and J. Samuel Fitch, eds., *Armies and Politics in Latin America.* New York: Holmes and Meier.

O'Donnell, Guillermo. 1994. "Delegative Democracy." *Journal of Democracy* 5: 55–69.

O'Donnell, Guillermo. 1998. "Horizontal Accountability in New Democracies." *Journal of Democracy* 9: 112–126.

O'Donnell, Guillermo. 2007. "The Perpetual Crises of Democracy." *Journal of Democracy* 18: 5–11.

Okin, Sarah M. 1999. *Is Multiculturalism Bad for Women?* Princeton: Princeton University Press.

O'Leary, Brendan. 2001. "Nationalism and Ethnicity." In Daniel Chirot and Martin Seligman, eds., *Ethnopolitical Warfare.* Washington, DC: American Psychological Association Press.

Ottaway, Marina, and Thomas Carothers. 2000. *Funding Virtue: Civil Society Aid and Democracy Promotion.* Washington, DC: Carnegie Endowment for International Peace.

Ottaway, Marina, and Thomas Carothers. 2004. "Think Again: Middle East Democracy." *Foreign Policy* 145: 22–28.

Ottemoeller, Dan. 1998. "Popular Perceptions of Democracy: Elections and Attitudes in Uganda." *Comparative Political Studies* 31: 98–124.

Owen, John M. 1997. "Perceptions and the Limits of Liberal Peace: The Mexican-American and Spanish American Wars." In Miriam Fendius Elman, ed., *Paths to Peace: Is Democracy the Answer?* Cambridge, MA: MIT Press.

Pappas, Takis S. 2005. "Shared culture, individual strategy, and collective action: explaining Slobodan Milošević's charismatic rise to power." *Southeast European and Black Sea Studies* 5: 191–211.

Patrucco, Armand. 1973. *The Critics of the Italian Parliamentary System, 1860–1915.* Dusseldorf: Bertelsmann Universitätsverlag.

Paxton, Pamela, and Rumi Morishima. 2005. "Does Democracy Aid Promote Democracy?" The John Glenn Institute for Public Service and Public Policy, Ohio State University.

Perry, Charles M., and Dimitris Keridis. 2004. *Defense Reform, Modernization, and Military Cooperation in Southeastern Europe*. Dulles, VA: Brassey's.

Pew Foundation. 2007. "Global Unease with Major World Powers." Pew Global Attitudes Project, released June 27. <pewglobal.org>.

Pew Global Attitudes Survey 17. 2005. Andrew Kohut, Director. *Islamic Extremism Common Concern for Muslim and Western Publics*.

Phillips, David L. 2005. *Losing Iraq: Inside the Postwar Reconstruction Fiasco*. New York: Basic Books.

Pierson, Paul. 1993. "When Effect Becomes Cause." *World Politics* 45: 595–628.

Plumb, J. H. 1973. *The Growth of Political Stability in England 1675–1725*. Harmondsworth, UK: Penguin.

Pocock, J. G. A. 1975. *The Machievellian Moment*. Princeton: Princeton University Press.

Poggi, Gianfranco. 1978. *The Development of the Modern State*. Stanford, CA: Stanford University Press.

Potter, David M., and Don E. Fehrenbacher. 1976. *The Impending Crisis*. New York: Harper Collins.

Przeworski, Adam. 1991. *Democracy and the Market*. Cambridge: Cambridge University Press.

Przeworski, Adam. 2007. "Is the Science of Comparative Politics Possible?" In Carles Boix and Susan C. Stokes, eds., *Oxford Handbook of Comparative Politics*. New York: Oxford University Press.

Przeworski, Adam, Michael E. Alvarez, Jose Antonio Cheibub, and Fernando Limongi. 2000. *Democracy and Development: Political Institutions and Well-being in the World, 1950–1990*. Cambridge: Cambridge University Press.

Puddington, Arch. 2007. "The 2006 Freedom House Survey." *Journal of Democracy* 18: 125–137.

Putnam, Robert D. 1993. *Making Democracy Work: Civic Traditions in Modern Italy*. Princeton, NJ: Princeton University Press.

Putnam, Robert D. 1994. *Making Democracy Work: Civic Traditions in Modern Italy*. Princeton, NJ: Princeton University Press.

Pycroft, Christopher. 1994. "Angola – 'the Forgotten Tragedy.'" *Journal of Southern African Studies* 20: 241–262.

Rabello de Castro, Paulo, and Marcio Ronci. 1991. "Sixty Years of Populism in Brazil." In Rudiger Dornbusch and Sebastian Edwards, eds., *The Macroeconomics of Populism in Latin America*. Chicago: University of Chicago Press.

Ramos, A. J., R. C. Oates, and T. L. McMahon. 1992. "The U.S. Southern Command: A Strategy for the Future." *Military Review*, November: 32–39.

Rasch, Bjorn Erik, and Roger D. Congleton. 2006. "Amendment Procedures and Constitutional Stability." In Roger D. Congleton and Brigitta Swedenborg, eds., *Democratic Constitutional Design and Public Policy*. Cambridge, MA: MIT Press.

Rasler, Karen A., and William R. Thompson. 2005. *Puzzles of the Democratic Peace: Theory, Geopolitics, and the Transformation of World Politics*. 1st ed. New York: Palgrave Macmillan, 2005.

Reed, John S. 1983. *Southerners*. Chapel Hill, NC: University of North Carolina Press.

Reilly, Ben. 2002. "Electoral Systems for Divided Societies." *Journal of Democracy* 13: 156–170.

Reilly, Benjamin. 2004. "Elections in Post-Conflict Societies." In Edward Newman and Roland Rich, eds., *The UN Role in Promoting Democracy: Between Ideals and Reality* Tokyo: United Nations University Press.

Reilly, Ben, and Andrew Reynolds. 1999. *Electoral Systems and Conflict in Divided Societies*. Washington, DC: National Academy Press.

Remington, Thomas, and Steven Smith. 1996. "Political Goals, Institutional Context, and the Choice of an Electoral System: The Russian Parliamentary Election Law." *American Journal of Political Science* 40: 1253–1279.

Reynolds, Andrew. 1999. "Women in the Legislatures and Executives of the World: Knocking at the Highest Glass Ceiling." *World Politics* 51: 547–572.

Reynolds, Andrew. 2005. "Constitutional Medicine." *Journal of Democracy* 16: 54–68.

Reynolds, Andrew. 2006. "The Curious Case of Afghanistan." *Journal of Democracy* 17: 104–117.

Riker, William H. 1982. *Liberalism against Populism*. Prospect Heights, IL: Waveland Press.

Riker, William. 1982. "The Two-Party System and Duverger's Law: An Essay on the History of Political Science." *The American Political Science Review* 76: 753–766.

Riley, Dylan. 2005. "Civic Associations and Authoritarian Regimes in Interwar Europe: Italy and Spain in Comparative Perspective." *American Sociological Review* 70: 288–310.

Rizvi, Hasan-Askari. 2000. *Military, State and Society in Pakistan*. New York: St. Martin's.

Robespierre, Maximilien. 1967. *Oeuvres de Maximilien Robespierre*. 10 vols. M. Bouloisou et al., eds. Paris: Presses Universitaires de France.

Rodman, Kenneth A. 1994. "Public and Private Sanctions against South Africa." *Political Science Quarterly* 109: 313–334.

Rose, Richard. 2007. "Learning to Support New Regimes in Europe." *Journal of Democracy* 18: 111–125.

Rose, Richard, Neil Munro, and Stephen White. 2001. "Voting in a Floating Party System: The 1999 Duma Election." *Europe-Asia Studies* 53: 419–443.

Rotberg, Robert I., ed. 2004. *Crafting the New Nigeria*. Boulder, CO: Lynne Rienner.

Rousseau, Jean Jacques. 1959–95. *Oeuvres complètes*. 5 vols. Gagnebin and Raymond, eds. Paris: Pléiade.

Rudolph, Susan H., and Lloyd I. Rudolph. 2002. "New Dimensions of Indian Democracy." *Journal of Democracy* 13: 52–66.

Rummel, R. J. 1994. *Death by Government*. New Brunswick: Transaction Press.

Russett, Bruce M. 1993. *Grasping the Democratic Peace: Principles for a Post-Cold War World*. Princeton, NJ: Princeton University Press.

Russett, Bruce, and John Oneal. 2001. *Triangulating Peace: Democracy, Interdependence, and International Organizations*. New York: W.W. Norton.

Samuels, David. 2004. "Presidentialism and Accountability for the Economy in Comparative Perspective." *American Political Science Review* 98: 425–436.

Samuels, Kristi. 2006. "Post-Conflict Peace-Building and Constitution-Making." *Chicago Journal of International Law* 2: 663–682.

Sartori, Giovanni. 1968. "Political Development and Political Engineering." In John Montgomery and Alfred O. Hirschmann, eds., *Public Policy 17*. Cambridge: Harvard University Press.

Sartori, Giovanni. 1986. "The Influence of Electoral Systems: Faulty Laws or Faulty Method?" In Bernard Grofman and Arend Lijphart, eds., *Electoral Laws and Their Political Consequences*. New York: Agathon.

Schedler, Andreas. 2002. "The Menu of Manipulation." *Journal of Democracy* 13: 36–50.

Schmitter, Philippe. 2004. "The Ambiguous Virtues of Accountability." *Journal of Democracy* 15: 47–60.

Schmitter, Philippe C. 2006. "A Balance Sheet of the Vices and Virtues of Populism." Paper presented at the "The Challenge of the New Populism" conference, Sofia, Bulgaria, May 10–11.

Schmitter, Philippe, and Terry Lynn Karl. 1991. "What Democracy Is ... and Is Not." *Journal of Democracy* 2: 75–88.

Schoultz, Lars. 1981. *Human Rights and United States Policy toward Latin America*. Princeton, NJ: Princeton University Press.

Schoultz, Lars. 1987. *National Security and United States Policy toward Latin America*. Princeton, NJ: Princeton University Press.

Schoultz, Lars. 1998. *Beneath the United States: A History of U.S. Policy Toward Latin America*. Cambridge, MA: Harvard University Press.

Schuller, Wolfgang. 1995. "Zur Entstehung der griechischen Demokratie ausserhalb Athens." In Konrad Kinzl, ed., *Demokratia: Der Weg zur Demokratie bei den Griechen*. Darmstadt: Wissenschaftliche Buchgesellschaft.

Schumpeter, Joseph. 1976. *Capitalism, Socialism, and Democracy*. New York: Harper and Row.

Schwindt-Bayer, L. 2006. "Still Supermadres? Gender and the Policy Priorities of Latin American Legislators." *American Journal of Political Science* 50: 570–585.

Scott, James M., and Carie A. Steele. 2005. "Assisting Democrats or Resisting Dictators? The Nature and Impact of Democracy Support by the United States National Endowment for Democracy, 1990–99." *Democratization* 12: 439–460.

Seligman, Adam. 1992. *The Idea of Civil Society*. New York: The Free Press.

Seligman, Adam. 1995. *The Idea of Civil Society*. Princeton: Princeton University Press.

Seligman, Adam 2004. *Modest Claims*. Notre Dame: Notre Dame University Press.

Seton-Watson, Christopher. 1967. *Italy from Liberalism to Fascism*. London: Methuen.

Sheehan, James. 1995. *German Liberalism in the Nineteenth Century*. Atlantic Highlands, NJ: Humanities Press.

Shepherd, Robin. 2005. "Russia's Misplaced Pride Holds Back Its Democracy." *Financial Times*, 25 November.

Shils, Edward. 1963. "The Theory of Mass Society." In Philip G. Olson, ed., *America as a Mass Society: Changing Community and Identity*. New York: Free Press.

Shils, Edward. 1975. *Centre and Periphery: Essays in MacroSociology*. Chicago: University of Chicago Press.

Shugart, Matthew S. 1995. "The Electoral Cycle and Institutional Sources of Divided Government." *American Political Science Review* 89: 327–343.

Simon, Jeffrey. 2003. *Hungary and NATO: Problems in Civil-Military Relations*. Lanham, MD: Rowman & Littlefield.

Sisson, Richard, and Leo Rose. 1990. *War and Secession: Pakistan, India, and the Creation of Bangladesh*. Berkeley, CA: University of California Press.

Skach, Cindy. 2005. *Borrowing Constitutional Designs: Constitutional Law in Weimar Germany and the French Fifth Republic*. Princeton, NJ: Princeton University Press.

Skinner, Quinten. 1990. "The Republican Ideal of Political Liberty." In G. Bock, Q. Skinner, and M. Viroli, eds. *Machiavelli and Republicanism*. Cambridge: Cambridge University Press.

Smith, Anthony D. 1986. *The Ethnic Origin of Nations*. Oxford, UK: Blackwell.

Smith, Anthony D. 2001. *Nationalism*. Cambridge, UK: Polity Press.

Smith, William C. 1989. *Authoritarianism and the Crisis of the Argentine Political Economy*. Stanford: Stanford University Press.

Snyder, Jack. 2000. *From Voting to Violence: Democratization and Nationalist Conflict*. New York: W. W. Norton.

Sogge, David. 2002. *Give and Take: What's the Matter with Foreign Aid?* London: Zed Books.

Sola, Lourdes. 1994. "The State, Structural Reform, and Democratization in Brazil." In William C. Smith, Carlos H. Acuna, and Edwardo A Gamarra, eds. *Democracy, Markets, and Structural Reform in Latin America*. Miami: North-South Center.

Soyinka, Wole. 1996. *The Open Sore of a Continent: A Personal Narrative of the Nigerian Crisis*. New York: Oxford University Press.

Stedman, Stephen John. 1997. "Spoiler Problems in Peace Processes." *International Security* 22: 5–53.

Steinberg, Jonathan. 1996. *Why Switzerland?* Cambridge, UK: Cambridge University Press.

Stepan, Alfred. 1988. *Rethinking Military Politics: Brazil and the Southern Cone*. Princeton, NJ: Princeton University Press.

Stepan, Alfred. 2004. "Religion, Democracy, and the 'Twin Tolerations.'" *Journal of Democracy* 11: 37–57.

Stone, Suzanne. 1991. "Sinaitic and Noahide Law: Legal Pluralism in Jewish Law." *Cardozo Law Review* 12: 1157–1214.

Stratégie gouvernance de la coopération française. 2007. Paris: Ministère des Affaires étrangères.

Sturzenegger, Federico A. 1991. "Description of a Populist Experience: Argentina, 1973–1976." In Rudiger Dornbusch and Sebastian Edwards, eds., *The Macroeconomics of Populism in Latin America*. Chicago: University of Chicago Press.

Svensson, J. 1999. "Aid, Growth and Democracy." *Economics and Politics* 11: 275–298.

Swayd, Samy. 2006. *Historical Dictionary of the Druzes*. Lanham, MD: Scarecrow Press.

Taagepera, Rein, and Matthew Shugart. 1989. *Seats and Votes*. New Haven: Yale University Press.

Talbot, Ian. 2000. *India and Pakistan*. London: Arnold.

Tambiah, Stanley J. 1992. *Buddhism Betrayed? Religion, Politics and Violence in Sri Lanka*. Chicago, IL: University of Chicago Press.

Tannenbaum, Edward. 1972. *The Fascist Experience: Italian Society and Culture, 1922–1945*. New York: Basic Books.

Tarrow, Sidney. 1996. "Making Social Science Work across Space and Time: A Critical Reflection on Robert Putnam's Making Democracy Work." *American Political Science Review* 90: 389–397.

Tate, Katherine. 2003. *Black Faces in the Mirror: African Americans and Their Representatives in the U.S. Congress*. Princeton: Princeton University Press.

Tavits, Margit, and Taavi Annus. 2006. "Learning to Make Votes Count: The Role of Democratic Experience." *Electoral Studies* 25: 72–90.

Taylor, Brian D. 2003. *Politics and the Russian Army: Civil-Military Relations, 1689–2000*. New York: Cambridge University Press.

Taylor, Charles. 1985. "What is Human Agency." *Human Agency and Language: Philosophical Paper*. Vol. 1. Cambridge: Cambridge University Press.

Taylor, Charles. 1992. *Multiculturalism and the Politics of Recognition*. Princeton: Princeton University Press.

Tessler, Mark, and Eleanor Gao. 2005. "Gauging Arab Support for Democracy." *Journal of Democracy* 16: 83–97.

Thayer, John. 1964. *Italy and the Great War: Politics and Culture, 1870–1915*. Madison, WI: University of Wisconsin Press.

Tilly, Charles, ed. 1974. *The Formation of the National States in Western Europe*. Princeton, NJ: Princeton University Press.

Tilly, Charles. 2004. *Contention and Democracy in Europe 1650–2000*. New York: Cambridge University Press.

Tolbert, C., and G. Steuernagel. 2001. "Women Lawmakers, State Mandates and Women's Health." *Women & Politics* 22: 1–39.

Traub, James. 2007. "Persuading Them." *New York Times Magazine*, November 25.

Trinkunas, Harold A. 2005. *Crafting Civilian Control of the Military in Venezuela: A Comparative Perspective*. Chapel Hill: University of North Carolina Press.

Trofimov, Yaroslav. 2001. Complex Foe: Brandishing Weapons and Aid, Hezbollah Tests U.S. Resolve. *Wall Street Journal*, 17 December, 1, 6.

Trounstine, Jessica. 2006. "Dominant Regimes and the Demise of Urban Democracy." *Journal of Politics* 68: 879–893.

Tsebelis, George. 1995. "Decision-Making in Political Systems: Veto Players in Presidentialism, Parliamentarism, Multicameralism and Multipartyism." *British Journal of Poltical Science* 25: 289–325.

Tsebelis, George. 1999. "Veto Players and Law Production in Parliamentary Democracies: An Empirical Analysis." *American Political Science Review* 93: 591–608.

Tsebelis, George, and Jeannette Money. 1997. *Bicameralism.* New York: Cambridge University Press.

Tufte, Edward R. 1997. *Visual Explanations: Images and Quantities, Evidence and Narrative.* Cheshire, CT: Graphics Press.

Uddin, Sufia. 2006. *Constructing Bangladesh.* Chapel Hill, NC: University of North Carolina Press.

U.K. Ministry of Defence. 1997. "Review of Parliamentary Oversight of the Romanian Ministry of National Defence and the Democratic Control of Its Armed Forces." London: U.K. Ministry of Defence, February.

Ullman, Richard. 1999. "The U.S. and the World: An Interview with George Kennan." *New York Review of Books* 46: 4, 6.

UNDP (United Nations Development Programme). 2003. *Human Development Report 2002.* New York: UNDP.

U.S. Government. 2001. *U.S. Assistance to Partnership for Peace* – Report to Congressional Committees, GAO 01-734. Washington, DC: U.S. Government Accounting Office, July.

Varshney, Ashutosh. 2001. "Ethnic Conflict and Civil Society – India and Beyond." *World Politics* 53: 362–398.

Varshney, Ashutosh. 2003. *Ethnic Conflict and Civic Life: Hindus and Muslims in India.* New Haven: Yale University Press.

Veremis, Thanos. 1997. *The Military in Greek Politics: From Independence to Democracy.* Montréal: Black Rose Books.

Wall Street Journal, September 20, 2006.

Walter, E. V. 1964. "'Mass Society:' The Late Stages of an Idea." *Social Research* 31: 391–410.

Wang, Zhengxu. 2007. "Public Support for Democracy in China." *Journal of Contemporary China* 16: 561–579.

Way, Lucan A. 2005. "Authoritarian State Building and the Sources of Regime Competitiveness in the Fourth Wave: The Cases of Belarus, Moldova, Russia, and Ukraine." *World Politics* 57: 231–261.

Weber, Eugen. 1976. *Peasants into Frenchmen.* Stanford, CA: Stanford University Press.

Wehler, Hans-Ulrich. 1974. "Der Aufstieg des Organisierten Kapitalismus und Interventionsstaates in Deutschland." In Heinrich August Winkler, ed., *Organizierter Kapitalismus: Voraussetzungen und Anfänge.* Göttingen: Vandenhoeck und Ruprecht.

Weiner, Myron. 1987. "Empirical Democratic Theory." In Myron Weiner and Ergun Ozbudun, eds., *Competitive Elections in Developing Countries.* Durham, NC: Duke University Press.

Weiner, Myron, and Ergun Özbudun. 1987. *Competitive Elections in Developing Countries*. Durham, NC: Duke University Press.

Weingast, Barry. 1997. "The Political Foundations of Democracy and the Rule of Law." *American Political Science Review* 91: 245–263.

Welch, Claude E., Jr. 1976. "Civilian Control of the Military: Myth and Reality." In Claude E. Welch, ed., *Civilian Control of the Military: Theory and Cases from Developing Countries*. Albany: State University of New York Press.

Weldon, Steven A. 2006. "The Institutional Context of Tolerance for Ethnic Minorities: A Comparative, Multilevel Analysis of Western Europe." *American Journal of Political Science* 50: 331–349.

Welsh, Jennifer. 1995. *Edmund Burke and International Relations: The Commonwealth of Europe and the Crusade against the French Revolution*. New York: St. Martins.

Whittington, Keith. 1998. "Revisiting Tocqueville's America. Society, Politics and Associations in the Nineteenth Century." *American Behaviorial Scientist* 42: 21–32.

Wickham, Carrie Rosefsky. 2002. *Mobilizing Islam: Religion, Activism, and Political Change in Egypt*. New York: Columbia University Press.

Widner, Jennifer. 2007. *Constitution Writing and Conflict Resolution Project*. Princeton, NJ: Princeton University <http://www.princeton.edu/~pcwcr/>.

Widner, Jennifer. 2007. "The Effects of Constitution Writing Procedures on Choice of Terms and Patterns of Violence: Some Data, Some Observations, and Many Reasons for Modesty." *Working Paper for Stanford Workshop in Comparative Politics*.

Wilkinson, Steven. 2004. *Votes and Violence: Electoral Competition and Ethnic Riots in India*. New York: Cambridge University Press.

Williams, Bernard. 1996. "Toleration: An Impossible Virtue." In M. Heyd, ed., *Toleration: An Elusive Virtue*. Princeton: Princeton University Press.

Wilson, Jeyaratnam A. 2000. *Sri Lankan Tamil Nationalism*. Vancouver, Canada: University of British Columbia Press.

Windsor, Jennifer. 2003. "Promoting Democratization Can Combat Terrorism." *Washington Quarterly* 26: 43–58.

Winkler, Heinrich August. 1972. *Mittelstand, Demokratie und Nationalsozialismus: Die politische Entwicklung von Handwerk und Kleinhandel in der Weimarer Republik*. Cologne: Kiepenheuer & Witsch.

Wolin, Sheldon. 1996. "Transgression, Equality, and Voice." In Josiah Ober and Charles Hedrick, eds., *Demokratia: A Conversation on Democracies, Ancient and Modern*. Princeton: Princeton University Press.

Woodward, E. L. 1938. *The Age of Reform*. Oxford, UK: Clarendon Press.

Woodward, Susan. 1995. *Balkan Tragedy*. Washington, DC: Brookings Institution.

World Bank. 2000. New Paths to Social Development: Community and Global Networks in Action. Working Paper 22339, May 31.

World Values Survey <www.worldvaluessurvey.org>.

Yang, Dali. 2007. "China's Long March to Freedom." *Journal of Democracy* 18: 58–64.

Young, Thomas-Durrell. 2006. "Military Professionalism in a Democracy." In Thomas C. Bruneau and Scott D. Tollefson, eds., *Who Guards the Guardians and How: Democratic Civil-Military Relations*. Austin: University of Texas Press.

Zakaria, Fareed. 1997. "The Rise of Illiberal Democracy." *Foreign Affairs* 76: 22–43.

Zaki, Moheb. 1995. *Civil Society and Democratization in Egypt*. Cairo: Konrad Adenauer Stiftung.

Zijderveld, Anton C. 1998. "Civil Society, Pillarization, and the Welfare State." In Robert Hefner, ed., *Democratic Civility*. New Brunswick, NJ: Transaction Publishers.

Zimmern, Alfred. 1961. *The Greek Commonwealth: Politics and Economics in Fifth Century Athens*. 5th ed. Oxford: Oxford University Press.

Zubaida, Sami. 1992. "Islam, the State, and Democracy: Contrasting Conceptions of Society in Egypt." *Middle East Report* 179: 2–10.

Index